T0245295

MATHEMATICAL METHODS IN DATA SCIENCE

MATHEMATICAL METHODS IN DATA SCIENCE

JINGLI REN

HAIYAN WANG

SCIENCE PRESS

Elsevier
Radarweg 29, PO Box 211, 1000 AE Amsterdam, Netherlands
The Boulevard, Langford Lane, Kidlington, Oxford OX5 1GB, United Kingdom
50 Hampshire Street, 5th Floor, Cambridge, MA 02139, United States

Copyright © 2023 China Science Publishing & Media Ltd. Published by Elsevier Inc. All rights reserved.

No part of this publication may be reproduced or transmitted in any form or by any means, electronic or mechanical, including photocopying, recording, or any information storage and retrieval system, without permission in writing from the publisher. Details on how to seek permission, further information about the Publisher's permissions policies and our arrangements with organizations such as the Copyright Clearance Center and the Copyright Licensing Agency, can be found at our website: www.elsevier.com/permissions.

This book and the individual contributions contained in it are protected under copyright by the Publisher (other than as may be noted herein).

Notices

Knowledge and best practice in this field are constantly changing. As new research and experience broaden our understanding, changes in research methods, professional practices, or medical treatment may become necessary.

Practitioners and researchers must always rely on their own experience and knowledge in evaluating and using any information, methods, compounds, or experiments described herein. In using such information or methods they should be mindful of their own safety and the safety of others, including parties for whom they have a professional responsibility.

To the fullest extent of the law, neither the Publisher nor the authors, contributors, or editors, assume any liability for any injury and/or damage to persons or property as a matter of products liability, negligence or otherwise, or from any use or operation of any methods, products, instructions, or ideas contained in the material herein.

ISBN: 978-0-443-18679-0

For information on all Elsevier publications
visit our website at https://www.elsevier.com/books-and-journals

Publisher: Glyn Jones
Editorial Project Manager: Naomi Robertson
Production Project Manager: Punithavathy Govindaradjane
Cover Designer: Matthew Limbert

Typeset by VTeX

Working together
to grow libraries in
developing countries

www.elsevier.com • www.bookaid.org

Contents

Preface

Data science is an interdisciplinary field that aims to use scientific approaches to extract meaning and insights from data. Today almost all kinds of organizations are generating exponential amounts of data. A closely related and overlapping field, machine learning, uses computer algorithms to find patterns and features in massive amounts of data in order to make decisions and predictions. To be able to truly understand data science and machine learning, it is important to appreciate the underlying mathematics and statistics, as well as computing algorithms. Mathematical knowledge in linear algebra, calculus, optimization, probability, and statistics is essential for data science. For historical reasons, courses in data science and machine learning tend to be taught in statistical and computer science departments, where the emphasis is on statistics and computer algorithms.

There are a number of books on mathematical methods in data science. Currently, all of these related books primarily focus on linear algebra, optimization, and statistical methods. However, ordinary and partial differential equation models play an increasingly important role in data science. For example, ordinary differential equation models, in particular, SIR (Susceptible-Infected-Recovered) models, have been extensively used for infectious disease modeling and prediction. With the availability of an unprecedented amount of clinical, epidemiological, and social COVID-19 data, data-driven differential equation models have revealed new insights into the spread and control of COVID-19.

In this book, we will cover a broad range of mathematical tools used in data science, including calculus, linear algebra, optimization, network analysis, probability, and differential equations. In particular, the book introduces a new approach based on network analysis to integrate big data into the framework of ordinary and partial differential equations for data analysis and prediction. The techniques in linear algebra, probability, calculus and optimization, and network analysis in Chapters 1, 2, 3, 4 are necessary for understanding the applications of differential equations in data science. For example, eigenvalues are used in network clustering, and gradient descent is extensively used in the training of differential equations for various predictions. The material in Chapters 4, 5, and 6 are based on the two authors' published and unpublished works on analysis and prediction with data-driven ordinary and partial differential equations.

Data science is virtually used in every section in our society. This timely book is of great interest to a broad range of readers including advanced undergraduate students, graduate students, and researchers. Background preparations and necessary references are also included to ensure the book is accessible to general readers who are interested in data science.

Jingli Ren and Haiyan Wang

Acknowledgments

We would like to acknowledge the contributions to the papers from our collaborators: Yufang Wang, Feng Wang, Kuai Xu, Shuhua Zhang, Nao Yamamoto, Bohan Jiang, Liying Zhang, Dongchen Li, Xiaoxiang Guo, and Yun Kang. We would thank a number of students, Yangyang Hao, Zihan Nie, and Huinan Chang, for their help in preparing the draft of this book. We want to thank the editor for the support of the project from the beginning.

Jingli Ren is grateful to Professors Junzhi Cui, Lei Guo, Weihua Wang, and Weigao Ge for their support and guidance in her academic career, and would like to acknowledge that this project has been supported by research grants from the National Science Foundation of China (No. 52071298) and ZhongYuan Science and Technology Innovation Leadership Program (No. 214200510010).

CHAPTER 1

Linear algebra

Contents

1.1 Introduction

Linear algebra is a field of mathematics that is widely used in various disciplines. Linear algebra plays an important role in data science and machine learning. A solid understanding of linear algebra concepts can enhance the understanding of many data science and machine learning algorithms. This chapter introduces basic concepts of linear algebra that need data science including vector spaces, orthogonality, eigenvalues, matrix decomposition, and is further expanded to include linear regression and principal component analysis where linear algebra plays a central role for solving data science problems. More advanced concepts and applications of linear algebra can be found in many references [1–4,118].

Mathematical Methods in Data Science
https://doi.org/10.1016/B978-0-44-318679-0.00007-7

Copyright © 2023 China Science Publishing &
Media Ltd. Published by Elsevier Inc.
All rights reserved.

1.2 Elements of linear algebra

We begin with a brief review of basic concepts for linear algebra. We confine our discussions to $V = \mathbb{R}^n$.

1.2.1 Linear spaces

1.2.1.1 Linear combinations

A linear combination in linear algebra is a new vector constructed from a subset by multiplying each vector by a constant and adding the results. A linear subspace is a subset of all linear combination.

Definition 1.2.1 (Linear subspace). A linear subspace of V is a subset $U \subseteq V$ that is closed under vector addition and scalar multiplication. That is, for all $\mathbf{u}_1, \mathbf{u}_2 \in U$ and $\alpha \in \mathbb{R}$, it holds that

$$\mathbf{u}_1 + \mathbf{u}_2 \in U, \quad \text{and} \quad \alpha \mathbf{u}_1 \in U. \tag{1.2.1}$$

In particular, $\mathbf{0}$ is always in a linear subspace. As we can see below, a span of a set of vectors is a linear subspace.

Definition 1.2.2 (Span). Let $\mathbf{w}_1, \ldots, \mathbf{w}_m \in V$. The span of $\{\mathbf{w}_1, \ldots, \mathbf{w}_m\}$, denoted $\mathrm{span}(\mathbf{w}_1, \ldots, \mathbf{w}_m)$, is the set of all linear combinations of the $\mathbf{w}_j$'s. That is,

$$\mathrm{span}(\mathbf{w}_1, \ldots, \mathbf{w}_m) = \left\{ \sum_{j=1}^{m} \alpha_j \mathbf{w}_j : \alpha_1, \ldots, \alpha_m \in \mathbb{R} \right\}. \tag{1.2.2}$$

A list of vectors that span a linear subspace U is also referred to as a spanning set of U. We can verify that a span is a linear subspace.

Lemma 1.2.3 (Every span is a linear subspace). *Let $W = \mathrm{span}(\mathbf{w}_1, \ldots, \mathbf{w}_m)$. Then W is a linear subspace.*

Proof. Let $\mathbf{u}_1, \mathbf{u}_2 \in W$, and $\alpha \in \mathbb{R}$. Then for $i = 1, 2$,

$$\mathbf{u}_i = \sum_{j=1}^{m} \beta_{i,j} \mathbf{w}_j,$$

and

$$\alpha \mathbf{u}_1 + \mathbf{u}_2 = \alpha \sum_{j=1}^{m} \beta_{1,j} \mathbf{w}_j + \sum_{j=1}^{m} \beta_{2,j} \mathbf{w}_j = \sum_{j=1}^{m} (\alpha \beta_{1,j} + \beta_{2,j}) \mathbf{w}_j.$$

We conclude that $\alpha \mathbf{u}_1 + \mathbf{u}_2 \in W$. $\qquad \square$

Often it is useful to study the column space of a matrix.

Definition 1.2.4 (Column space). Let $A \in \mathbb{R}^{n \times m}$ be an $n \times m$ matrix with columns $\mathbf{a}_1, \ldots, \mathbf{a}_m \in \mathbb{R}^n$. The column space of A, denoted $\mathrm{col}(A)$, is the span of the columns of A, that is, $\mathrm{col}(A) = \mathrm{span}(\mathbf{a}_1, \ldots, \mathbf{a}_m) \in \mathbb{R}^n$.

1.2.1.2 Linear independence and dimension

For many problems in applications including data science, it is desirable to avoid redundancy in the description of a linear subspace. The concept is central to the definition of dimension of a linear space.

Definition 1.2.5 (Linear independence). A list of vectors $\mathbf{u}_1, \ldots, \mathbf{u}_m$ is linearly independent if none of them can be written as a linear combination of the others, that is,

$$\forall i, \quad \mathbf{u}_i \notin \mathrm{span}(\{\mathbf{u}_j : j \neq i\}).$$

A list of vectors is called linearly dependent if it is not linearly independent.

Lemma 1.2.6. *The vectors* $\mathbf{u}_1, \ldots, \mathbf{u}_m$ *are linearly independent if and only if*

$$\sum_{j=1}^{m} \alpha_j \mathbf{u}_j = \mathbf{0} \implies \alpha_j = 0, \ \forall j.$$

Equivalently, $\mathbf{u}_1, \ldots, \mathbf{u}_m$ *are linearly dependent if and only if there exist* α_j*'s, not all zero, such that* $\sum_{j=1}^{m} \alpha_j \mathbf{u}_j = \mathbf{0}$.

Proof. The equivalence follows by contradiction. We prove the second statement. Assume $\mathbf{u}_1, \ldots, \mathbf{u}_m$ are linearly dependent. Then $\mathbf{u}_i = \sum_{j \neq i} \alpha_j \mathbf{u}_j$ for some i. Taking $\alpha_i = -1$ gives $\sum_{j=1}^{m} \alpha_j \mathbf{u}_j = \mathbf{0}$. On the other hand, assume $\sum_{j=1}^{m} \alpha_j \mathbf{u}_j = \mathbf{0}$ with α_j's not all zero. In particular, $\alpha_i \neq 0$ for some i. Then $\mathbf{u}_i = \frac{1}{\alpha_i} \sum_{j \neq i} \alpha_j \mathbf{u}_j$. □

For matrix form, let $\mathbf{a}_1, \ldots, \mathbf{a}_m \in \mathbb{R}^n$ and

$$A = \begin{pmatrix} | & & | \\ \mathbf{a}_1 & \cdots & \mathbf{a}_m \\ | & & | \end{pmatrix}.$$

Then linearly independence can be formulated as if there is a non-trivial solution of a linear system. It is clear that $A\mathbf{x}$ is the following linear combination of the columns of A: $\sum_{j=1}^{m} x_j \mathbf{a}_j$. Then $\mathbf{a}_1, \ldots, \mathbf{a}_m$ are linearly independent if and only if $A\mathbf{x} = \mathbf{0} \implies \mathbf{x} = \mathbf{0}$. Equivalently, $\mathbf{a}_1, \ldots, \mathbf{a}_m$ are linearly dependent if and only if $\exists \mathbf{x} \neq \mathbf{0}$ such that $A\mathbf{x} = \mathbf{0}$.

We now look at the concept of bases, which give a minimal representation of a subspace. A basis is a set of vectors that generates all elements of the vector space and the vectors in the set are linearly independent.

Definition 1.2.7 (Basis of a space). Let U be a linear subspace of V. A basis of U is a list of vectors $\mathbf{u}_1, \ldots, \mathbf{u}_m$ in U that: (1) span U, that is, $U = \text{span}(\mathbf{u}_1, \ldots, \mathbf{u}_m)$; and (2) are linearly independent.

We denote by $\mathbf{e}_1, \ldots, \mathbf{e}_n$ the standard basis of $\mathbb{R}^n$, where $\mathbf{e}_i$ has a one in coordinate i and zeros in all other coordinates. One of the first key properties of a basis is that it provides a unique representation of the vectors in the subspace. Indeed, let U be a linear subspace and $\mathbf{u}_1, \ldots, \mathbf{u}_m$ be a basis of U. Suppose that $\mathbf{w} \in U$ can be written as $\mathbf{w} = \sum_{j=1}^m \alpha_j \mathbf{u}_j$ and $\mathbf{w} = \sum_{j=1}^m \alpha'_j \mathbf{u}_j$. Then subtracting one equation from the other we arrive at $\sum_{j=1}^m (\alpha_j - \alpha'_j) \mathbf{u}_j = \mathbf{0}$. By linear independence, we have $\alpha_j - \alpha'_j = 0$ for each j.

A vector space can have several bases; however, all of the bases have the same number of elements, called the dimension of the vector space. When applied to a matrix A, the dimension of the column space of A is called the (column) rank of A. We state it as the following theorem.

Theorem 1.2.8 (Dimension theorem). *Let U be a linear subspace of V. Any basis of U always has the same number of elements. All bases of U have the same length, that is, the same number of elements. We call this number the dimension of U and denote it $\dim(U)$.*

The following lemma further describes the property of a linearly dependent set, which is used to prove the dimension theorem. It states that, given a linearly dependent list of vectors, one of the vectors is in the span of the previous ones and we can remove it without changing the span.

Lemma 1.2.9 (Characterization of linearly dependent sets). *Let $\mathbf{u}_1, \ldots, \mathbf{u}_m$ be a linearly dependent list of vectors with a linearly independent subset, $\mathbf{u}_i, i \in \{1, \ldots, k\}, k < m$. Then there is an $i > k$ such that:*
1. $\mathbf{u}_i \in \text{span}(\mathbf{u}_1, \ldots, \mathbf{u}_{i-1})$;
2. $\text{span}(\{\mathbf{u}_j : j \in \{1, \ldots, m\}\}) = \text{span}(\{\mathbf{u}_j : j \in \{1, \ldots, m\}, j \neq i\})$.

Proof (Characterization of linearly dependent sets). For 1, by linear dependence, $\sum_{j=1}^m \alpha_j \mathbf{u}_j = \mathbf{0}$ with not all α_j's zero. Further, because $\mathbf{u}_i, i \in \{1, \ldots, k\}$,

$k < m$ is independent, and not all $\alpha_{k+1}, \ldots, \alpha_m$ are zero. Take the largest index among the α_j's that are non-zero, say i. Then rearranging gives

$$\mathbf{u}_i = -\sum_{j=1}^{i-1} \frac{\alpha_j}{\alpha_i} \mathbf{u}_j.$$

For 2, we note that for any $\mathbf{w} \in \mathrm{span}(\{\mathbf{u}_j : j \in \{1, \ldots, m\}\})$ we can write it as $\mathbf{w} = \sum_{j=1}^{m} \beta_j \mathbf{u}_j$ and we can replace $\mathbf{u}_i$ by the equation above, producing a representation of $\mathbf{w}$ in terms of $\{\mathbf{u}_j : j \in \{1, \ldots, m\}, j \neq i\}$. $\square$

We are now able to prove the dimension theorem.

Proof (Dimension theorem). Suppose we have two bases $\{\mathbf{w}_i : i \in \{1, \ldots, n\}\}$ and $\{\mathbf{u}_j : j \in \{1, \ldots, m\}\}$ of U. It suffices to show that $n \geq m$. First, we consider the list $\{\mathbf{u}_1, \mathbf{w}_1, \ldots, \mathbf{w}_n\}$. Because the $\mathbf{w}_i$'s are spanning, adding $\mathbf{u}_1 \neq \mathbf{0}$ to them necessarily produces a linearly dependent list. By the lemma for the characterization of linearly dependent sets, we can remove one of the $\mathbf{w}_i$'s without changing the span. The new list B has length n again. Then we add $\mathbf{u}_2$ to B immediately after $\mathbf{u}_1$. By the lemma for the characterization of linearly dependent sets, one of the vectors in this list is in the span of the previous ones. It cannot be $\mathbf{u}_2$ as $\{\mathbf{u}_1, \mathbf{u}_2\}$ are linearly independent by assumption. So it must be one of the remaining $\mathbf{w}_i$'s. We remove that one, without changing the span by the linear dependence lemma again. This process can be continued until we have added all the $\mathbf{u}_j$'s, as otherwise a subset of $\{\mathbf{u}_j : j \in \{1, \ldots, m\}\}$ would span U, which is a contradiction. Hence $n \geq m$. $\square$

1.2.2 Orthogonality

In many applications, the use of orthonormal bases can greatly simplify mathematical representations and reveal more insights of the underlying problems. We begin with the following definitions and lemmas.

1.2.2.1 Orthonormal bases

Definition 1.2.10 (Norm and inner product). $\langle \mathbf{u}, \mathbf{v} \rangle = \mathbf{u} \cdot \mathbf{v} = \sum_{1}^{n} u_i v_i$ and $\|\mathbf{u}\| = \sqrt{\sum_{1}^{n} u_i^2}$.

Definition 1.2.11. A list of vectors $\{\mathbf{u}_1, \ldots, \mathbf{u}_m\}$ is orthonormal if the $\mathbf{u}_i$'s are pairwise orthogonal and each has norm 1, that is, for all i and all $j \neq i$, $\langle \mathbf{u}_i, \mathbf{u}_j \rangle = 0$, and $\|\mathbf{u}_i\| = 1$.

We generalize the Pythagorean theorem with orthogonal vectors.

Lemma 1.2.12 (Pythagorean theorem). *Let* $\mathbf{u}, \mathbf{v} \in V$ *be orthogonal. Then* $\|\mathbf{u} + \mathbf{v}\|^2 = \|\mathbf{u}\|^2 + \|\mathbf{v}\|^2$.

Proof (Pythagorean theorem). Using $\|\mathbf{w}\|^2 = \langle \mathbf{w}, \mathbf{w} \rangle$, we get

$$\|\mathbf{u} + \mathbf{v}\|^2 = \langle \mathbf{u} + \mathbf{v}, \mathbf{u} + \mathbf{v} \rangle = \langle \mathbf{u}, \mathbf{u} \rangle + 2 \langle \mathbf{u}, \mathbf{v} \rangle + \langle \mathbf{v}, \mathbf{v} \rangle = \|\mathbf{u}\|^2 + \|\mathbf{v}\|^2. \quad \square$$

Many useful results can be derived from Pythagorean theorem, for example, we have the following.

Lemma 1.2.13 (Cauchy–Schwarz). *For any* $\mathbf{u}, \mathbf{v} \in V$, $|\langle \mathbf{u}, \mathbf{v} \rangle| \leq \|\mathbf{u}\| \|\mathbf{v}\|$.

Proof (Cauchy–Schwarz). Let $\mathbf{q} = \frac{\mathbf{v}}{\|\mathbf{v}\|}$ be the unit vector in the direction of $\mathbf{v}$. We want to show $|\langle \mathbf{u}, \mathbf{q} \rangle| \leq \|\mathbf{u}\|$. Decompose $\mathbf{u}$ into its projection onto $\mathbf{q}$ and what is left is the following:

$$\mathbf{u} = \langle \mathbf{u}, \mathbf{q} \rangle \mathbf{q} + \{\mathbf{u} - \langle \mathbf{u}, \mathbf{q} \rangle \mathbf{q}\}.$$

The two terms on the right-hand side are orthogonal, so the Pythagorean theorem gives

$$\|\mathbf{u}\|^2 = \left\| \langle \mathbf{u}, \mathbf{q} \rangle \mathbf{q} \right\|^2 + \left\| \mathbf{u} - \langle \mathbf{u}, \mathbf{q} \rangle \mathbf{q} \right\|^2 \geq \left\| \langle \mathbf{u}, \mathbf{q} \rangle \mathbf{q} \right\|^2 = \langle \mathbf{u}, \mathbf{q} \rangle^2.$$

Taking a square root gives the claim. $\quad \square$

Now we have the following properties for orthonormal lists.

Lemma 1.2.14. *Let* $\{\mathbf{u}_1, \ldots, \mathbf{u}_m\}$ *be an orthonormal list of vectors.*
1. $\| \sum_{j=1}^{m} \alpha_j \mathbf{u}_j \|^2 = \sum_{j=1}^{m} \alpha_j^2$ *for any* $\alpha_j \in \mathbb{R}$, $j \in \{1, \ldots, m\}$;
2. $\{\mathbf{u}_1, \ldots, \mathbf{u}_m\}$ *are linearly independent.*

Proof. For 1, noting that $\|\mathbf{x}\|^2 = \langle \mathbf{x}, \mathbf{x} \rangle$ and $\langle \beta \mathbf{x}_1 + \mathbf{x}_2, \mathbf{x}_3 \rangle = \beta \langle \mathbf{x}_1, \mathbf{x}_3 \rangle + \langle \mathbf{x}_2, \mathbf{x}_3 \rangle$, we have

$$\left\| \sum_{j=1}^{m} \alpha_j \mathbf{u}_j \right\|^2 = \left\langle \sum_{i=1}^{m} \alpha_i \mathbf{u}_i, \sum_{j=1}^{m} \alpha_j \mathbf{u}_j \right\rangle = \sum_{i=1}^{m} \alpha_i \left\langle \mathbf{u}_i, \sum_{j=1}^{m} \alpha_j \mathbf{u}_j \right\rangle$$

$$= \sum_{i=1}^{m} \sum_{j=1}^{m} \alpha_i \alpha_j \langle \mathbf{u}_i, \mathbf{u}_j \rangle,$$

which $\sum_{i=1}^{m} \alpha_i^2$, where we used orthonormality in the rightmost equation, that is, $\langle \mathbf{u}_i, \mathbf{u}_j \rangle$ is 1 if $i = j$ and 0 otherwise.

For 2, suppose $\sum_{i=1}^m \beta_i \mathbf{u}_i = \mathbf{0}$. Then we must have by 1 that $\sum_{i=1}^m \beta_i^2 = 0$. That implies $\beta_i = 0$ for all i. Hence the $\mathbf{u}_i$'s are linearly independent. $\qquad\square$

Given a basis $\{\mathbf{u}_1, \ldots, \mathbf{u}_m\}$ of a subspace $\mathcal{U}$, we know that: for any $\mathbf{w} \in \mathcal{U}$, $\mathbf{w} = \sum_{i=1}^m \alpha_i \mathbf{u}_i$ for some α_i's. It is not immediately obvious in general how to find these α_i's. In the orthonormal case, it is straightforward.

Theorem 1.2.15 (Orthonormal basis expansion). *Let $\mathbf{q}_1, \ldots, \mathbf{q}_m$ be an orthonormal basis of $\mathcal{U}$ and let $\mathbf{u} \in \mathcal{U}$. Then*

$$\mathbf{u} = \sum_{j=1}^m \langle \mathbf{u}, \mathbf{q}_j \rangle \, \mathbf{q}_j.$$

Proof. Because $\mathbf{u} \in \mathcal{U}$, $\mathbf{u} = \sum_{i=1}^m \alpha_i \mathbf{q}_i$ for some α_i. Take the inner product with $\mathbf{q}_j$ and use orthonormality:

$$\langle \mathbf{u}, \mathbf{q}_j \rangle = \left\langle \sum_{i=1}^m \alpha_i \mathbf{q}_i, \mathbf{q}_j \right\rangle = \sum_{i=1}^m \alpha_i \langle \mathbf{q}_i, \mathbf{q}_j \rangle = \alpha_j. \qquad\square$$

1.2.2.2 Best approximation theorem

Many optimization applications can be converted to the following best approximation problem. We have a linear subspace $\mathcal{U} \subseteq V$ and a vector $\mathbf{v} \notin \mathcal{U}$. We want to find the vector $\mathbf{v}^*$ in $\mathcal{U}$ that is closest to $\mathbf{v}$ in the norm as in Fig. 1.1, that is, we want to solve

$$\min_{\mathbf{v}^* \in \mathcal{U}} \|\mathbf{v}^* - \mathbf{v}\|.$$

Example 1.2.16. Consider the two-dimensional case with a one-dimensional subspace, say $\mathcal{U} = \mathrm{span}(\mathbf{u}_1)$ with $\|\mathbf{u}_1\| = 1$. The geometrical intuition of the best approximation theorem is demonstrated in Fig. 1.1. The solution $\mathbf{v}^*$ has the property that the difference $\mathbf{v} - \mathbf{v}^*$ makes a right angle with $\mathbf{u}_1$, that is, it is orthogonal to it.

Letting $\mathbf{v}^* = \alpha^* \mathbf{u}_1$, the geometrical condition above translates into

$$0 = \langle \mathbf{u}_1, \mathbf{v} - \mathbf{v}^* \rangle = \langle \mathbf{u}_1, \mathbf{v} - \alpha^* \mathbf{u}_1 \rangle = \langle \mathbf{u}_1, \mathbf{v} \rangle - \alpha^* \langle \mathbf{u}_1, \mathbf{u}_1 \rangle = \langle \mathbf{u}_1, \mathbf{v} \rangle - \alpha^*.$$

which implies that

$$\mathbf{v}^* = \langle \mathbf{u}_1, \mathbf{v} \rangle \, \mathbf{u}_1.$$

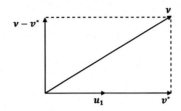

Figure 1.1

By the Pythagorean theorem, we then have for any $\alpha \in \mathbb{R}$,

$$\|\mathbf{v} - \alpha\,\mathbf{u}_1\|^2 = \|\mathbf{v} - \mathbf{v}^* + \mathbf{v}^* - \alpha\,\mathbf{u}_1\|^2 = \|\mathbf{v} - \mathbf{v}^* + (\alpha^* - \alpha)\,\mathbf{u}_1\|^2$$
$$= \|\mathbf{v} - \mathbf{v}^*\|^2 + \|(\alpha^* - \alpha)\,\mathbf{u}_1\|^2$$

and, therefore,

$$\|\mathbf{v} - \alpha\,\mathbf{u}_1\|^2 \geq \|\mathbf{v} - \mathbf{v}^*\|^2.$$

This confirms the optimality of $\mathbf{v}^*$.

The argument in the example above carries through in higher dimension, leading to the following fundamental result.

Definition 1.2.17 (Orthogonal projection). Let $\mathscr{U} \subseteq V$ be a linear subspace with orthonormal basis $\mathbf{q}_1, \ldots, \mathbf{q}_m$. The orthogonal projection of $\mathbf{v} \in V$ on $\mathscr{U}$ is defined as

$$\mathscr{P}_{\mathscr{U}}\mathbf{v} = \sum_{j=1}^{m} \langle \mathbf{v}, \mathbf{q}_j \rangle\, \mathbf{q}_j.$$

Theorem 1.2.18 (Best approximation theorem). *Let $\mathscr{U} \subseteq V$ be a linear subspace with orthonormal basis $\mathbf{q}_1, \ldots, \mathbf{q}_m$ and let $\mathbf{v} \in V$. For any $\mathbf{u} \in \mathscr{U}$,*

$$\|\mathbf{v} - \mathscr{P}_{\mathscr{U}}\mathbf{v}\| \leq \|\mathbf{v} - \mathbf{u}\|.$$

Furthermore, if $\mathbf{u} \in \mathscr{U}$ and the inequality above is an equality, then $\mathbf{u} = \mathscr{P}_{\mathscr{U}}\mathbf{v}$.

The visualization of the theorem is shown in Fig. 1.2. In addition, we note the following.

Lemma 1.2.19 (Orthogonal decomposition). *Let $\mathscr{U} \subseteq V$ be a linear subspace with orthonormal basis $\mathbf{q}_1, \ldots, \mathbf{q}_m$ and let $\mathbf{v} \in V$. For any $\mathbf{u} \in \mathscr{U}$, $\langle \mathbf{v} - \mathscr{P}_{\mathscr{U}}\mathbf{v}, \mathbf{u} \rangle = 0$. In particular, $\mathbf{v}$ can be decomposed as $(\mathbf{v} - \mathscr{P}_{\mathscr{U}}\mathbf{v}) + \mathscr{P}_{\mathscr{U}}\mathbf{v}$ where the two terms are orthogonal.*

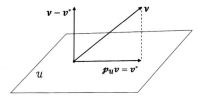

Figure 1.2 Best approximation theorem.

Proof (Orthogonal decomposition). We can write any $\mathbf{u} \in \mathscr{U}$ as $\sum_{j=1}^{m} \alpha_j \mathbf{q}_j$ for some α_j's. Then

$$\langle \mathbf{v} - \mathscr{P}_{\mathscr{U}} \mathbf{v}, \mathbf{u} \rangle = \left\langle \mathbf{v} - \sum_{j=1}^{m} \langle \mathbf{v}, \mathbf{q}_j \rangle \, \mathbf{q}_j, \, \sum_{j=1}^{m} \alpha_j' \mathbf{q}_j \right\rangle$$

$$= \sum_{j=1}^{m} \langle \mathbf{v}, \mathbf{q}_j \rangle \, \alpha_j' - \sum_{j=1}^{m} \alpha_j' \langle \mathbf{v}, \mathbf{q}_j \rangle = 0$$

where we used the orthonormality of the $\mathbf{q}_j$'s in the rightmost equality. The second claim follows from $\mathscr{P}_{\mathscr{U}} \mathbf{v} \in \mathscr{U}$. $\qquad\square$

We return to the proof of our main theorem.

Proof (Best approximation theorem). For any $\mathbf{u} \in \mathscr{U}$, the vector $\mathbf{u}' = \mathscr{P}_{\mathscr{U}} \mathbf{v} - \mathbf{u}$ is also in $\mathscr{U}$. By the orthogonal decomposition lemma and Pythagoras,

$$\|\mathbf{v} - \mathbf{u}\|^2 = \|\mathbf{v} - \mathscr{P}_{\mathscr{U}} \mathbf{v} + \mathscr{P}_{\mathscr{U}} \mathbf{v} - \mathbf{u}\|^2$$

$$= \|\mathbf{v} - \mathscr{P}_{\mathscr{U}} \mathbf{v}\|^2 + \|\mathscr{P}_{\mathscr{U}} \mathbf{v} - \mathbf{u}\|^2 \geq \|\mathbf{v} - \mathscr{P}_{\mathscr{U}} \mathbf{v}\|^2.$$

Furthermore, equality holds only if $\|\mathscr{P}_{\mathscr{U}} \mathbf{v} - \mathbf{u}\|^2 = 0$, which holds only if $\mathbf{u} = \mathscr{P}_{\mathscr{U}} \mathbf{v}$ by the point-separating property of the norm. $\qquad\square$

The map $\mathscr{P}_{\mathscr{U}}$ is linear, that is, $\mathscr{P}_{\mathscr{U}} (\alpha \mathbf{x} + \mathbf{y}) = \alpha \, \mathscr{P}_{\mathscr{U}} \mathbf{x} + \mathscr{P}_{\mathscr{U}} \mathbf{y}$ for all $\alpha \in \mathbb{R}$ and $\mathbf{x}, \mathbf{y} \in \mathbb{R}^n$. Indeed,

$$\mathscr{P}_{\mathscr{U}} (\alpha \mathbf{x} + \mathbf{y}) = \sum_{j=1}^{m} \langle \alpha \mathbf{x} + \mathbf{y}, \mathbf{q}_j \rangle \, \mathbf{q}_j = \sum_{j=1}^{m} \left\{ \alpha \, \langle \mathbf{x}, \mathbf{q}_j \rangle + \langle \mathbf{y}, \mathbf{q}_j \rangle \right\} \mathbf{q}_j$$

$$= \alpha \, \mathscr{P}_{\mathscr{U}} \mathbf{x} + \mathscr{P}_{\mathscr{U}} \mathbf{y}.$$

As a result, it can be encoded as an $n \times m$ matrix Q. Let

$$Q = \begin{pmatrix} | & & | \\ \mathbf{q}_1 & \cdots & \mathbf{q}_m \\ | & & | \end{pmatrix}$$

and note that computing

$$Q^T \mathbf{v} = \begin{pmatrix} \langle \mathbf{v}, \mathbf{q}_1 \rangle \\ \cdots \\ \langle \mathbf{v}, \mathbf{q}_m \rangle \end{pmatrix}$$

lists the coefficients in the expansion of $\mathscr{P}_{\mathcal{U}} \mathbf{v}$ over the basis $\mathbf{q}_1, \ldots, \mathbf{q}_m$. Hence we see that

$$\mathscr{P} = QQ^T.$$

On the other hand,

$$Q^T Q = \begin{pmatrix} \langle \mathbf{q}_1, \mathbf{q}_1 \rangle & \cdots & \langle \mathbf{q}_1, \mathbf{q}_m \rangle \\ \langle \mathbf{q}_2, \mathbf{q}_1 \rangle & \cdots & \langle \mathbf{q}_2, \mathbf{q}_m \rangle \\ \vdots & \ddots & \vdots \\ \langle \mathbf{q}_m, \mathbf{q}_1 \rangle & \cdots & \langle \mathbf{q}_m, \mathbf{q}_m \rangle \end{pmatrix} = I_{m \times m}$$

where $I_{m \times m}$ denotes the $m \times m$ identity matrix.

1.2.3 Gram–Schmidt process

The Gram–Schmidt algorithm is used to obtain an orthonormal basis. Let $\mathbf{a}_1, \ldots, \mathbf{a}_m$ be linearly independent. We intend to find an orthonormal basis of $\mathrm{span}(\mathbf{a}_1, \ldots, \mathbf{a}_m)$. The process takes advantage of the properties of the orthogonal projection derived above. In essence, we add the vectors $\mathbf{a}_i$ one by one, but only after taking out their orthogonal projection on the previously included vectors. The outcome spans the same subspace and orthogonal decomposition ensures orthogonality.

Theorem 1.2.20 (Gram–Schmidt). *Let $\mathbf{a}_1, \ldots, \mathbf{a}_m$ in R^n be linearly independent. Then there exist an orthonormal basis $\mathbf{q}_1, \ldots, \mathbf{q}_m$ of $\mathrm{span}(\mathbf{a}_1, \ldots, \mathbf{a}_m)$.*

Proof. The inductive step is the following. Assume that we have constructed orthonormal vectors $\mathbf{q}_1, \ldots, \mathbf{q}_{i-1}$ such that

$$U_{i-1} := \mathrm{span}(\mathbf{q}_1, \ldots, \mathbf{q}_{i-1}) = \mathrm{span}(\mathbf{a}_1, \ldots, \mathbf{a}_{i-1}).$$

Since we have an orthonormal basis for U_{i-1}, we can compute the orthogonal projection of $\mathbf{a}_i$,

$$\mathscr{P}_{U_{i-1}}\mathbf{a}_i = \sum_{j=1}^{i-1} \langle \mathbf{a}_i, \mathbf{q}_j \rangle \, \mathbf{q}_j.$$

And we set

$$\mathbf{b}_i = \mathbf{a}_i - \mathscr{P}_{U_{i-1}}\mathbf{a}_i \quad \text{and} \quad \mathbf{q}_i = \frac{\mathbf{b}_i}{\|\mathbf{b}_i\|}.$$

Here, we used that $\|\mathbf{b}_i\| > 0$; otherwise, $\mathbf{a}_i$ would be equal to its projection $\mathscr{P}_{U_{i-1}}\mathbf{a}_i \in \mathrm{span}(\mathbf{a}_1, \ldots, \mathbf{a}_{i-1})$, which would contradict linear independence of the $\mathbf{a}_j$'s. By the orthogonal decomposition result, $\mathbf{q}_i$ is orthogonal to $\mathrm{span}(\mathbf{q}_1, \ldots, \mathbf{q}_{i-1})$ and, unrolling the calculations above, $\mathbf{a}_i$ is the following linear combination of $\mathbf{q}_1, \ldots, \mathbf{q}_i$:

$$\mathbf{a}_i = \sum_{j=1}^{i-1} \langle \mathbf{a}_i, \mathbf{q}_j \rangle \, \mathbf{q}_j + \left\| \mathbf{a}_i - \sum_{j=1}^{i-1} \langle \mathbf{a}_i, \mathbf{q}_j \rangle \, \mathbf{q}_j \right\| \mathbf{q}_i.$$

Hence $\mathbf{q}_1, \ldots, \mathbf{q}_i$ forms an orthonormal list with $\mathrm{span}(\mathbf{a}_1, \ldots, \mathbf{a}_i) \subseteq \mathrm{span}(\mathbf{q}_1, \ldots, \mathbf{q}_i)$. The opposite inclusion holds by construction. Moreover, because $\mathbf{q}_1, \ldots, \mathbf{q}_i$ are orthonormal, they are linearly independent so we must form a basis of their span so that induction goes through. $\square$

1.2.4 Eigenvalues and eigenvectors

Eigenvalues and eigenvectors are key concepts in many applications. As before, we work on $\mathbb{R}^d$.

Definition 1.2.21 (Eigenvalues and eigenvectors). Let $A \in \mathbb{R}^{d \times d}$ be a square matrix. Then $\lambda \in \mathbb{R}$ is an eigenvalue of A if there exists a non-zero vector $\mathbf{x} \neq \mathbf{0}$ such that

$$A\mathbf{x} = \lambda \mathbf{x}. \tag{1.2.3}$$

The vector $\mathbf{x}$ is referred to as an eigenvector.

As the next example shows, not every matrix has an eigenvalue.

Example 1.2.22 (No real eigenvalues). Set $d = 2$ and let

$$A = \begin{pmatrix} 0 & -1 \\ 1 & 0 \end{pmatrix}.$$

For λ to be an eigenvalue, there must be an non-zero eigenvector $\mathbf{x} = (x_1, x_2)^T$ such that

$$A\mathbf{x} = \lambda\mathbf{x}$$

or put differently

$$-x_2 = \lambda x_1 \quad \text{and} \quad x_1 = \lambda x_2.$$

Replacing these equations into each other, it must be that

$$-x_2 = \lambda^2 x_2 \quad \text{and} \quad x_1 = -\lambda^2 x_1.$$

Because x_1, x_2 cannot both be 0, λ must satisfy the equation

$$\lambda^2 = -1$$

for which there is no real solution.

As we can see from below, $A \in \mathbb{R}^{d \times d}$ has at most d distinct eigenvalues.

Lemma 1.2.23 (Number of eigenvalues). *Let $A \in \mathbb{R}^{d \times d}$ and let $\lambda_1, \ldots, \lambda_m$ be distinct eigenvalues of A with corresponding non-zero eigenvectors $\mathbf{x}_1, \ldots, \mathbf{x}_m$. Then $\mathbf{x}_1, \ldots, \mathbf{x}_m$ are linearly independent. As a result, $m \le d$.*

Proof. Assume by contradiction that $\mathbf{x}_1, \ldots, \mathbf{x}_m$ are linearly dependent. By linear dependence, there is $k \le m$ such that

$$\mathbf{x}_k \in \text{span}(\mathbf{x}_1, \ldots, \mathbf{x}_{k-1})$$

where $\mathbf{x}_1, \ldots, \mathbf{x}_{k-1}$ are linearly independent. In particular, there are $a_1, \ldots, a_{k-1}$ such that

$$\mathbf{x}_k = a_1\mathbf{x}_1 + \cdots + a_{k-1}\mathbf{x}_{k-1}.$$

Transform the equation above in two ways: (1) multiply both sides by λ_k and (2) apply A. Then subtract the resulting equations. That leads to

$$\mathbf{0} = a_1(\lambda_k - \lambda_1)\mathbf{x}_1 + a_{k-1}(\lambda_k - \lambda_{k-1})\mathbf{x}_{k-1}.$$

Because the λ_i's are distinct and $\mathbf{x}_1, \ldots, \mathbf{x}_{k-1}$ are linearly independent, we must have $a_1 = \cdots = a_{k-1} = 0$. But that implies that $\mathbf{x}_k = \mathbf{0}$, a contradiction. For the second claim, if there were more than d distinct eigenvalues, then there would be more than d corresponding linearly independent eigenvectors by the first claim, a contradiction. $\square$

1.2.4.1 Diagonalization of symmetric matrices

We will use the notation $\text{diag}(\lambda_1, \ldots, \lambda_d)$ for the diagonal matrix with diagonal entries $\lambda_1, \ldots, \lambda_d$.

Example 1.2.24 (Diagonal (and similar) matrices). Let A be similar to a matrix $D = \text{diag}(\lambda_1, \ldots, \lambda_d)$ with distinct diagonal entries, that is, there exists a non–singular matrix P such that

$$A = PDP^{-1}.$$

Let $\mathbf{p}_1, \ldots, \mathbf{p}_d$ be the columns of P. Then

$$AP = PD,$$

which implies that

$$A\mathbf{p}_i = \lambda_i \mathbf{p}_i.$$

Theorem 1.2.25. *If A is symmetric, then any two eigenvectors from different eigenspaces are orthogonal.*

Proof. Let $\mathbf{u}_1$ and $\mathbf{u}_2$ be eigenvectors that correspond to distinct eigenvalues, say, λ_1 and λ_2. To show that $\mathbf{u}_1 \cdot \mathbf{u}_2 = 0$, we compute

$$
\begin{aligned}
\lambda_1 \mathbf{u}_1 \cdot \mathbf{u}_2 &= (\lambda_1 \mathbf{u}_1)^T \mathbf{u}_2 = (A\mathbf{u}_1)^T \mathbf{u}_2 && \text{Since } \mathbf{u}_1 \text{ is an eigenvector} \\
&= \left(\mathbf{u}_1^T A^T\right) \mathbf{u}_2 = \mathbf{u}_1^T (A\mathbf{u}_2) && \text{Since } A^T = A \\
&= \mathbf{u}_1^T (\lambda_2 \mathbf{u}_2) && \text{Since } \mathbf{u}_2 \text{ is an eigenvector} \\
&= \lambda_2 \mathbf{u}_1^T \mathbf{u}_2 = \lambda_2 \mathbf{u}_1 \cdot \mathbf{u}_2
\end{aligned}
$$

Hence $(\lambda_1 - \lambda_2) \mathbf{u}_1 \cdot \mathbf{u}_2 = 0$. But $\lambda_1 - \lambda_2 \neq 0$, so $\mathbf{u}_1 \cdot \mathbf{u}_2 = 0$. □

A matrix A is said to be orthogonally diagonalizable if there are an orthogonal matrix P (with $P^{-1} = P^T$) and a diagonal matrix D such that

$$A = PDP^T = PDP^{-1} \qquad (1.2.4)$$

To orthogonally diagonalize an $n \times n$ matrix, we must be able to find n linearly independent and orthonormal eigenvectors. If A is orthogonally diagonalizable, then

$$A^T = \left(PDP^T\right)^T = P^{TT} D^T P^T = PDP^T = A$$

Thus A is symmetric. The following results reveal more properties of a symmetric matrix, which implies that every symmetric matrix is orthogonally diagonalizable.

Theorem 1.2.26 (The spectral theorem for symmetric matrices). *An $n \times n$ symmetric matrix A has the following properties:*

- *A has n real eigenvalues, counting multiplicities.*
- *If λ is an eigenvalue of A with multiplicity k, then the eigenspace for λ is k-dimensional.*
- *The eigenspaces are mutually orthogonal, in the sense that eigenvectors corresponding to different eigenvalues are orthogonal.*
- *A is orthogonally diagonalizable.*

Proof. We only give the idea of proof. If $\mathbf{u}_1$ is a unit eigenvector corresponding to λ_1, now start with $\mathbf{u}_1$ and find $[\mathbf{u}_1, ..., \mathbf{u}_n]$ to be an orthonormal basis by the Gram–Schmidt process and let $U = [\mathbf{u}_1, ..., \mathbf{u}_n]$. Then

$$U^T A U = \begin{pmatrix} \lambda_1 & * \\ 0 & A_1 \end{pmatrix}$$

Note that A is symmetric and we must have

$$U^T A U = \begin{pmatrix} \lambda_1 & 0 \\ 0 & A_1 \end{pmatrix}$$

Now A_1 must be symmetric and have the remaining eigenvalues and continuing this process, we arrive at

$$U^T A U = \begin{pmatrix} \lambda_1 & \cdots & 0 \\ \vdots & \ddots & \vdots \\ 0 & \cdots & \lambda_n \end{pmatrix}$$

This observation will clearly lead to the conclusions of the theorem.   □

Suppose that $A = PDP^{-1}$, where the columns of P are orthonormal eigenvectors $\mathbf{v}_1, ..., \mathbf{v}_n$ of A and the corresponding eigenvalues $\lambda_1, ..., \lambda_n$ are in the diagonal matrix D. Since $P^{-1} = P^T$,

$$A = PDP^T = \begin{pmatrix} \mathbf{v}_1 & \cdots & \mathbf{v}_n \end{pmatrix} \begin{pmatrix} \lambda_1 & \cdots & 0 \\ \vdots & \ddots & \vdots \\ 0 & \cdots & \lambda_n \end{pmatrix} \begin{pmatrix} \mathbf{v}_1^T \\ \vdots \\ \mathbf{v}_n^T \end{pmatrix}$$

$$= \begin{pmatrix} \lambda_1 \mathbf{v}_1 & \cdots & \lambda_n \mathbf{v}_n \end{pmatrix} \begin{pmatrix} \mathbf{v}_1^T \\ \vdots \\ \mathbf{v}_n^T \end{pmatrix}$$

Using the column–row expansion of a product, we can write

$$A = \lambda_1 \mathbf{v}_1 \mathbf{v}_1^T + \lambda_2 \mathbf{v}_2 \mathbf{v}_2^T + \cdots + \lambda_n \mathbf{v}_n \mathbf{v}_n^T. \tag{1.2.5}$$

This representation of A is called a spectral decomposition of A because it breaks up A into pieces determined by the spectrum (eigenvalues) of A. Each $\mathbf{v}_i \mathbf{v}_i^T$ is an $n \times n$ matrix of rank 1. For example, every column of $\lambda_1 \mathbf{v}_1 \mathbf{v}_1^T$ is a multiple of $\mathbf{v}_1$. Furthermore, each matrix $\mathbf{v}_j \mathbf{v}_j^T$ is a **projection matrix** in the sense that for each $\mathbf{x}$ in $\mathbb{R}^n$, the vector $(\mathbf{v}_j \mathbf{v}_j^T) \mathbf{x}$ is the orthogonal projection of $\mathbf{x}$ onto the subspace spanned by $\mathbf{v}_j$.

1.2.4.2 Constrained optimization

The following result is useful for many optimization problems.

Theorem 1.2.27. *Let A be $n \times n$ symmetric matrix A with an orthogonal diagonalization $A = PDP^{-1}$. The columns of P are orthonormal eigenvectors $\mathbf{v}_1, ..., \mathbf{v}_n$ of A. Assume that the diagonals of D are arranged so that $\lambda_1 \leq \lambda_2, ... \leq \lambda_n$. Then*

$$min_{\mathbf{x} \neq 0} \frac{\mathbf{x}^T A \mathbf{x}}{\mathbf{x}^T \mathbf{x}} = \lambda_1$$

is achieved when $\mathbf{x} = \mathbf{v_1}$ *and*

$$max_{\mathbf{x} \neq 0} \frac{\mathbf{x}^T A \mathbf{x}}{\mathbf{x}^T \mathbf{x}} = \lambda_n$$

is achieved when $\mathbf{x} = \mathbf{v_n}$.

Proof. From the assumption, we have

$$A = P \begin{pmatrix} \lambda_1 & & \\ & \ddots & \\ & & \lambda_n \end{pmatrix} P^T$$

and

$$P = \begin{bmatrix} \mathbf{v_1} & \cdots & \mathbf{v_n} \end{bmatrix},$$

Rearranging the terms gives

$$P^T A P = \begin{pmatrix} \lambda_1 & & \\ & \ddots & \\ & & \lambda_n \end{pmatrix}.$$

In addition, note that

$$A\mathbf{v_i} = \lambda_i \mathbf{v_i},$$

$$\mathbf{x} = P\mathbf{y},$$

and

$$\sum x_i^2 = \sum y_i^2.$$

It is easy to see that

$$\frac{\mathbf{x}^T A \mathbf{x}}{\sum x_i^2} = \frac{\mathbf{y}^T P^T A P \mathbf{y}}{\sum y_i^2} = \frac{\lambda_1 y_1^2 + \cdots + \lambda_n y_n^2}{\sum y_i^2}$$

$$\geq \lambda_1 \text{ (equality holds when } \mathbf{y} = \begin{pmatrix} 1 \\ 0 \\ \vdots \\ 0 \end{pmatrix})$$

$$\leq \lambda_n \text{ (equality holds when } \mathbf{y} = \begin{pmatrix} 0 \\ \vdots \\ 0 \\ 1 \end{pmatrix})$$

Note that

$$\mathbf{v_1} = P \begin{pmatrix} 1 \\ 0 \\ \vdots \\ 0 \end{pmatrix}$$

and

$$\mathbf{v_n} = P \begin{pmatrix} 0 \\ 0 \\ \vdots \\ 1 \end{pmatrix}.$$ □

1.3 Linear regression

Linear regression is used frequently in practical applications because of its simplicity. The models depend linearly on their unknown parameters and, therefore, are easier to fit than models which are non-linearly related to their parameters. As a result, the statistical properties of the resulting estimators are easier to determine. In this section, we first discuss QR decomposition, the least-squares problem, and return to linear regression.

1.3.1 QR decomposition

QR decomposition is a useful procedure to solve the linear least squares problem. First, we use the Gram–Schmidt algorithm to obtain an orthonormal basis $\text{span}(\mathbf{a}_1, \ldots, \mathbf{a}_m)$ from a linearly independent set of $\text{span}(\mathbf{a}_1, \ldots, \mathbf{a}_m)$. In order to derive QR decomposition, let

$$A = \begin{pmatrix} | & & | \\ \mathbf{a}_1 & \cdots & \mathbf{a}_m \\ | & & | \end{pmatrix} \quad \text{and} \quad Q = \begin{pmatrix} | & & | \\ \mathbf{q}_1 & \cdots & \mathbf{q}_m \\ | & & | \end{pmatrix},$$

where A, Q are $n \times m$ matrices. The output of the Gram–Schmidt algorithm above can then be written in the following compact form, known as a QR decomposition in Fig. 1.3,

$$A = QR,$$

where column i of the $m \times m$ matrix R contains the coefficients of the linear combination of $\mathbf{q}_j$'s that produces $\mathbf{a}_i$. Q is a $\mathbb{R}^{n \times m}$ matrix with $Q^T Q = I_{m \times m}$. It may be easier to verify $A = QR$ by

$$A^T = R^T Q^T.$$

By the proof of Gram–Schmidt, $\mathbf{a}_i \in \text{span}(\mathbf{q}_1, \ldots, \mathbf{q}_i)$. So column i of R has only zeros below the diagonal. Hence R has a special structure; it is upper triangular.

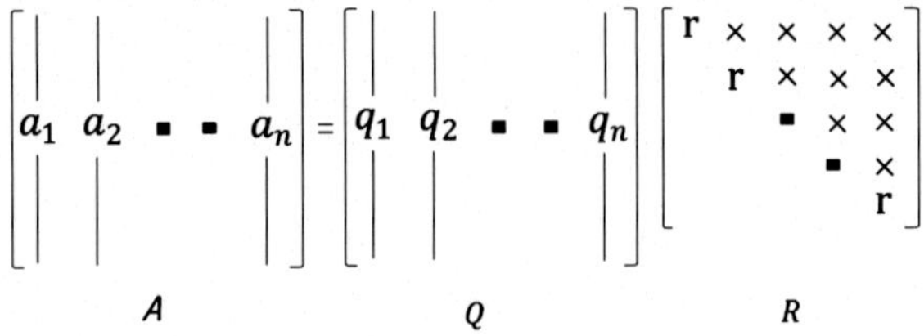

$$\begin{bmatrix} | & | & & | \\ a_1 & a_2 & \bullet\ \bullet & a_n \\ | & | & & | \end{bmatrix} = \begin{bmatrix} | & | & & | \\ q_1 & q_2 & \bullet\ \bullet & q_n \\ | & | & & | \end{bmatrix} \begin{bmatrix} r & \times & \times & \times & \times \\ & r & \times & \times & \times \\ & & \bullet & \times & \times \\ & & & \bullet & \times \\ & & & & r \end{bmatrix}$$

$$\quad\quad\quad A \quad\quad\quad\quad\quad\quad Q \quad\quad\quad\quad\quad\quad R$$

Figure 1.3 QR decomposition.

1.3.2 Least-squares problems

Let $A \in \mathbb{R}^{n \times m}$ be an $n \times m$ matrix and $\mathbf{b} \in \mathbb{R}^n$ be a vector. We try to solve the system $A\mathbf{x} = \mathbf{b}$, which is often inconsistent. We are looking to use the $A\mathbf{x}$ to approximate $\mathbf{b}$. It is reasonable to assume that matrix A has linearly independent columns. If $n = m$, that is, if A is a square matrix, we can use the matrix inverse to solve the system. But we are particularly interested in the over-determined case where $n > m$. We cannot use the matrix inverse then. One possibility to make sense of the problem in that case is to cast it as the least-squares problem:

$$\min_{\mathbf{x} \in \mathbb{R}^m} \|A\mathbf{x} - \mathbf{b}\|.$$

In order to use the orthogonal decomposition result, we write

$$A = \begin{pmatrix} | & & | \\ \mathbf{a}_1 & \cdots & \mathbf{a}_m \\ | & & | \end{pmatrix} = \begin{pmatrix} a_{1,1} & \cdots & a_{1,m} \\ a_{2,1} & \cdots & a_{2,m} \\ \vdots & \ddots & \vdots \\ a_{n,1} & \cdots & a_{n,m} \end{pmatrix} \quad \text{and} \quad \mathbf{b} = \begin{pmatrix} b_1 \\ \vdots \\ b_n \end{pmatrix}$$

Now we seek a linear combination of the columns of A that minimizes the objective

$$\left\| \sum_{j=1}^{m} x_j \mathbf{a}_j - \mathbf{b} \right\|^2 = \sum_{i=1}^{n} \left(\sum_{j=1}^{m} x_j a_{i,j} - b_i \right)^2 = \sum_{i=1}^{n} (\hat{y}_i - b_i)^2,$$

where

$$\hat{y}_i = \sum_{j=1}^{m} x_j a_{i,j}.$$

Now apply our characterization of the orthogonal projection on the column space of A. Let

$$\hat{\mathbf{b}} = \mathscr{P}_{\text{col}(A)}\mathbf{b}.$$

Because $\hat{\mathbf{b}}$ is in the column space of A, the equation $A\mathbf{x} = \hat{\mathbf{b}}$ is consistent and there is an $\hat{x}$ such that

$$A\hat{\mathbf{x}} = \hat{\mathbf{b}}. \tag{1.3.1}$$

Since $\hat{\mathbf{b}}$ is the closed point in $\text{col}(A)$ to $\mathbf{b}$ a vector $\hat{\mathbf{x}}$ is a least-square solution of $A\mathbf{x} = \mathbf{b}$ if and only (1.3.1) holds. The following theorem provides an alternative description of the solution.

Theorem 1.3.1 (Normal equations). *Let $A \in \mathbb{R}^{n \times m}$ be an $n \times m$ matrix with linearly independent columns and let $\mathbf{b} \in \mathbb{R}^n$ be a vector. The solution to the least-squares problem*

$$\min_{\mathbf{x} \in \mathbb{R}^m} \|A\mathbf{x} - \mathbf{b}\|,$$

satisfies

$$A^T A\mathbf{x} = A^T \mathbf{b},$$

which is known as the normal equations.

Proof. Let $U = \text{col}(A) = \text{span}(\mathbf{a}_1, \ldots, \mathbf{a}_m)$. By the best approximation theorem, the orthogonal projection $\hat{\mathbf{b}} = A\hat{\mathbf{x}}$ of $\mathbf{b}$ on U is the unique solution to the least-squares problem. By the orthogonal decomposition, it must satisfy $\langle \mathbf{b} - \hat{\mathbf{b}}, \mathbf{u} \rangle = 0$ for all $\mathbf{u} \in U$. Because the $\mathbf{a}_i$'s are a basis of U, it suffices that $\langle \mathbf{b} - A\hat{\mathbf{x}}, \mathbf{a}_i \rangle = 0$ for all $i \in \{1, \ldots, m\}$. In matrix form,

$$A^T(A\hat{\mathbf{x}} - \mathbf{b}) = \mathbf{0},$$

as claimed, after rearranging. $\qquad\qquad\qquad\qquad\qquad\qquad\qquad\qquad \Box$

When A has linearly independent columns, in view of the QR decomposition, it can be shown that $A^T A$ is invertible and the solution of the normal equation is

$$(A^T A)^{-1} A^T \mathbf{b}.$$

However, that approach has numerical issues, we solve the problem via QR decomposition:

- Construct an orthonormal basis of col(A) through a QR decomposition:

$$A = QR.$$

- Form the orthogonal projection matrix,

$$\mathscr{P}_{\mathrm{col}(A)} = QQ^T.$$

- Apply the projection to $\mathbf{b}$ and observe that $\mathbf{x}^*$ satisfies

$$A\mathbf{x}^* = QQ^T\mathbf{b}.$$

- Use the QR decomposition for A to get

$$QR\mathbf{x}^* = QQ^T\mathbf{b}.$$

- Note $Q^T Q = I_{m \times m}$ and multiply both sides by Q^T to get

$$R\mathbf{x}^* = Q^T\mathbf{b}.$$

- Because R is upper triangular, solving this system for $\mathbf{x}^*$ is straightforward. This is done via back substitution.

Theorem 1.3.2 (Least squares via QR). *Let $A \in \mathbb{R}^{n \times m}$ be an $n \times m$ matrix with linearly independent columns, let $\mathbf{b} \in \mathbb{R}^n$ be a vector, and let $A = QR$ be a QR decomposition of A, where Q is a $\mathbb{R}^{n \times m}$ matrix with $Q^T Q = I_{m \times m}$ and R is upper triangular. The solution to the least-squares problem*

$$\min_{\mathbf{x} \in \mathbb{R}^m} \|A\mathbf{x} - \mathbf{b}\|,$$

satisfies

$$R\mathbf{x}^* = Q^T\mathbf{b}.$$

1.3.3 Linear regression

Given input data points $\{(\mathbf{x}_i, y_i)\}_{i=1}^n$ with each $\mathbf{x}_i = (x_{i1}, ..., x_{id})^T$, we seek an affine function to fit the data. The common approach involves finding coefficients β_j's that minimize the criterion

$$\sum_{i=1}^n (y_i - \hat{y}_i)^2,$$

where

$$\hat{y}_i = \beta_0 + \sum_{j=1}^{d} \beta_j x_{ij}$$

can be viewed as the predicted values of the linear model with coefficients β_j. The minimization problem can be formulated in matrix form. Let

$$\mathbf{y} = \begin{pmatrix} y_1 \\ y_2 \\ \vdots \\ y_n \end{pmatrix}, \qquad A = \begin{pmatrix} 1 & \mathbf{x}_1^T \\ 1 & \mathbf{x}_2^T \\ \vdots & \vdots \\ 1 & \mathbf{x}_n^T \end{pmatrix} \quad \text{and} \quad \boldsymbol{\beta} = \begin{pmatrix} \beta_0 \\ \beta_1 \\ \vdots \\ \beta_d \end{pmatrix}.$$

Then the problem is transformed to

$$\min_{\boldsymbol{\beta}} \|\mathbf{y} - A\boldsymbol{\beta}\|^2.$$

This is exactly the least-squares problem that we discuss in the last section.

1.4 Principal component analysis

Principal component analysis is commonly used for dimensionality reduction by projecting each data point onto only the first few principal components to obtain lower-dimensional data while preserving as much of the data's variation as possible. Its underlying mathematics can be explained with singular value decomposition.

1.4.1 Singular value decomposition

Let A be an $m \times n$ matrix. Then $A^T A$ is symmetric and can be orthogonally diagonalized. Let $\mathbf{v}_1, \ldots, \mathbf{v}_n$ be an orthonormal basis for $\mathbb{R}^n$ consisting of eigenvectors of $A^T A$, and let $\lambda_1, \ldots, \lambda_n$ be the associated eigenvalues of $A^T A$. Then, for $1 \le i \le n$,

$$
\begin{aligned}
\|A\mathbf{v}_i\|^2 = (A\mathbf{v}_i)^T A\mathbf{v}_i &= \mathbf{v}_i^T A^T A\mathbf{v}_i \\
&= \mathbf{v}_i^T (\lambda_i \mathbf{v}_i) && \text{since } \mathbf{v}_i \text{ is an eigenvectors of } A^T A \\
&= \lambda_i && \text{since } \mathbf{v}_i \text{ is a unit vector}
\end{aligned}
$$

$$(1.4.1)$$

So the eigenvalues of A are all non-negative. By renumbering, if necessary, we may assume that the eigenvalues are arranged so that

$$\lambda_1 \geq \lambda_2 \geq \cdots \lambda_n \geq 0.$$

The singular values of A are the square roots of the eigenvalues of $A^T A$, denoted by $\sigma_1, ..., \sigma_n$, and they are arranged in decreasing order. That is, $\sigma_i = \sqrt{\lambda_i}$ for $1 \leq i \leq n$. The singular values of A are the lengths of the vectors $A\mathbf{v}_1, ..., A\mathbf{v}_n$.

Theorem 1.4.1. *If an $m \times n$ matrix A has r non-zero singular values, $\sigma_1, ..., \sigma_r \geq 0$ with $\sigma_{r+1} = \cdots = \sigma_n = 0$, then the dimension of col$(A) = r$.*

Proof. Let $\mathbf{v}_1, ..., \mathbf{v}_n$ be an orthonormal basis of $\mathbb{R}^n$ of $A^T A$, ordered so that the corresponding eigenvalues of $A^T A$ satisfy $\lambda_1 \geq \cdots \lambda_n$. Then for $i \neq j$,

$$(A\mathbf{v}_i)^T (A\mathbf{v}_j) = \mathbf{v}_i^T A^T A\mathbf{v}_j = \mathbf{v}_i^T (\lambda_j \mathbf{v}_j) = 0$$

since $\mathbf{v}_i$ and $\lambda_j \mathbf{v}_j$ are orthogonal. Thus $\{A\mathbf{v}_1, ..., A\mathbf{v}_n\}$ is an orthogonal set. Let r be the number of non-zero singular values of A; that is, r is the number of non-zero eigenvalues of $A^T A$. We see that $A\mathbf{v}_i \neq \mathbf{0}$ if and only if $1 \leq i \leq r$. Then $[A\mathbf{v}_1, ..., A\mathbf{v}_r]$ is linearly independent and clearly is in col(A). Furthermore, for any $\mathbf{y}$ in col(A)—say, $\mathbf{y} = A\mathbf{x}$—we may write $\mathbf{x} = c_1 \mathbf{v}_1 + \cdots + c_n \mathbf{v}_n$, and

$$\begin{aligned} \mathbf{y} = A\mathbf{x} &= c_1 A\mathbf{v}_1 + \cdots + c_r A\mathbf{v}_r + c_{r+1} A\mathbf{v}_{r+1} + \cdots + c_n A\mathbf{v}_n \\ &= c_1 A\mathbf{v}_1 + \cdots + c_r A\mathbf{v}_r + \mathbf{0} + \cdots + 0. \end{aligned}$$

Thus y is in span of $\{A\mathbf{v}_1, ..., A\mathbf{v}_r\}$, which shows that $\{A\mathbf{v}_1, ..., A\mathbf{v}_r\}$ is an (orthogonal) basis for col(A). Hence the dimension of col$(A) = r$. $\square$

The decomposition of A involves an $m \times n$ diagonal matrix Σ of the form

$$\Sigma = \begin{bmatrix} D & 0 \\ 0 & 0 \end{bmatrix}$$

where D is an $r \times r$ diagonal matrix for some r not exceeding the smaller of m and n. (If r equals m or n or both, some or all of the zero matrices will not appear.)

Theorem 1.4.2 (The singular value decomposition). *Let A be an $m \times n$ matrix with the dimension of col$(A) = r$. Then there exists an $m \times n$ matrix Σ,* *where the diagonal entries in D are the first r singular values of A, $\sigma_1 \geq \sigma_2 \geq \cdots \geq \sigma_r \geq 0$, and there exist an $m \times m$ orthogonal matrix U and an $n \times n$ orthogonal matrix V such that*

$$A = U \sum V^T.$$

Any factorization $A = U \sum V^T$, with U and V orthogonal and $\sum$, is called a singular value decomposition **SVD** of A. The matrices U and V are not unique, but the diagonal entries of $\sum$ are necessarily the singular values of A. The column of U in such a decomposition are called **left singular vectors** of A, and the column of V are called **right singular vectors** of A. This type of matrix factorization is illustrated in Fig. 1.4.

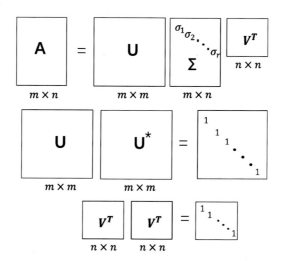

Figure 1.4 Singular value decomposition visualization.

Proof. Let λ_i be and $\mathbf{v}_i$ be as in the proof of Theorem 1.4.1. Then $\sigma_i = \sqrt{\lambda_i} = \|A\mathbf{v}_i\| \geq 0$ for $1 \leq i \leq r$, and $\{A\mathbf{v}_1, ..., A\mathbf{v}_r\}$ is an orthogonal basis for col(A). For $1 \leq i \leq r$, define

$$\mathbf{u}_i = \frac{1}{\|A\mathbf{v}_i\|} A\mathbf{v}_i = \frac{1}{\sigma_i} A\mathbf{v}_i$$

so that

$$A\mathbf{v}_i = \sigma_i \mathbf{u_i} \quad (1 \leq i \leq r). \tag{1.4.2}$$

Then $\mathbf{u}_1, ...\mathbf{u}_r$ is an orthonormal basis of $\mathrm{lcol}(A)$. Extend this set to an orthonormal basis $\mathbf{u}_1, ...\mathbf{u}_m$ of $\mathbb{R}^m$, and let

$$U = \begin{pmatrix} \mathbf{u}_1 & \mathbf{u}_2 & \cdots & \mathbf{u}_m \end{pmatrix} \quad \text{and} \quad V = \begin{pmatrix} \mathbf{v}_1 & \mathbf{v}_2 & \cdots & \mathbf{v}_n \end{pmatrix}.$$

Then U and V are orthogonal matrices and

$$AV = \begin{bmatrix} A\mathbf{v}_1 & \cdots & A\mathbf{v}_r & 0 & \cdots & 0 \end{bmatrix}$$
$$= \begin{bmatrix} \sigma_1\mathbf{u}_1 & \cdots & \sigma_r\mathbf{u}_r & 0 & \cdots & 0 \end{bmatrix}.$$

Let D be the diagonal matrix with diagonal entries $\sigma_1, ..., \sigma_r$. Then

$$U\sum = \begin{pmatrix} \mathbf{u}_1 & \mathbf{u}_2 & \cdots & \mathbf{u}_m \end{pmatrix} \left(\begin{array}{cccc|c} \sigma_1 & & & 0 & \\ & \sigma_2 & & & 0 \\ & & \ddots & & \\ 0 & & & \sigma_r & \\ \hline & & 0 & & 0 \end{array} \right)$$

$$= \begin{pmatrix} \sigma_1\mathbf{u}_1 & \cdots & \sigma_r\mathbf{u}_r & 0\cdots & 0 \end{pmatrix} = AV.$$

Since V is an orthogonal matrices, $U\sum V^T = AVV^T = A$. $\qquad\qquad \square$

1.4.2 Low-rank matrix approximations

In this section, we discuss low-rank approximations of matrices. We first introduce matrix norms, which allow us in particular to talk about the distance between two matrices.

Definition 1.4.3 (Induced norm). The 2-norm of a matrix $A \in \mathbb{R}^{n \times m}$ is

$$\|A\|_2 = \max_{0 \neq \mathbf{x} \in \mathbb{R}^m} \frac{\|A\mathbf{x}\|}{\|\mathbf{x}\|} = \max_{\mathbf{x} \neq 0, \|\mathbf{x}\|=1} \|A\mathbf{x}\| = \max_{\mathbf{x} \neq 0, \|\mathbf{x}\|=1} \mathbf{x}^T A^T A \mathbf{x} \qquad (1.4.3)$$

Let $A \in \mathbb{R}^{n \times m}$ be a matrix with SVD,

$$A = \sum_{j=1}^{r} \sigma_j \mathbf{u}_j \mathbf{v}_j^T. \qquad (1.4.4)$$

For $k < r$, truncate the sum at the kth term

$$A_k = \sum_{j=1}^{k} \sigma_j \mathbf{u}_j \mathbf{v}_j^T. \qquad (1.4.5)$$

The rank of A_k is exactly k. Indeed, by construction:

1. the vectors $\{\mathbf{u}_j : j = 1, \ldots, k\}$ are orthonormal, and
2. since $\sigma_j > 0$ for $j = 1, \ldots, k$ and the vectors $\{\mathbf{v}_j : j = 1, \ldots, k\}$ are orthonormal, $\{\mathbf{u}_j : j = 1, \ldots, k\}$ spans the column space of A_k.

Lemma 1.4.4 (Matrix norms and singular values). *Let $A \in \mathbb{R}^{n \times m}$ be a matrix with SVD,*

$$A = \sum_{j=1}^{r} \sigma_j \mathbf{u}_j \mathbf{v}_j^T,$$

where recalling that $\sigma_1 \geq \sigma_2 \geq \cdots \sigma_r > 0$ and letting A_k be the truncation defined above. Then

$$\|A - A_k\|_2^2 = \sigma_{k+1}^2.$$

Proof. For any $\mathbf{x} \neq 0$ and $\|\mathbf{x}\| = 1$,

$$\|(A - A_k)\mathbf{x}\|^2 = \left\| \sum_{j=k+1}^{r} \sigma_j \mathbf{u}_j (\mathbf{v}_j^T \mathbf{x}) \right\|^2 = \sum_{j=k+1}^{r} \sigma_j^2 \langle \mathbf{v}_j, \mathbf{x} \rangle^2$$

$$= \mathbf{x}^T (A - A_k)^T (A - A_k) \mathbf{x}.$$

Because the σ_j's are in decreasing order, this is maximized when $\langle \mathbf{v}_j, \mathbf{x} \rangle = 1$ if $j = k + 1$ and 0 otherwise. In view of Theorem 1.2.27, that is, we take $\mathbf{x} = \mathbf{v}_{k+1}$ and the norm is then σ_{k+1}^2, as claimed. $\qquad\square$

With additional effort, we can prove the following theorem [5].

Theorem 1.4.5 (Eckart–Young–Mirsky theorem; Low-rank approximation in the induced norm). *Let $A \in \mathbb{R}^{n \times m}$ be a matrix with SVD,*

$$A = \sum_{j=1}^{r} \sigma_j \mathbf{u}_j \mathbf{v}_j^T,$$

and let A_k be the truncation defined above with $k < r$. For any matrix $B \in \mathbb{R}^{n \times m}$ of rank at most k,

$$\|A - A_k\|_2 \leq \|A - B\|_2. \tag{1.4.6}$$

1.4.3 Principal component analysis

1.4.3.1 Covariance matrix

To prepare for principal component analysis, let $[\mathbf{X}_1 \cdots \mathbf{X}_N]$ be a $p \times N$ matrix of observation, such as described above. The **sample mean** M of the observation vectors $\mathbf{X}_1, \ldots, \mathbf{X}_n$ is given by

$$\mathbf{M} = \frac{1}{N} \left(\mathbf{X}_1 + \cdots + \mathbf{X}_N \right).$$

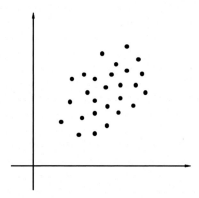

Figure 1.5 A scatter plot of observation vectors $\mathbf{X}_1, \ldots, \mathbf{X}_N$.

For the data in Fig. 1.5, the sample mean is the point in the "center" of the scatter plot. For $k = 1, \ldots, N$, let

$$\hat{\mathbf{X}}_k = \mathbf{X}_k - \mathbf{M}.$$

The columns of the $p \times N$ matrix

$$B = \left[\hat{\mathbf{X}}_1, \hat{\mathbf{X}}_2, \cdots \hat{\mathbf{X}}_N \right]$$

have a zero sample mean, and B is said to be in **mean–deviation form**. When the sample mean is subtracted from the data in Fig. 1.5, the resulting scatter plot has the form in Fig. 1.6.

The **(sample) covariance matrix** is the $p \times p$ matrix S defined by

$$S = \frac{1}{N-1} BB^T.$$

Since any matrix of the form BB^T is positive semidefinite, so is S.

1.4.3.2 Principal component analysis

Now assume that the columns of the $p \times N$ data matrix

$$X = [\mathbf{X}_1, \mathbf{X}_2, \cdots \mathbf{X}_N]$$

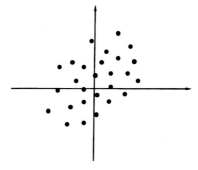

Figure 1.6 Weight-height data in mean-deviation form.

is already in mean-deviation form. The goal of principal component analysis (PCA) is to find k, $(k \leq p)$ orthonormal vectors $\mathbf{v}_1$, ..., $\mathbf{v}_k$, (top k principal components) that maximize the objective function,

$$\frac{1}{N}\sum_{i=1}^{N}\sum_{j=1}^{k}\langle \mathbf{X}_i \cdot \mathbf{v_j}\rangle^2, \tag{1.4.7}$$

$\langle \mathbf{X_i} \cdot \mathbf{v_j}\rangle$ is the length of projection of $\mathbf{X}_i$ on $\mathbf{v_j}$.

On the other hand, for each j, it is easy to see that

$$\mathbf{v_j}^T X X^T \mathbf{v_j} = (X^T \mathbf{v_j})^T (X^T \mathbf{v_j}) = \sum_{i=1}^{N}\langle \mathbf{X_i} \cdot \mathbf{v_j}\rangle^2 \tag{1.4.8}$$

where XX^T is a $p \times p$ matrix. As a result, for each $j \leq k$, the variance-maximization problem can be rephrased as

$$\operatorname{argmax}_{\mathbf{v}:||\mathbf{v}||=1}\mathbf{v_j}^T X X^T \mathbf{v_j}. \tag{1.4.9}$$

Assume that

$$XX^T = V\operatorname{diag}(\lambda_1, ..., \lambda_p)V^T, \text{ or } V^T XX^T V = (\lambda_1, ..., \lambda_p).$$

In view of Theorem 1.4.5, we conclude that the optimal choice of the first k eigenvectors of XX^T corresponding to the first k largest eigenvalues, which are also the first k columns of $V = [\mathbf{v}_1, \cdots, \mathbf{v}_p]$ of the covariance matrix XX^T, which are called the principal components of the data (in the matrices of observations). The first principal component is the eigenvector corresponding to the largest eigenvalue of XX^T, the second principal component is the eigenvector corresponding to the second largest eigenvalue, and so on.

The orthogonal $p \times p$ matrix $V = [\mathbf{v}_1, \cdots, \mathbf{v}_p]$ that determines a change of variable, $\mathbf{x} = V\mathbf{y}$, or

$$\begin{pmatrix} x_1 \\ x_2 \\ \vdots \\ x_p \end{pmatrix} = \begin{pmatrix} \mathbf{v}_1 & \mathbf{v}_2 & \cdots & \mathbf{v}_p \end{pmatrix} \begin{pmatrix} y_1 \\ y_2 \\ \vdots \\ y_p \end{pmatrix}$$

with the property that the new variables $y_1, \ldots, y_p$ are uncorrelated and are arranged in order of decreasing variance. Indeed, we have

$$\mathbf{x}^T XX^T \mathbf{x} = \mathbf{y}^T V^T XX^T V\mathbf{y} = \mathbf{y}^T \text{diag}(\lambda_1, \ldots, \lambda_p)\mathbf{y} = \sum_1^p \lambda_i y_i^2.$$

The orthogonal change of variable $\mathbf{x} = V\mathbf{y}$ that each observation vector $\mathbf{x}$ receives a "new name" $\mathbf{y}$, such that $\mathbf{x} = V\mathbf{y}$. Notice that $\mathbf{y} = V^{-1}\mathbf{x} = V^T\mathbf{x}$. Let $v_{1i}, \ldots, v_{pi}$ be the entries in $\mathbf{v}_i$. Since $\mathbf{v}_i^T$ the ith row of V^T the equation $\mathbf{y} = V^T\mathbf{x}$ shows that

$$y_i = \mathbf{v}_i^T \mathbf{x} = v_{1i}x_1 + v_{2i}x_2 + \cdots + v_{pi}x_p.$$

Thus y_i is a linear combination of the original variables $x_1, \ldots, x_p$, using the entries the eigenvector $\mathbf{v}_i$ as weights, which are called loadings.

1.4.3.3 Total variance

Given the columns of the $p \times N$ data matrix and assume it is already in mean–deviation form,

$$X = [\mathbf{X}_1, \mathbf{X}_2, \cdots \mathbf{X}_N],$$

and let covariance matrix S,

$$S = \frac{1}{N-1} XX^T.$$

The entries in $S = [S_{ij}]$, for $j = 1, \ldots, p$, the diagonal entry s_{jj} in S is called the **variance** of x_j, which is the first jth row of X. The variance of x_j measures the spread of the values of x_j. The total variance of the data is the sum of the variances on the diagonal of S. In general, the sum of the diagonal entries of a square matrix S is called the trace of the matrix, written $tr\,(S)$. Thus

$$\text{Total Variance} = tr\,(S)$$

Note that if

$$XX^T = V\text{diag}(\lambda_1, ..., \lambda_p)\,V^T, \ \text{or} \ V^T XX^T V = \text{diag}(\lambda_1, ..., \lambda_p),$$

then

$$\text{tr}\,(S) = \frac{1}{N-1}\sum_1^p \lambda_j.$$

because $\text{tr}\left(VSV^T\right) = \text{tr}\,(S)$. Thus the fraction of the variances of the first k term truncation is

$$\frac{\sum_1^k \lambda_j}{\sum_1^p \lambda_j}.$$

CHAPTER 2

Probability

Contents

2.1 Introduction

Probability concerns the study of uncertainty and is often used to quantify uncertainty in the data analysis and prediction, uncertainty in the data science and machine learning model. Probability is a key mathematical concept that is essential for modeling and understanding various model performances. Data science and machine learning rely heavily on probabilistic models. This section will provide the necessary probability background for learning and understanding data science concepts. It will introduce the concept of probability, provide an overview of probability distribution, conditional probability, random variables, and describe how to compute

Copyright © 2023 China Science Publishing &
Media Ltd. Published by Elsevier Inc.
All rights reserved.

expectation and variance. In addition, it includes maximum likelihood estimation. Further, probability and their applications can be found in many references [3,6,7].

2.2 Probability distribution

A probability distribution is the mathematical function that gives the probabilities of occurrence of different possible outcomes for an experiment. We will discuss both discrete and continuous probability distributions.

2.2.1 Probability axioms

2.2.1.1 Sample spaces and events

We start with an **experiment,** which is any activity or process whose outcome is subject to uncertainty. In general, the word *experiment* may represent a planned or carefully controlled laboratory testing situation. In probability, we use it here in a much wider sense. Thus experiments that may be of interest include tossing a coin once or several times, selecting a card or cards from a deck, weighing a loaf of bread, ascertaining the commuting time from home to work on a particular morning, obtaining blood types from a group of individuals, or measuring blood pressures of human beings.

Definition 2.2.1. The **sample space** of an experiment, denoted by S, is the set of all possible outcomes of that experiment.

In probability, we will be interested not only in the individual outcomes of S but also in various collections of outcomes from S. In fact, it is often more meaningful to study the collection of outcomes.

Definition 2.2.2. An **event** is any collection (subset) of outcomes contained in the sample space S. An event is **simple** if it consists of exactly one outcome and **compound** if it consists of more than one outcome.

Definition 2.2.3. Given an experiment and a sample space S, the **probability distribution** is a function which assigns to each event A a number $P(A)$, called the **probability of the event** A, which will give a precise measure of the chance that A will occur. The probability assignments should satisfy the following axioms (basic properties) of probability:
- For any event A, $1 \geq P(A) \geq 0$
- $P(S) = 1$

- If $A_1, A_2, A_3, \ldots$ is an infinite collection of disjoint events, then

$$P(A_1 \cup A_2 \cup A_3 \cup \cdots) = \sum_{i=1}^{\infty} P(A_i)$$

- For any event A, $P(A) + P(A') = 1$, from which $P(A) = 1 - P(A')$
- When events A and B are mutually exclusive, $P(A \cup B) = P(A) + P(B)$
- For any two events A and B,

$$P(A \cup B) = P(A) + P(B) - P(A \cap B)$$

Example 2.2.4. In a simply and yet common experiment consisting of N outcomes, it is reasonable to assign equal probabilities to all N simple events. That is, if there are N equally likely outcomes, the probability for each is $1/N$. Now consider an event A, with $N(A)$ denoting the number of outcomes contained in A and we have

$$P(A) = \frac{N(A)}{N}$$

2.2.2 Conditional probability

Conditional probability is defined as the likelihood of an event or outcome occurring, based on the occurrence of a previous event or outcome. The conditional probability is expressed as a ratio of unconditional probabilities: The numerator is the probability of the intersection of the two events, whereas the denominator is the probability of the conditioning event B. Given that B has occurred, the relevant sample space is no longer S but consists of outcomes in B; A has occurred if and only if one of the outcomes in the intersection occurred, so the conditional probability of A given B is proportional to $P(A \cap B)$. A Venn diagram illuminates this relationship in Fig. 2.1.

Definition 2.2.5. For any two events A and B with $P(B) > 0$, the **conditional probability of A given that B has occurred** is defined by

$$P(A \mid B) = \frac{P(A \cap B)}{P(B)} \qquad (2.2.1)$$

Conditional probability gives a rise to the multiplication rule,

$$P(A \cap B) = P(A \mid B) \cdot P(B).$$

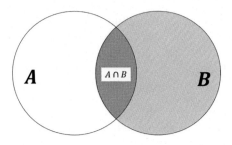

Figure 2.1 Conditional probability.

This rule is important because it is often the case that $P(A \cap B)$ is desired, whereas both $P(B)$ and $P(A \mid B)$ can be specified from the problem description.

Often it is interesting to know if A and B are independent events, meaning that the occurrence or nonoccurrence of one event has no bearing on the chance that the other will occur.

Definition 2.2.6. Two events A and B are **independent** if $P(A \mid B) = P(A)$ (or $P(A \cap B) = P(A) \cdot P(B)$), and are **dependent** otherwise.

The notion of independence of two events can be extended to collections of more than two events.

Definition 2.2.7. Events $A_1, \ldots, A_n$ are **mutually independent** if for every $k(k = 2, 3, \ldots, n)$ and every subset of indices $i_1, i_2, \ldots, i_k$,

$$P\left(A_{i_1} \cap A_{i_2} \cap \ldots \cap A_{i_k}\right) = P\left(A_{i_1}\right) \cdot P\left(A_{i_2}\right) \cdots \cdots P\left(A_{i_k}\right).$$

2.2.3 Discrete random variables

A random variable is understood as a measurable function defined on a probability space that maps from the sample space to the real numbers. It is often convenient to associate each outcome of an experiment with a number. A random variable is described informally as a variable whose values depend on outcomes of a random phenomenon as shown in Fig. 2.2.

Definition 2.2.8. For a given sample space S of some experiment, a **random variable** is any rule that associates a number with each outcome in S. Mathematically, a random variable is a function whose domain is the sample space and whose range is the set of real numbers.

There are two different types of random variables.

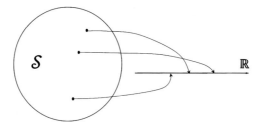

Figure 2.2 A random variable.

Definition 2.2.9. A **discrete** random variable is a random variable whose possible values either constitute a finite set or else can be listed in an infinite sequence. A random variable is **continuous** if *both* of the following apply:
1. Its set of possible values consists all numbers in a single interval on the number line.
2. $P(X = c) = 0$ for any possible value individual c.

In practice, we wish to know the total probability of 1 is distributed among (allocated to) the various possible X values. A probability mass function (pmf) is a function that gives the probability that a discrete random variable is exactly equal to some value. The pmf of a probability distribution specifies the probability of observing that value when the experiment is performed.

Definition 2.2.10. The **probability distribution** or **probability mass function** (pmf) of a discrete random variable is defined for every number x by

$$p(x) = P(X = x) = P(\text{all } s \in S : X(s) = x).$$

Definition 2.2.11. The cumulative distribution function (cdf) $F(x)$ of a discrete random variable X with pmf $p(x)$ is defined for every number x by

$$F(x) = P(X \leq x) = \sum_{y:y\leq x} p(y). \tag{2.2.2}$$

Example 2.2.12. In many cases, there are only two possible values associated with the random variable. Any random variable whose only possible values are 0 and 1 is called a **Bernoulli random variable**. Given Bernoulli experiments with outcomes: S (success) and F (failure). The binomial random variable X associated with independent Bernoulli experiment consisting of n trials is defined as

$$X = \text{the number of S's among the } n \text{ trials.}$$

The probability of success is constant p from trial to trial. The pmf of X has the form

$$b(x; n, p) = \begin{cases} \binom{n}{x}p^x(1-p)^{n-x}, & x = 0, 1, 2, 3, \ldots, n \\ 0, & \text{otherwise} \end{cases}$$

The cdf of X has the form

$$B(x; n, p) = P(X \le x) = \sum_{y \le x} b(x; n, p) = \sum_{y=0}^{x} \binom{n}{y}p^x(1-p)^{n-x}. \qquad (2.2.3)$$

Example 2.2.13. The Poisson distribution is a discrete probability distribution that describes the probability of a given number of events occurring in a fixed interval of time or space if these events occur with a known constant mean rate and independently of the time since the last event. A discrete random variable X is said to have a Poisson distribution with parameter μ if the pmf of X is the following. The pmf of X has the form

$$p(x; \mu) = \frac{e^{-\mu}\mu^x}{x!}, \quad x = 0, 1, 2, 3, \ldots.$$

2.2.3.1 The expected value and variance of X

The expected value of a random variable X is a generalization of the weighted average, and is intuitively the arithmetic mean of a large number of independent realizations of X.

Definition 2.2.14. Let X be a discrete random variable with set of possible values D and pmf $p(x)$. The **expected value** or **mean value** of X, denoted by $E(X)$ or μ_X or just μ, is

$$E(X) = \mu_X = \sum_{x \in D} x \cdot p(x).$$

Example 2.2.15. Let $X = 1$ be a Bernoulli random variable with pmf $p(1) = p$, $p(0) = 1 - p$, and from which $E(X) = 0 \times p(0) + 1 \times p(1) = p$. That is, the expected value of X is just the probability that X takes on the value 1.

Sometimes we need to compute the expected value of some function $h(X)$ rather than on just $E(X)$.

Proposition 2.2.16. *If the random variable X has a set of possible values D and pmf $p(x)$, then the expected value of any function $h(X)$, denoted by $E[h(X)]$ or $\mu_{h(X)}$, is computed by*

$$E[h(X)] = \sum_{D} h(x) \cdot p(x).$$

In particular,

$$E(aX + b) = a \cdot E(X) + b.$$

Variances measure how far a set of numbers is spread out from their average value.

Definition 2.2.17. Let X have pmf $p(x)$ and expected value μ. Then the **variance** of X, denoted by $V(X)$ or σ_X^2, or just σ^2, is

$$V(X) = \sum_{D} (x - \mu)^2 \cdot p(x) = E\left[(X - \mu)^2\right].$$

The **standard deviation** (SD) of X is

$$\sigma_X = \sqrt{\sigma_X^2}.$$

It is easy to verify the following.

Proposition 2.2.18.

$$V(aX + b) = \sigma_{aX+b}^2 = a^2 \cdot \sigma_X^2 \quad \text{and} \quad \sigma_{aX+b} = |a| \cdot \sigma_x.$$

In particular,

$$\sigma_{aX} = |a| \cdot \sigma_X, \quad \sigma_{X+b} = \sigma_X. \tag{2.2.4}$$

It is useful to know expected values and variances of the two important distributions.

Proposition 2.2.19.
- If X is a binomial random variable with parameters n, p, then, $E(X) = np$, $V(X) = np(1 - p)$, $\sigma_X = \sqrt{np(1 - p)}$.
- If X is a Poisson distribution with parameter μ, then $E(X) = \mu$, $V(X) = \mu$.

2.2.4 Continues random variables

A random variable X is continuous if possible values comprise either a single interval on the number line or a union of disjoint intervals.

Definition 2.2.20. Let X be a continuous random variable. Then a **probability distribution** or **probability density function** (pdf) of X is a function $f(x)$ such that for any two numbers a and b with $a \leq b$,

$$P(a \leq X \leq b) = \int_a^b f(x)dx.$$

That is, the probability that X takes on a value in the interval $[a, b]$ is the area above this interval and under the graph of the density function, as illustrated in Fig. 2.3. $f(x)$ must satisfy the following two conditions:

1. $f(x) \geq 0$ for all x
2. $\int_{-\infty}^{\infty} f(x)dx = $ Total area under the entire graph of $f(x)$
   $= 1$

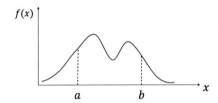

Figure 2.3 $P(a \leq X \leq b) = $ the area under the density curve between a and b.

2.2.4.1 Expected values and variances

We define the expected values and variances for continuous random variables as for discrete variables.

Definition 2.2.21. The **expected** or **mean value** of a continuous random variable X with pdf $f(x)$ is

$$\mu_X = E(X) = \int_{-\infty}^{\infty} x \cdot f(x)dx.$$

Definition 2.2.22. The **variance** of a continuous random variable X with pdf $f(x)$ and the variance is μ is

$$\sigma_X^2 = V(X) = \int_{-\infty}^{\infty} (x - \mu)^2 \cdot f(x)dx = E\left[(X - \mu)^2\right].$$

The **standard deviation** (SD) of X is $\sigma_X = \sqrt{V(X)}$.

It is easy to verify the following.

Proposition 2.2.23. *The expected values and variance have the following properties:*
- *If X is a continuous random variable with pdf $f(x)$ and $h(X)$ is any function of X, then*

$$E[h(X)] = \mu_{h(X)} = \int_{-\infty}^{\infty} h(x) \cdot f(x)\,dx$$

-

$$V(X) = E\left(X^2\right) - [E(X)]^2$$

Definition 2.2.24. X is said to have an **exponential distribution** with parameter $\lambda (\lambda > 0)$ if the pdf of X is

$$f(x; \lambda) = \begin{cases} \lambda e^{-\lambda x} & x \geq 0 \\ 0 & \text{otherwise} \end{cases} \qquad (2.2.5)$$

The expected value of an exponentially distributed random variable X is

$$E(X) = \int_0^{\infty} x \lambda e^{-\lambda x}\,dx.$$

Obtaining this expected value necessitates doing an integration by parts. The variance of X can be computed using the fact that $V(X) = E\left(X^2\right) - [E(X)]^2$. The determination of $E\left(X^2\right)$ requires integrating by parts twice in succession. The results of these integrations are as follows:

$$\mu = \frac{1}{\lambda} \qquad \sigma^2 = \frac{1}{\lambda^2}.$$

Both the mean and standard deviation of the exponential distribution equal $1/\lambda$.

2.2.4.2 The normal distribution

Normal distributions are often used in the natural and social sciences to represent real-valued random variables whose distributions are not known.

Definition 2.2.25. A continuous random variable X is said to have a **normal distribution** with parameters μ and σ (or μ and σ^2), where

$-\infty < \mu < \infty$ and $0 < \sigma$, if the pdf of X is

$$f(x; \mu, \sigma) = \frac{1}{\sqrt{2\pi}\sigma} e^{-(x-\mu)^2/(2\sigma^2)} \quad -\infty < x < \infty. \quad (2.2.6)$$

This is illustrated in Fig. 2.4.

The computation of $P(a \leq X \leq b)$ when X is a normal random variable with parameters μ and σ requires evaluating

$$\int_a^b \frac{1}{\sqrt{2\pi}\sigma} e^{-(x-\mu)^2/(2\sigma^2)} dx. \quad (2.2.7)$$

Definition 2.2.26. The normal distribution with parameter values $\mu = 0$ and $\sigma = 1$ is called the standard normal distribution. A random variable having a standard normal distribution is called a **standard normal random variable** and will be denoted by Z. The pdf of Z is

$$f(z; 0, 1) = \frac{1}{\sqrt{2\pi}} e^{-z^2/2} \quad -\infty < z < \infty.$$

The graph of $f(z; 0, 1)$ is called the standard normal (or z) curve, as is shown in Fig. 2.4. Its inflection points are at 1 and -1. The cdf of Z is $P(Z \leq z) = \int_{-\infty}^z f(y; 0, 1) dy$, which we will denote by $\Phi(z)$.

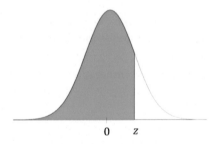

$$0 \quad z$$

Figure 2.4 Standard normal cumulative areas.

A normal distribution, $X \sim N\left(\mu, \sigma^2\right)$ can be converted to the **standardized variable** is $(X - \mu)/\sigma$.

Proposition 2.2.27. *If X has a normal distribution with mean μ and standard deviation σ, then*

$$Z = \frac{X - \mu}{\sigma}$$

has a standard normal distribution. Thus

$$P(a \le X \le b) = P\left(\frac{a-\mu}{\sigma} \le Z \le \frac{b-\mu}{\sigma}\right)$$
$$= \Phi\left(\frac{b-\mu}{\sigma}\right) - \Phi\left(\frac{a-\mu}{\sigma}\right)$$
$$P(X \le a) = \Phi\left(\frac{a-\mu}{\sigma}\right) \quad P(X \ge b) = 1 - \Phi\left(\frac{b-\mu}{\sigma}\right)$$

The proposition can be proved by writing the cdf of $Z = (X - \mu)/\sigma$ as

$$P(Z \le z) = P(X \le \sigma z + \mu) = \int_{-\infty}^{\sigma z + \mu} f(x; \mu, \sigma)dx.$$

Using a result from calculus, this integral can be differentiated with respect to z to yield the desired pdf $f(z; 0, 1)$.

2.3 Independent variables and random samples

2.3.1 Joint probability distributions

In real life, we are often interested in several random variables that are re-lated to each other. Joint probability is the probability of two or more events happening together. A joint probability distribution shows a probability dis-tribution for two (or more) random variables.

2.3.1.1 Two discrete random variables

The probability mass function (pmf) of a single discrete random variable X can be extended to two variables X, Y for describing how much probability mass is placed on each possible pair of values (x, y).

Definition 2.3.1. Let X and Y be two discrete random variable's defined on the sample space S of an experiment. The **joint probability mass function** $p(x, y)$ is defined for each pair of numbers (x, y) by

$$p(x, y) = P(X = x \text{ and } Y = y).$$

It must be the case that $p(x, y) \ge 0$ and $\sum_x \sum_y p(x, y) = 1$.

The marginal distribution of a subset of a collection of random vari-ables is the probability distribution of the variables contained in the subset without reference to the values of the other variable.

Definition 2.3.2. The **marginal probability mass function of** X, denoted by $p_X(x)$, is given by

$$p_X(x) = \sum_{y:p(x,y)>0} p(x,y) \quad \text{for each possible value } x.$$

Similarly, the **marginal probability mass function of** Y is

$$p_Y(y) = \sum_{x:p(x,y)>0} p(x,y) \quad \text{for each possible value } y.$$

2.3.1.2 Two continuous random variables

The joint continuous distribution is the continuous analogue of a joint discrete distribution. For that reason, all of the conceptual ideas will be equivalent, and the formulas will be the continuous counterparts of the discrete formulas. The probability that the pair (X, Y) of continuous random variables falls in a two-dimensional set A (such as a rectangle) is obtained by integrating a function called the joint density function.

Definition 2.3.3. Let X and Y be continuous random variables. A joint probability density function $f(x, y)$ for these two variables is a function satisfying $f(x, y) \geq 0$ and $\int_{-\infty}^{\infty} \int_{-\infty}^{\infty} f(x, y) dxdy = 1$. Then for any two-dimensional set A,

$$P[(X, Y) \in A] = \iint_A f(x, y) dxdy.$$

In particular, if A is the two-dimensional rectangle $\{(x, y) : a \leq x \leq b, c \leq y \leq d\}$ then

$$P[(X, Y) \in A] = P(a \leq X \leq b, c \leq Y \leq d) = \int_a^b \int_c^d f(x, y) dydx.$$

If $f(x, y)$ is a surface at height $f(x, y)$ above the point (x, y) in a three-dimensional coordinate system. Then $P[(X, Y) \in A]$ is the volume underneath this surface and above the region A, analogous to the area under a curve in the case of a single random variable. This is illustrated in Fig. 2.5. The marginal probability density function of continuous random variables can be defined analogously.

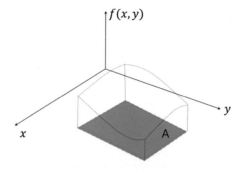

Figure 2.5 $P[(X, Y) \in A] =$ volume under density surface above A.

Definition 2.3.4. The **marginal probability density functions** of X and Y, denoted by $f_X(x)$ and $f_Y(y)$, respectively, are given by

$$f_X(x) = \int_{-\infty}^{\infty} f(x, y)\,dy \quad \text{for } -\infty < x < \infty$$
$$f_Y(y) = \int_{-\infty}^{\infty} f(x, y)\,dx \quad \text{for } -\infty < y < \infty$$

2.3.1.3 Independent random variables

The concept of independent random variables is very similar to independent events. In many situations, information about the observed value of one of the two variables X and Y gives information about the value of the other variable. Independent random variables describe a situation where the occurrence of one does not affect the probability of occurrence of the other (equivalently, does not affect the odds). One way of defining independence of two events is via the condition $P(A \cap B) = P(A) \cdot P(B)$. Here is an analogous definition for the independence of two random variables.

Definition 2.3.5. Two random variables X and Y are said to be **independent** if for every pair of x and y values,

$$p(x, y) = p_X(x) \cdot p_Y(y) \quad \text{when } X \text{ and } Y \text{ are discrete}$$

or

$$f(x, y) = f_X(x) \cdot f_Y(y) \quad \text{when } X \text{ and } Y \text{ are continuous.}$$

If the above is not satisfied for all (x, y), then X and Y are said to be **dependent**.

Example 2.3.6. Suppose that the lifetimes of two components are independent of one another and that the first lifetime, X_1, has an exponential distribution with parameter λ_1, whereas the second, X_2, has an exponential distribution with parameter λ_2. Then the joint pdf is

$$f(x_1, x_2) = f_{X_1}(x_1) \cdot f_{X_2}(x_2)$$

$$= \begin{cases} \lambda_1 e^{-\lambda_1 x_1} \cdot \lambda_2 e^{-\lambda_2 x_2} = \lambda_1 \lambda_2 e^{-\lambda_1 x_1 - \lambda_2 x_2} & x_1 > 0, x_2 > 0 \\ 0 & \text{otherwise} \end{cases}$$

Let $\lambda_1 = 1/1100$ and $\lambda_2 = 1/1300$, so that the expected lifetimes are 1100 hours and 1300 hours, respectively. The probability that both component lifetimes are at least 1400 hours is

$$P(1400 \leq X_1, 1400 \leq X_2) = P(1400 \leq X_1) \cdot P(1400 \leq X_2)$$

$$= e^{-\lambda_1(1400)} \cdot e^{-\lambda_2(1400)}$$

$$= (.28)(.34) = .0952$$

We can extend the concept of a joint distribution of two variables to more than two random variables.

Definition 2.3.7. If $X_1, X_2, \ldots, X_n$ are all discrete random variables, the joint pmf of the variables is the function

$$p(x_1, x_2, \ldots, x_n) = P(X_1 = x_1, X_2 = x_2, \ldots, X_n = x_n).$$

If the variables are continuous, the joint pdf of $X_1, \ldots, X_n$ is the function $f(x_1, x_2, \ldots, x_n)$ such that for any n intervals $[a_1, b_1], \ldots, [a_n, b_n]$,

$$P(a_1 \leq X_1 \leq b_1, \ldots, a_n \leq X_n \leq b_n) = \int_{a_1}^{b_1} \cdots \int_{a_n}^{b_n} f(x_1, \ldots, x_n) \, dx_n \ldots dx_1$$

Definition 2.3.8. The random variables $X_1, X_2, \ldots, X_n$ are said to be **in-dependent** if for *every* subset $X_{i_1}, X_{i_2}, \ldots, X_{i_k}$ of the variables (each pair, each triple, and so on), the joint pmf or pdf of the subset is equal to the product of the marginal pmf's or pdf's.

2.3.2 Correlation and dependence

Correlations are useful because they can indicate a predictive relationship that can be exploited in practice. Covariance is a measure of the joint variability of two random variables.

2.3.2.1 Correlation for random variables

When two random variables X and Y are not independent, it is frequently of interest to assess how strongly they are related to one another.

Definition 2.3.9. Let X and Y be jointly distributed random variables with pmf $p(x, y)$ or pdf $f(x, y)$ according to whether the variables are discrete or continuous. The **covariance** between two random variables X and Y is

$$\text{Cov}(X, Y) = E[(X - \mu_X)(Y - \mu_Y)]$$

$$= \begin{cases} \sum_x \sum_y (x - \mu_X)(y - \mu_Y) p(x, y), & X, Y \text{ discrete} \\ \int_{-\infty}^{\infty} \int_{-\infty}^{\infty} (x - \mu_X)(y - \mu_Y) f(x, y) dx dy, & X, Y \text{ continuous} \end{cases}$$

Fig. 2.6 has three cases when the covariance is positive, negative, and near zero. Since $X - \mu_X$ and $Y - \mu_Y$ are the deviations of the two variables from their respective mean values the covariance is the expected product of deviations. Note that $\text{Cov}(X, X) = E[(X - \mu_X)^2] = V(X)$.

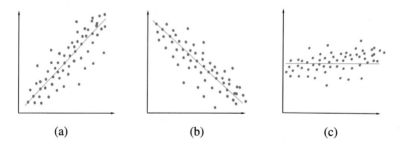

(a)   (b)   (c)

Figure 2.6 (a) Positive covariance; (b) Negative covariance; (c) Covariance near zero.

The correlation coefficient is the covariance of the two variables divided by the product of their standard deviations, which is a measure of linear correlation between two variables or sets of data.

Definition 2.3.10. The **correlation coefficient** of X and Y, denoted by $\text{Corr}(X, Y)$, $\rho_{X,Y}$, or just ρ, is defined by

$$\rho_{X,Y} = \frac{\text{Cov}(X, Y)}{\sigma_X \cdot \sigma_Y}$$

Proposition 2.3.11. *Correlation coefficients have the following properties:*
1. *If X and Y are independent, then $\rho = 0$, but $\rho = 0$ does not imply independence.*
2. *$|\rho| \le 1$, $\rho = 1$ or -1 if $Y = aX + b$ for some numbers a and b with $a \neq 0$.*

2.3.2.2 Correlation for samples

Correlation coefficient, when applied to a sample, is commonly represented by r_{xy} and may be referred to as the sample correlation coefficient or the sample Pearson correlation coefficient. We can obtain a formula for r_{xy} by substituting estimates of the covariances and variances based on a sample into the formula above. Given paired data $\{(x_1, y_1), \ldots, (x_n, y_n)\}$ consisting of n pairs,

$$r_{xy} = \frac{\sum_{i=1}^{n}(x_i - \bar{x})(y_i - \bar{y})}{\sqrt{\sum_{i=1}^{n}(x_i - \bar{x})^2}\sqrt{\sum_{i=1}^{n}(y_i - \bar{y})^2}}$$

where $\bar{x} = \dfrac{1}{n}\sum_{i=1}^{n} x_i$ (the sample mean); and analogously for $\bar{y}$.

Fig. 2.7 shows the correlation coefficients of x and y for several data sets. Note that the correlation reflects the strength and direction of a linear relationship, but not the slope of that relationship, nor many aspects of nonlinear relationships.

| $0 < r < 1$ | $-1 < r < 0$ | $r = 0$ | $r = 1$ | $r = -1$ |

Figure 2.7 Correlation coefficients.

It is easy to verify the following result.

Proposition 2.3.12. *The correlation coefficient for samples has the following properties:*

- $r_{xy} = \dfrac{s_{xy}}{s_x s_y}$ *where the sample covariance*

$$s_{xy} = \frac{1}{n-1}\sum_{i=1}^{n}(x_i - \bar{x})(y_i - \bar{y})$$

and the sample standard deviation

$$s_x = \sqrt{\frac{1}{n-1}\sum_{i=1}^{n}(x_i - \bar{x})^2}$$

- *If* $y = ax + b$, *then* $r_{xy} = 1$ *or* -1 *if a is positive or negative.*

The proof of the second part comes from the observation: $s_{(ax)y} = as_{xy}$ and $s_{(x+a)y} = s_{xy}$ because $\bar{ax} = a\bar{x}$; if $y = x + a$, $s_x = s_y$; and if $y = ax$, $s_y = |a|s_x$; and $s_{xx} = s_x^2$. If $y = ax + b$, then $r_{xy} = 1$ or -1 if a is positive or negative.

2.3.3 Random samples

2.3.3.1 Random samples

A simple random sample is a randomly selected subset of a population and often is used in practice.

Definition 2.3.13. The random variables $X_1, X_2, \ldots, X_n$ are said to form a (simple) **random sample** of size n if:
1. The X_i's are independent random variables.
2. Every X_i has the same probability distribution.

We can draw conclusions about the population mean μ using the sample mean $\bar{X} = \frac{1}{n}(X_1 + \cdots + X_n)$. Some of the most frequently used inferential procedures are based on properties of the sampling distribution of $\bar{X}$. We review these relationships between $E(\bar{X})$ and μ and also among $V(\bar{X})$, σ^2, and n.

Proposition 2.3.14. *Let $X_1, X_2, \ldots, X_n$ be a random sample from a distribution with mean value μ and standard deviation σ. Then:*
1. *$E(\bar{X}) = \mu_{\bar{X}} = \mu$;*
2. *$V(\bar{X}) = \sigma_{\bar{X}}^2 = \sigma^2/n$ and $\sigma_{\bar{X}} = \sigma/\sqrt{n}$.*
In addition, with $T_o = X_1 + \cdots + X_n$ (the sample total), $E(T_o) = n\mu$, $V(T_o) = n\sigma^2$, and $\sigma_{T_o} = \sqrt{n}\sigma$.

2.3.3.2 The central limit theorem

The central limit theorem (CLT) indicates that the properly normalized sum of independent random variables tends toward a normal distribution even if the original variables themselves are not normally distributed. The theorem is a key concept in probability theory because it implies that probabilistic and statistical methods that work for normal distributions can be applicable to many problems involving other types of distributions. The formal statement of this result is the most important theorem of probability.

Theorem 2.3.15 (The central limit theorem (CLT)). *Let $X_1, X_2, \ldots, X_n$ be a random sample from a distribution with mean μ and variance σ^2. Then if n is sufficiently large, $\bar{X}$ has approximately a normal distribution with $\mu_{\bar{X}} = \mu$ and $\sigma_{\bar{X}}^2 = \sigma^2/n$, and T_o also has approximately a normal distribution with $\mu_{T_o} = n\mu$, $\sigma_{T_o}^2 = n\sigma^2$. The larger the value of n, the better the approximation.*

2.4 Maximum likelihood estimation

2.4.1 MLE for random samples

Maximum likelihood estimation (MLE) is an effective approach of estimating the parameters of a probability distribution through maximizing a likelihood function. The point in the parameter space that maximizes the likelihood function is called the maximum likelihood estimate. The logic of maximum likelihood is both intuitive and flexible. As a result, the method has become a dominant means of statistical inference.

Definition 2.4.1. Let $X_1, X_2, \ldots, X_n$ have joint pmf or pdf

$$f(x_1, x_2, \ldots, x_n; \theta_1, \ldots, \theta_m) \qquad (2.4.1)$$

where the parameters $\theta_1, \ldots, \theta_m$ have unknown values. When $x_1, \ldots, x_n$ are the observed sample values and (2.4.1) is regarded as a function of $\theta_1, \ldots, \theta_m$, it is called the **likelihood function**. The maximum likelihood estimates (mle's) $\hat{\theta}_1, \ldots, \hat{\theta}_m$ are those values of the θ_i's that maximize the likelihood function, so that

$$f\left(x_1, \ldots, x_n; \hat{\theta}_1, \ldots, \hat{\theta}_m\right) \geq f(x_1, \ldots, x_n; \theta_1, \ldots, \theta_m) \text{ for all } \theta_1, \ldots, \theta_m.$$

When the X_i's are substituted in place of the x_i's, **the maximum likelihood estimators** result.

Example 2.4.2. Let $X_1, \ldots, X_n$ be a random sample from a normal distribution. The likelihood function is

$$f\left(x_1, \ldots, x_n; \mu, \sigma^2\right) = \frac{1}{\sqrt{2\pi\sigma^2}} e^{-(x_1-\mu)^2/(2\sigma^2)} \cdots \cdot \frac{1}{\sqrt{2\pi\sigma^2}} e^{-(x_n-\mu)^2/(2\sigma^2)}$$

$$= \left(\frac{1}{2\pi\sigma^2}\right)^{n/2} e^{-\Sigma(x_i-\mu)^2/(2\sigma^2)}$$

So

$$\ln\left[f\left(x_1, \ldots, x_n; \mu, \sigma^2\right)\right] = -\frac{n}{2} \ln\left(2\pi\sigma^2\right) - \frac{1}{2\sigma^2} \sum (x_i - \mu)^2$$

To find the maximizing values of μ and σ^2, we must take the partial derivatives of $\ln(f)$ with respect to μ and σ^2, equate them to zero, and solve the resulting two equations. First, taking derivative with respect to μ, we have

$$\frac{\partial \ln\left[f\left(x_1, \ldots, x_n; \mu, \sigma^2\right)\right]}{\partial \mu} = -\frac{1}{\sigma^2} \sum (x_i - \mu)$$

Equating the derivative zero and solving for μ result in the following:

$$\hat{\mu} = \frac{1}{n}\sum x_i.$$

Similarly, taking derivative with respect to σ^2,

$$\frac{\partial \ln\left[f\left(x_1, \ldots, x_n; \mu, \sigma^2\right)\right]}{\partial \sigma^2} = -\frac{n}{2\sigma^2} + \frac{1}{2\sigma^4}\sum (x_i - \mu)^2$$

and

$$\sigma^2 = \frac{\sum (x_i - \mu)^2}{n}.$$

Therefore, the resulting mle's are

$$\hat{\mu} = \bar{X} \quad \hat{\sigma}^2 = \frac{\sum \left(X_i - \bar{X}\right)^2}{n}.$$

2.4.2 Linear regression

Given input data points $\{(\mathbf{x}_i, y_i)\}_{i=1}^n$, we seek an affine function to fit the data and each $\mathbf{x}_i = (x_{i1}, \ldots, x_{ip})$. The common approach involves finding coefficients $\beta_j, j = 1 \ldots, p$'s that minimize the criterion

$$\sum_{i=1}^n \left(y_i - \hat{y}_i\right)^2,$$

where

$$\hat{y}_i = \beta_0 + \beta_1 x_{i1} + \ldots + \beta_p x_{ip}$$

Now we wish to discuss it from a probabilistic point of view by the maximum likelihood estimation. Consider that we have n points, each of which is drawn in an independent and identically distributed (i.i.d.) way from the normal distribution. For a given, μ, σ^2, the probability of those n points being drawn define the likelihood function, which are just the multiplication of n normal probability density functions (pdf) (because they are independent):

$$\mathscr{P}(\mu \mid y) = \prod_{i=1}^n P_Y\left(y_i \mid \mu, \sigma^2\right) = \prod_{i=1}^n \frac{1}{\sigma\sqrt{2\pi}} e^{-\frac{(y_i - \mu)^2}{2\sigma^2}} \qquad (2.4.2)$$

Now understand that y is a random variable,

$$y_i = \hat{y}_i + \varepsilon,$$

where $\varepsilon \sim N\left(0, \sigma^2\right)$. Thus y_i is a normal variable with mean as a linear function of $\mathbf{x}$ and a fixed standard deviation:

$$y_i \sim N\left(\hat{y}_i, \sigma^2\right). \tag{2.4.3}$$

As a result, for each y_i, we choose μ in the normal distributions in (2.4.2) as

$$\mu_i = \hat{y}_i.$$

Hence we derive the maximum likelihood estimate

$$
\begin{aligned}
\hat{\beta} = \arg\max \mathscr{P}(\beta \mid y) &= \arg\max_{\beta} \prod_{i=1}^{n} \frac{1}{\sigma\sqrt{2\pi}} e^{-\frac{(y_i - \hat{y}_i)^2}{2\sigma^2}} \\
&= \arg\max_{\beta} \log\left(\prod_{i=1}^{n} \frac{1}{\sigma\sqrt{2\pi}} e^{-\frac{(y_i - \hat{y}_i)^2}{2\sigma^2}}\right) \\
&= \arg\max_{\beta} \sum_{i=1}^{n} \log\left(\frac{1}{\sigma\sqrt{2\pi}}\right) + \log\left(e^{-\frac{(y_i - \hat{y}_i)^2}{2\sigma^2}}\right) \\
&= \arg\max_{\beta} \sum_{i=1}^{n} \log\left(e^{-\frac{(y_i - \hat{y}_i)^2}{2\sigma^2}}\right) \\
&= \arg\max_{\beta} \sum_{i=1}^{n} -\frac{(y_i - \hat{y}_i)^2}{2\sigma^2} \\
&= \arg\min_{\beta} \sum_{i=1}^{n} (y_i - \hat{y}_i)^2,
\end{aligned} \tag{2.4.4}
$$

which is exactly the least square problem we discussed before.

CHAPTER 3

Calculus and optimization

Contents

3.1 Introduction

Many algorithms in data science and machine learning optimize an objective function with respect to a set of desired model parameters that control how well a model explains the data. Finding good parameters can be expressed as an optimization problem. Many optimization problems rely on the concept of derivative in calculus. This chapter introduces basic concepts

Copyright © 2023 China Science Publishing &
Media Ltd. Published by Elsevier Inc.
All rights reserved.
51

for data science and includes limits, derivatives, convexity, and gradient descent and further expanded to include logistic regression, k-means, support vector machines, and neural networks. Further calculus and optimizations and their applications can be found in many references [3,8–11,31,118].

3.2 Continuity and differentiation

3.2.1 Limits and continuity

Limits are essential to calculus and mathematical analysis, and are used to define continuity, derivatives, and integrals. In this chapter, we will use the Euclidean norm $\|\mathbf{x}\| = \sqrt{\sum_{i=1}^{d} x_i^2}$ for $\mathbf{x} = (x_1, \ldots, x_d)^T \in \mathbb{R}^d$. The open r-ball around $\mathbf{x} \in \mathbb{R}^d$ is the set of points within Euclidean distance r of $\mathbf{x}$, that is,

$$B_r(\mathbf{x}) = \{\mathbf{y} \in \mathbb{R}^d : \|\mathbf{y} - \mathbf{x}\| < r\}.$$

A point $\mathbf{x} \in \mathbb{R}^d$ is a limit point (or accumulation point) of a set $A \subseteq \mathbb{R}^d$ if every open ball around $\mathbf{x}$ contains an element $\mathbf{a}$ of A such that $\mathbf{a} \neq \mathbf{x}$ as in Fig. 3.1. A set A is closed if every limit point of A belongs to A. A set A is open if there is a $B_r(\mathbf{x}) \subseteq A$ for all $x \in A$ as in Fig. 3.2. A set $A \subseteq \mathbb{R}^d$ is bounded if there exists an $r > 0$ such that $A \subseteq B_r(\mathbf{0})$, where $\mathbf{0} = (0, \ldots, 0)^T$.

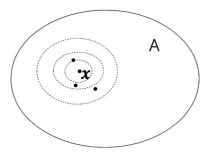

Figure 3.1 Point of accumulation.

Definition 3.2.1 (Limits of a function). Let $f : D \to \mathbb{R}$ be a real-valued function on $D \subseteq \mathbb{R}^d$. Then f is said to have a limit $L \in \mathbb{R}$ as $\mathbf{x}$ approaches $\mathbf{a}$ if: for any $\varepsilon > 0$, there exists a $\delta > 0$ such that $|f(\mathbf{x}) - L| < \varepsilon$ for all $\mathbf{x} \in D \cap B_\delta(\mathbf{a}) \setminus \{\mathbf{a}\}$. This is written as

$$\lim_{\mathbf{x} \to \mathbf{a}} f(\mathbf{x}) = L.$$

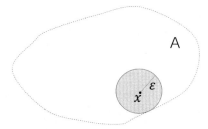

Figure 3.2 Open set example.

Continuous function is a function that does not have any abrupt changes in value, known as discontinuities. The definition of continuity of a function can be visualized in Fig. 3.3. Note that we explicitly exclude **a** itself from having to satisfy the condition $|f(\mathbf{x}) - L| < \varepsilon$. In particular, we may have $f(\mathbf{a}) \neq L$. We also do not restrict **a** to be in D.

Definition 3.2.2 (Continuous function). Let $f : D \to \mathbb{R}$ be a real-valued function on $D \subseteq \mathbb{R}^d$. Then f is said to be continuous at $\mathbf{a} \in D$ if

$$\lim_{\mathbf{x} \to \mathbf{a}} f(\mathbf{x}) = f(\mathbf{a}).$$

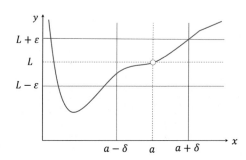

Figure 3.3 Example of continuous function.

Fig. 3.3 is an example of a continuous function. Functions are often obtained from the composition of simpler ones. We will use the standard notation $h = g \circ f$ for the function $h(\mathbf{x}) = g(f(\mathbf{x}))$ as in Fig. 3.4.

Lemma 3.2.3 (Composition of continuous functions). *Let* $\mathbf{f} : D_1 \to \mathbb{R}^m$, *where* $D_1 \subseteq \mathbb{R}^d$, *and let* $\mathbf{g} : D_2 \to \mathbb{R}^p$, *where* $D_2 \subseteq \mathbb{R}^m$. *Assume that* $\mathbf{f}$ *is continuous at* $\mathbf{x}_0$ *and that* $\mathbf{g}$ *is continuous* $\mathbf{f}(\mathbf{x}_0)$. *Then* $g \circ f$ *is continuous at* $\mathbf{x}_0$.

The extremum lemma is very useful. We will not prove it here. Its proof can be found in many books.

Definition 3.2.4 (Extremum). Suppose $f : D \to \mathbb{R}$ is defined on a set $D \subseteq \mathbb{R}^d$. We say that f attains a maximum value M at $\mathbf{z}^*$ if $f(\mathbf{z}^*) = M$ and $M \geq f(\mathbf{x})$ for all $\mathbf{x} \in D$. Similarly, we say f attains a minimum value m at $\mathbf{z}_*$ if $f(\mathbf{z}_*) = m$ and $m \leq f(\mathbf{x})$ for all $\mathbf{x} \in D$.

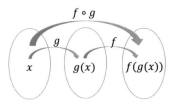

Figure 3.4 Composition of functions.

Theorem 3.2.5 (Extreme value). *Let $f : D \to \mathbb{R}$ be a real-valued, continuous function on a nonempty, closed, bounded set $D \subseteq \mathbb{R}^d$. Then f attains a maximum and a minimum on D.*

3.2.2 Derivatives

3.2.2.1 Single-variable case

The derivative of a function of a real variable measures the sensitivity to change the function value (output value) with respect to another variable. We begin by reviewing the single-variable case.

Definition 3.2.6 (Derivative). Let $f : D \to \mathbb{R}$ where $D \subseteq \mathbb{R}$ and let $x_0 \in D$ be an interior point of D. The derivative of f at x_0 is

$$f'(x_0) = \frac{df(x_0)}{dx} = \lim_{h \to 0} \frac{f(x_0 + h) - f(x_0)}{h},$$

provided the limit exists.

The definition of derivative of a function can be illustrated in Fig. 3.5. The following proposition indicates that the differentiation is a linear operator.

Proposition 3.2.7. *Let f and g have derivatives at x and let α and β be constants. The following results hold:*

$$[\alpha f(x) + \beta g(x)]' = \alpha f'(x) + \beta g'(x).$$

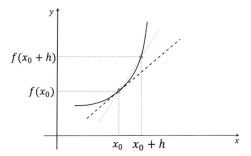

Figure 3.5 Derivative.

The following lemma encapsulates a key insight about the derivative of f at x_0; it tells us where to find extreme values.

Lemma 3.2.8. *Let $f : D \to \mathbb{R}$ with $D \subseteq \mathbb{R}$ and let $x_0 \in D$ be an interior point of D where $f'(x_0)$ exists. If $f'(x_0) > 0$, then there is an open ball $B_\delta(x_0) \subseteq D$ around x_0 such that for each x in $B_\delta(x_0)$:*
  (a) $f(x) > f(x_0)$ if $x > x_0$,
  (b) $f(x) < f(x_0)$ if $x < x_0$.
If instead $f'(x_0) < 0$, the opposite holds.

Proof. Take $\varepsilon = f'(x_0)/2$. By definition of the derivative, there is $\delta > 0$ such that

$$f'(x_0) - \frac{f(x_0 + h) - f(x_0)}{h} < \varepsilon$$

for all $0 < h < \delta$. Rearranging gives

$$f(x_0 + h) > f(x_0) + [f'(x_0) - \varepsilon]h > f(x_0)$$

by our choice of ε. The other direction is similar.   □

One immediate implication of Lemma 3.2.8 is the mean value theorem as in Fig. 3.7, which will lead us later to Taylor's theorem. First, we need to prove an important special case: Rolle theorem as in Fig. 3.6.

Theorem 3.2.9 (Rolle). *Let $f : [a, b] \to \mathbb{R}$ be a continuous function and assume that its derivative exists on (a, b). If $f(a) = f(b)$, then there is $a < c < b$ such that $f'(c) = 0$.*

Proof. If $f(x) = f(a)$ for all $x \in (a, b)$, then $f'(x) = 0$ on (a, b) and we are done. So assume there is $y \in (a, b)$ such that $f(y) \neq f(a)$. Assume without

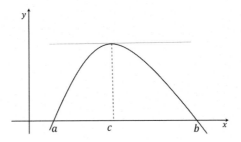

Figure 3.6 Rolle.

loss of generality that $f(y) > f(a)$ (otherwise consider the function $-f$). By the extreme value theorem, f attains a maximum value at some $c \in [a, b]$. By our assumption, a and b cannot be the location of the maximum and it must be that $c \in (a, b)$.

We claim that $f'(c) = 0$. We argue by contradiction. Suppose $f'(c) > 0$. By Lemma 3.2.8, there is a $\delta > 0$ such that $f(x) > f(c)$ for all $x \in B_\delta(c)$, a contradiction. A similar argument holds if $f'(c) < 0$. That concludes the proof. $\qquad\square$

Theorem 3.2.10 (Mean value). *Let $f : [a, b] \to \mathbb{R}$ be a continuous function and assume that its derivative exists on (a, b). Then there is $a < c < b$ such that*

$$f(b) = f(a) + (b - a)f'(c),$$

or put differently

$$\frac{f(b) - f(a)}{b - a} = f'(c).$$

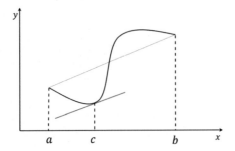

Figure 3.7 Mean value.

Proof. The mean value theorem is shown in Fig. 3.7. Let $\phi(x) = f(x) - f(a) - \frac{f(b)-f(a)}{b-a}(x-a)$. Note that $\phi(a) = \phi(b) = 0$ and $\phi'(x) = f'(x) - \frac{f(b)-f(a)}{b-a}$ for all $x \in (a,b)$. Thus, by Rolle, there is $c \in (a,b)$ such that $\phi'(c) = 0$. That implies $\frac{f(b)-f(a)}{b-a} = f'(c)$ and plugging into $\phi(b)$ gives the result.   □

In a similar manner, one can also define higher-order derivatives. Note that, if f' exists in D, then it is itself a function of x. Then the second derivative at x_0, an interior point of D is

$$f''(x_0) = \frac{d^2 f(x_0)}{dx^2} = \lim_{h \to 0} \frac{f'(x_0 + h) - f'(x_0)}{h},$$

provided the limit exists.

3.2.2.2 General case

Many functions in data science involves several independent variables. For functions of several variables, we have the following generalization. As before, we let $\mathbf{e}_i \in \mathbb{R}^d$ be the ith standard basis vector.

Definition 3.2.11 (Partial derivative). Let $f : D \to \mathbb{R}$ where $D \subseteq \mathbb{R}^d$ and let $\mathbf{x}_0 \in D$ be an interior point of D. The partial derivative of f at $\mathbf{x}_0$ with respect to x_i is

$$\frac{\partial f(\mathbf{x}_0)}{\partial x_i} = \lim_{h \to 0} \frac{f(\mathbf{x}_0 + h\mathbf{e}_i) - f(\mathbf{x}_0)}{h},$$

provided the limit exists. If $\frac{\partial f(\mathbf{x}_0)}{\partial x_i}$ exists and is continuous in an open ball around $\mathbf{x}_0$ for all i, then we say that f continuously differentiable at $\mathbf{x}_0$.

Definition 3.2.12 (Jacobian). Let $\mathbf{f} = (f_1, \ldots, f_m) : D \to \mathbb{R}^m$ where $D \subseteq \mathbb{R}^d$ and let $\mathbf{x}_0 \in D$ be an interior point of D where $\frac{\partial f_j(\mathbf{x}_0)}{\partial x_i}$ exists for all i, j. The Jacobian of $\mathbf{f}$ at $\mathbf{x}_0$ is the $d \times m$ matrix

$$\mathbf{J_f}(\mathbf{x}_0) = \begin{pmatrix} \frac{\partial f_1(\mathbf{x}_0)}{\partial x_1} & \cdots & \frac{\partial f_1(\mathbf{x}_0)}{\partial x_d} \\ \vdots & \ddots & \vdots \\ \frac{\partial f_m(\mathbf{x}_0)}{\partial x_1} & \cdots & \frac{\partial f_m(\mathbf{x}_0)}{\partial x_d} \end{pmatrix}.$$

For a real-valued function $f : D \to \mathbb{R}$, the Jacobian reduces to the row vector

$$\mathbf{J}_f(\mathbf{x}_0) = \nabla f(\mathbf{x}_0)^T,$$

where the vector

$$\nabla f(\mathbf{x}_0) = \left(\frac{\partial f(\mathbf{x}_0)}{\partial x_1}, \ldots, \frac{\partial f(\mathbf{x}_0)}{\partial x_d} \right)^T$$

is the gradient of f at $\mathbf{x}_0$.

Example 3.2.13. Consider the affine function

$$f(\mathbf{x}) = \mathbf{q}^T \mathbf{x} + r,$$

where $\mathbf{x} = (x_1, \ldots, x_d)^T$, $\mathbf{q} = (q_1, \ldots, q_d)^T \in \mathbb{R}^d$. The partial derivatives of the linear term are given by

$$\frac{\partial}{\partial x_i}[\mathbf{q}^T \mathbf{x}] = \frac{\partial}{\partial x_i}\left[\sum_{j=1}^d q_j x_j \right] = q_i.$$

So the gradient of f is

$$\nabla f(\mathbf{x}) = \mathbf{q}.$$

Example 3.2.14. Consider the quadratic function

$$f(\mathbf{x}) = \mathbf{x}^T P \mathbf{x} + \mathbf{q}^T \mathbf{x} + r,$$

where $\mathbf{x} = (x_1, \ldots, x_d)^T$, $\mathbf{q} = (q_1, \ldots, q_d)^T \in \mathbb{R}^d$ and $P \in \mathbb{R}^{d \times d}$. The partial derivatives of the quadratic term are given by

$$\frac{\partial}{\partial x_i}[\mathbf{x}^T P \mathbf{x}] = \frac{\partial}{\partial x_i}\left[\sum_{j,k=1}^d P_{jk} x_j x_k \right]$$

$$= \frac{\partial}{\partial x_i}\left[P_{ii} x_i^2 + \sum_{j=1,j\neq i}^d P_{ji} x_j x_i + \sum_{k=1,k\neq i}^d P_{ik} x_i x_k \right]$$

$$= 2 P_{ii} x_i + \sum_{j=1,j\neq i}^d P_{ji} x_j + \sum_{k=1,k\neq i}^d P_{ik} x_k$$

$$= \sum_{j=1}^d [P^T]_{ij} x_j + \sum_{k=1}^d [P]_{ik} x_k.$$

So the gradient of f is

$$\nabla f(\mathbf{x}) = [P + P^T]\mathbf{x} + \mathbf{q}.$$

In calculus, the chain rule is a formula that expresses the derivative of the composition of two or more differentiable functions in terms of the derivative of each of them. The chain rule gives a convenient formula for the Jacobian of a composition. We will use the vector notation $\mathbf{h} = \mathbf{g} \circ \mathbf{f}$ for the function $\mathbf{h}(\mathbf{x}) = \mathbf{g}(\mathbf{f}(\mathbf{x}))$.

Theorem 3.2.15 (Chain rule). *Let* $\mathbf{f}: D_1 \to \mathbb{R}^m$, *where* $D_1 \subseteq \mathbb{R}^d$, *and let* $\mathbf{g}: D_2 \to \mathbb{R}^p$, *where* $D_2 \subseteq \mathbb{R}^m$. *Assume that* $\mathbf{f}$ *is continuously differentiable at* $\mathbf{x}_0$, *an interior point of* D_1, *and that* $\mathbf{g}$ *is continuously differentiable at* $\mathbf{f}(\mathbf{x}_0)$, *an interior point of* D_2. *Then*

$$\mathbf{J}_{\mathbf{g} \circ \mathbf{f}}(\mathbf{x}_0) = \mathbf{J}_{\mathbf{g}}(\mathbf{f}(\mathbf{x}_0)) \mathbf{J}_{\mathbf{f}}(\mathbf{x}_0)$$

as a product of matrices.

Proof. To simplify the notation, we begin with a special case. Suppose that f is a real-valued function of $\mathbf{x} = (x_1, \ldots, x_m)$ whose components are themselves functions of $t \in \mathbb{R}$. Assume f is continuously differentiable at $\mathbf{x}(t)$. To compute the total derivative $\frac{df(t)}{dt}$, let $\Delta x_k = x_k(t + \Delta t) - x_k(t)$, $x_k = x_k(t)$ and

$$\Delta f = f(x_1 + \Delta x_1, \ldots, x_m + \Delta x_m) - f(x_1, \ldots, x_m).$$

We seek to compute the limit $\lim_{\Delta t \to 0} \frac{\Delta f}{\Delta t}$. To relate this limit to partial derivatives of f, we rewrite Δf as a telescoping sum where each term involves variation of a single variable x_k. That is,

$$\begin{aligned}
\Delta f =& [f(x_1 + \Delta x_1, \ldots, x_m + \Delta x_m) - f(x_1, x_2 + \Delta x_2, \ldots, x_m + \Delta x_m)] \\
& + [f(x_1, x_2 + \Delta x_2, \ldots, x_m + \Delta x_m) - f(x_1, x_2, x_3 + \Delta x_3, \ldots, x_m + \Delta x_m)] \\
& + \cdots + [f(x_1, \cdots, x_{m-1}, x_m + \Delta x_m) - f(x_1, \ldots, x_m)].
\end{aligned}$$

Applying the mean value theorem to each term gives

$$\begin{aligned}
\Delta f =& \Delta x_1 \frac{\partial f(x_1 + \theta_1 \Delta x_1, x_2 + \Delta x_2, \ldots, x_m + \Delta x_m)}{\partial x_1} \\
& + \Delta x_2 \frac{\partial f(x_1, x_2 + \theta_2 \Delta x_2, x_3 + \Delta x_3, \ldots, x_m + \Delta x_m)}{\partial x_2} \\
& + \cdots + \Delta x_m \frac{\partial f(x_1, \cdots, x_{m-1}, x_m + \theta_m \Delta x_m)}{\partial x_m},
\end{aligned}$$

where $0 < \theta_k < 1$ for $k = 1, \ldots, m$. Dividing by Δt, taking the limit $\Delta t \to 0$ and using the fact that f is continuously differentiable, we get

$$\frac{df(t)}{dt} = \sum_{k=1}^{m} \frac{\partial f(\mathbf{x}(t))}{\partial x_k} \frac{dx_k(t)}{dt}.$$

Going back to the general case, the same argument shows that

$$\frac{\partial h_i(\mathbf{x}_0)}{\partial x_j} = \sum_{k=1}^{m} \frac{\partial g_i(\mathbf{f}(\mathbf{x}_0))}{\partial f_k} \frac{\partial f_k(\mathbf{x}_0)}{\partial x_j},$$

where the notation $\frac{\partial g}{\partial f_k}$ indicates the partial derivative of g with respect to its kth component. In matrix form, the claim follows. $\square$

3.2.2.3 Further derivatives

The directional derivative of a multivariate differentiable (scalar) function along a given vector intuitively measure the rate of change of a function along the direction.

Definition 3.2.16 (Directional derivative). Let $f : D \to \mathbb{R}$ where $D \subseteq \mathbb{R}^d$, let $\mathbf{x}_0 \in D$ be an interior point of D, and let $\mathbf{v} \in \mathbb{R}^d$ be a unit vector. The directional derivative of f at $\mathbf{x}_0$ in the direction $\mathbf{v}$ is

$$\frac{\partial f(\mathbf{x}_0)}{\partial \mathbf{v}} = \lim_{h \to 0} \frac{f(\mathbf{x}_0 + h\mathbf{v}) - f(\mathbf{x}_0)}{h},$$

provided the limit exists.

Note that taking $\mathbf{v} = \mathbf{e}_i$ recovers the ith partial derivative

$$\frac{\partial f(\mathbf{x}_0)}{\partial \mathbf{e}_i} = \lim_{h \to 0} \frac{f(\mathbf{x}_0 + h\mathbf{e}_i) - f(\mathbf{x}_0)}{h} = \frac{\partial f(\mathbf{x}_0)}{\partial x_i}.$$

Conversely, a general directional derivative can be expressed in terms of the partial derivatives.

Theorem 3.2.17 (Directional derivative from gradient). *Let $f : D \to \mathbb{R}$ where $D \subseteq \mathbb{R}^d$, let $\mathbf{x}_0 \in D$ be an interior point of D, and let $\mathbf{v} \in \mathbb{R}^d$ be a unit vector. Assume that f is continuously differentiable at $\mathbf{x}_0$. Then the directional derivative of f at $\mathbf{x}_0$ in the direction $\mathbf{v}$ is given by*

$$\frac{\partial f(\mathbf{x}_0)}{\partial \mathbf{v}} = \mathbf{J}_f(\mathbf{x}_0)\,\mathbf{v} = \nabla f(\mathbf{x}_0)^T \mathbf{v}.$$

Proof. Consider the composition $\beta(h) = f(\alpha(h))$ where $\alpha(h) = \mathbf{x}_0 + h\mathbf{v}$. Observe that $\alpha(0) = \mathbf{x}_0$ and $\beta(0) = f(\mathbf{x}_0)$. Then, by definition of the derivative,

$$\frac{d\beta(0)}{dh} = \lim_{h\to 0}\frac{\beta(h)-\beta(0)}{h} = \lim_{h\to 0}\frac{f(\mathbf{x}_0+h\mathbf{v})-f(\mathbf{x}_0)}{h} = \frac{\partial f(\mathbf{x}_0)}{\partial \mathbf{v}}.$$

Applying the chain rule, we arrive at

$$\frac{d\beta(0)}{dh} = \mathbf{J}_\beta(0) = \mathbf{J}_f(\alpha(0))\mathbf{J}_\alpha(0) = \mathbf{J}_f(\mathbf{x}_0)\mathbf{J}_\alpha(0).$$

It remains to compute $\mathbf{J}_\alpha(0)$. By the linearity of derivatives,

$$\frac{\partial \alpha_i(h)}{\partial h} = [x_{0,i}+hv_i]' = v_i,$$

where we denote $\alpha = (\alpha_1,\ldots,\alpha_d)^T$ and $\mathbf{x}_0 = (x_{0,1},\ldots,x_{0,d})^T$. So $\mathbf{J}_\alpha(0) = \mathbf{v}$ and we get finally

$$\frac{d\beta(0)}{dh} = \mathbf{J}_f(\mathbf{x}_0)\mathbf{v},$$

as claimed. $\qquad\square$

We can also take higher-order derivatives. We will restrict ourselves to the second order.

Definition 3.2.18 (Second partial derivatives and Hessian). Let $f : D \to \mathbb{R}$ where $D \subseteq \mathbb{R}^d$ and let $\mathbf{x}_0 \in D$ be an interior point of D. Assume that f is continuously differentiable in an open ball around $\mathbf{x}_0$. Then $\partial f(\mathbf{x})/\partial x_i$ is itself a function of $\mathbf{x}$ and its partial derivative with respect to x_j, if it exists, is denoted by

$$\frac{\partial^2 f(\mathbf{x}_0)}{\partial x_j \partial x_i} = \lim_{h\to 0}\frac{\partial f(\mathbf{x}_0+h\mathbf{e}_j)/\partial x_i - \partial f(\mathbf{x}_0)/\partial x_i}{h}.$$

To simplify the notation, we write this as $\partial^2 f(\mathbf{x}_0)/\partial x_i^2$ when $j = i$. If $\partial^2 f(\mathbf{x})/\partial x_j \partial x_i$ and $\partial^2 f(\mathbf{x})/\partial x_i^2$ exist and are continuous in an open ball around $\mathbf{x}_0$ for all i,j, we say that f is twice continuously differentiable at $\mathbf{x}_0$.

The Jacobian of the gradient ∇f is called the Hessian and is denoted by

$$\mathbf{H}_f(\mathbf{x}_0) = \begin{pmatrix} \frac{\partial^2 f(\mathbf{x}_0)}{\partial x_1^2} & \cdots & \frac{\partial^2 f(\mathbf{x}_0)}{\partial x_d \partial x_1} \\ \vdots & \ddots & \vdots \\ \frac{\partial^2 f(\mathbf{x}_0)}{\partial x_1 \partial x_d} & \cdots & \frac{\partial^2 f(\mathbf{x}_0)}{\partial x_d^2} \end{pmatrix}.$$

When f is twice continuously differentiable at $\mathbf{x}_0$, its Hessian is a symmetric matrix.

Theorem 3.2.19 (Symmetry of the Hessian). *Let $f : D \to \mathbb{R}$ where $D \subseteq \mathbb{R}^d$ and let $\mathbf{x}_0 \in D$ be an interior point of D. Assume that f is twice continuously differentiable at $\mathbf{x}_0$. Then for all $i \neq j$,*

$$\frac{\partial^2 f(\mathbf{x}_0)}{\partial x_j \partial x_i} = \frac{\partial^2 f(\mathbf{x}_0)}{\partial x_i \partial x_j}.$$

Example 3.2.20. Consider again the quadratic function

$$f(\mathbf{x}) = \frac{1}{2}\mathbf{x}^T P \mathbf{x} + \mathbf{q}^T \mathbf{x} + r.$$

Recall that the gradient of f is

$$\nabla f(\mathbf{x}) = \frac{1}{2}[P + P^T]\mathbf{x} + \mathbf{q}.$$

Each component of ∇f is an affine function of $\mathbf{x}$, so by our previous result the gradient of ∇f is

$$\mathbf{H}_f = \frac{1}{2}[P + P^T].$$

Observe that this is indeed a symmetric matrix.

3.2.3 Taylor's theorem

Taylor's theorem gives an approximation of a differentiable function around a given point by a polynomial. We will make use of Taylor's theorem, a powerful generalization of the mean value theorem that provides polynomial approximations to a function around a point. We restrict ourselves to the case of a linear approximation with second-order error term, which will suffice for our purposes.

We begin by reviewing the single-variable case, which we will use to prove the general version.

Theorem 3.2.21 (Taylor). *Let $f : D \to \mathbb{R}$ where $D \subseteq \mathbb{R}$. Suppose f has a m times continuous derivative on $[a, b]$. Then*

$$f(b) = f(a) + (b-a)f'(a) + \frac{1}{2}(b-a)^2 f''(a) + \ldots + \frac{(b-a)^{m-1}}{(m-1)!}f^{(m-1)}(a) + R_m,$$

$$(3.2.1)$$

where $R_m = \frac{(b-a)^m}{(m)!} f^{(m)}(a + \theta(b-a))$ *for some* $0 < \theta < 1$. *In particular, for* $m = 2$, *we have*

$$f(b) = f(a) + (b-a)f'(a) + \frac{1}{2}(b-a)^2 f''(\xi) \qquad (3.2.2)$$

for some $a < \xi < b$.

Proof. We only look at the case when $m = 2$. Other cases can be proved similarly. Let

$$P(t) = \alpha_0 + \alpha_1(t-a) + \alpha_2(t-a)^2.$$

We choose the α_i's so that $P(a) = f(a)$, $P'(a) = f'(a)$, and $P(b) = f(b)$. The first two lead to the conditions

$$\alpha_0 = f(a), \quad \alpha_1 = f'(a).$$

Let $\phi(t) = f(t) - P(t)$. By construction, $\phi(a) = \phi(b) = 0$. By Rolle, there is a $\xi' \in (a, b)$ such that $\phi'(\xi') = 0$. Moreover, $\phi'(a) = 0$. Hence we can apply Rolle again— this time to ϕ' on $[a, \xi']$. It implies that there is $\xi \in (a, \xi')$ such that $\phi''(\xi) = 0$. The second derivative of ϕ at ξ is

$$0 = \phi''(\xi) = f''(\xi) - P''(\xi) = f''(\xi) - 2\alpha_2,$$

so $\alpha_2 = f''(\xi)/2$. Plugging into P and using $\phi(b) = 0$ gives the claim. $\qquad \square$

Again, in the case of several variables, we restrict ourselves to the second order. We start with an important special case: a multivariate mean value theorem.

Theorem 3.2.22 (Multivariate mean value). *Let* $f : D \to \mathbb{R}$ *where* $D \subseteq \mathbb{R}^d$. *Let* $\mathbf{x}_0 \in D$ *and* $\delta > 0$ *be such that* $B_\delta(\mathbf{x}_0) \subseteq D$. *If* f *is continuously differentiable on* $B_\delta(\mathbf{x}_0)$, *then for any* $\mathbf{x} \in B_\delta(\mathbf{x}_0)$,

$$f(\mathbf{x}) = f(\mathbf{x}_0) + \nabla f(\mathbf{x}_0 + \xi \mathbf{p})^T \mathbf{p}, \qquad (3.2.3)$$

for some $\xi \in (0, 1)$, *where* $\mathbf{p} = \mathbf{x} - \mathbf{x}_0$.

Proof. Let $\phi(t) = f(\boldsymbol{\alpha}(t))$ where $\boldsymbol{\alpha}(t) = \mathbf{x}_0 + t\mathbf{p}$. Observe that $\phi(0) = f(\mathbf{x}_0)$ and $\phi(1) = f(\mathbf{x})$. By the chain rule,

$$\phi'(t) = J_f(\boldsymbol{\alpha}(t)) J_{\boldsymbol{\alpha}}(t) = \nabla f(\boldsymbol{\alpha}(t))^T \mathbf{p} = \nabla f(\mathbf{x}_0 + t\mathbf{p})^T \mathbf{p}.$$

In particular, ϕ has a continuous first derivative on $[0, 1]$. By the mean value theorem in the single-variable case,

$$\phi(t) = \phi(0) + t\phi'(\xi)$$

for some $\xi \in (0, t)$. Plugging in the expressions for $\phi(0)$ and $\phi'(\xi)$ and taking $t = 1$ will result in the claim. $\quad\square$

Theorem 3.2.23 (Multivariate Taylor). *Let $f : D \to \mathbb{R}$ where $D \subseteq \mathbb{R}^d$. Let $\mathbf{x}_0 \in D$ and $\delta > 0$ be such that $B_\delta(\mathbf{x}_0) \subseteq D$. If f is three times continuously differentiable on $B_\delta(\mathbf{x}_0)$, then for any $\mathbf{x} \in B_\delta(\mathbf{x}_0)$,*

$$f(\mathbf{x}) = f(\mathbf{x}_0) + \nabla f(\mathbf{x}_0)^T \mathbf{p} + \frac{1}{2} \mathbf{p}^T \mathbf{H}_f(\mathbf{x}_0) \mathbf{p} + O(\|\mathbf{p}\|^3), \qquad (3.2.4)$$

where $\mathbf{p} = \mathbf{x} - \mathbf{x}_0$.

If f is twice continuously differentiable on $B_\delta(\mathbf{x}_0)$, then for any $\mathbf{x} \in B_\delta(\mathbf{x}_0)$,

$$f(\mathbf{x}) = f(\mathbf{x}_0) + \nabla f(\mathbf{x}_0)^T \mathbf{p} + \frac{1}{2} \mathbf{p}^T \mathbf{H}_f(\mathbf{x}_0 + \xi \mathbf{p}) \mathbf{p}, \qquad (3.2.5)$$

for some $\xi \in (0, 1)$, where $\mathbf{p} = \mathbf{x} - \mathbf{x}_0$.

Proof. We only prove the second case, the first case can be proved similarly. Let $\phi(t) = f(\boldsymbol{\alpha}(t))$ where $\boldsymbol{\alpha}(t) = \mathbf{x}_0 + t\mathbf{p}$. Observe that $\phi(0) = f(\mathbf{x}_0)$ and $\phi(1) = f(\mathbf{x})$. As observed in the proof of the multivariate mean value theorem, $\phi'(t) = \nabla f(\boldsymbol{\alpha}(t))^T \mathbf{p}$. By the chain rule,

$$\phi''(t) = \frac{\mathrm{d}}{\mathrm{d}t}\left[\sum_{i=1}^{d} \frac{\partial f(\boldsymbol{\alpha}(t))}{\partial x_i} p_i \right] = \sum_{i=1}^{d} \sum_{j=1}^{d} \frac{\partial^2 f(\boldsymbol{\alpha}(t))}{\partial x_j \partial x_i} p_j p_i = \mathbf{p}^T \mathbf{H}_f(\mathbf{x}_0 + t\mathbf{p}) \mathbf{p}.$$

In particular, ϕ has continuous first and second derivatives on $[0, 1]$. By Taylor's theorem in the single-variable case,

$$\phi(t) = \phi(0) + t\phi'(0) + \frac{1}{2} t^2 \phi''(\xi),$$

for some $\xi \in (0, t)$. Plugging in the expressions for $\phi(0)$, $\phi'(0)$, and $\phi''(\xi)$ and taking $t = 1$ gives the claim. $\quad\square$

Example 3.2.24. Consider the function $f(x_1, x_2) = x_1 x_2 + x_1^2 + e^{x_1} \cos x_2$. We apply Taylor's theorem with $\mathbf{x}_0 = (0, 0)$ and $\mathbf{x} = (x_1, x_2)$. The gradient is

$$\nabla f(x_1, x_2) = (x_2 + 2x_1 + e^{x_1} \cos x_2, x_1 - e^{x_1} \sin x_2)^T,$$

and the Hessian is

$$\mathbf{H}_f(x_1, x_2) = \begin{pmatrix} 2 + e^{x_1} \cos x_2 & 1 - e^{x_1} \sin x_2 \\ 1 - e^{x_1} \sin x_2 & -e^{x_1} \cos x_2 \end{pmatrix}.$$

So $f(0,0) = 1$ and $\nabla f(0,0) = (1,0)^T$. Thus, by Taylor's theorem,

$$f(x_1, x_2) \approx 1 + x_1 + \frac{1}{2}(3x_1^2 + 2x_1 x_2 - x_2^2).$$

3.3 Unconstrained optimization

In this section, we derive optimality conditions for unconstrained continuous optimization problems and start with local minimizers.

3.3.1 Necessary and sufficient conditions of local minimizers

We will be interested in unconstrained optimization of the form:

$$\min_{\mathbf{x} \in \mathbb{R}^d} f(\mathbf{x}), \tag{3.3.1}$$

where $f : \mathbb{R}^d \to \mathbb{R}$. In this subsection, we defined several notions of solution and derive characterizations. Ideally, we would like to find a global minimizer to the optimization problem above.

Definition 3.3.1 (Global minimizer). Let $f : \mathbb{R}^d \to \mathbb{R}$. The point $\mathbf{x}^* \in \mathbb{R}^d$ is a global minimizer of f over $\mathbb{R}^d$ if

$$f(\mathbf{x}) \geq f(\mathbf{x}^*), \quad \forall \mathbf{x} \in \mathbb{R}^d. \tag{3.3.2}$$

Often it is difficult to find a global minimizer unless some special structure is present. Therefore weaker notions of solution have been introduced. The relationship between global minimizer and local minimizer is shown in Fig. 3.8.

Definition 3.3.2 (Local minimizer). Let $f : \mathbb{R}^d \to \mathbb{R}$. The point $\mathbf{x}^* \in \mathbb{R}^d$ is a local minimizer of f over $\mathbb{R}^d$ if there is $\delta > 0$ such that

$$f(\mathbf{x}) \geq f(\mathbf{x}^*), \quad \forall \mathbf{x} \in B_\delta(\mathbf{x}^*) \setminus \{\mathbf{x}^*\}. \tag{3.3.3}$$

If the inequality is strict, we say that $\mathbf{x}^*$ is a strict local minimizer.

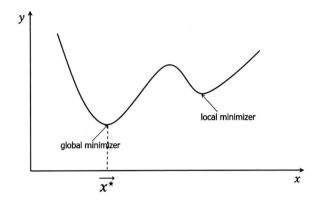

Figure 3.8 Global and local minimizers.

$\mathbf{x}^*$ is a local minimizer if there is open ball around $\mathbf{x}^*$ where it attains the minimum value. The difference between global and local minimizers is illustrated in Fig. 3.8. We will characterize local minimizers in terms of the gradient and Hessian of the function.

We first need to define what a descent direction is, which generalizes the case when the derivative of a one-dimensional function is negative.

Definition 3.3.3 (Descent direction). Let $f : \mathbb{R}^d \to \mathbb{R}$. A vector $\mathbf{v}$ is a descent direction for f at $\mathbf{x}_0$ if there is $\alpha^* > 0$ such that

$$f(\mathbf{x}_0 + \alpha\mathbf{v}) < f(\mathbf{x}_0), \quad \forall \alpha \in (0, \alpha^*). \tag{3.3.4}$$

In the continuously differentiable case, the directional derivative gives a criterion for descent directions.

Lemma 3.3.4 (Descent direction and directional derivative). *Let* $f : \mathbb{R}^d \to \mathbb{R}$ *be continuously differentiable at* $\mathbf{x}_0$. *A vector* $\mathbf{v}$ *is a descent direction for* f *at* $\mathbf{x}_0$ *if*

$$\frac{\partial f(\mathbf{x}_0)}{\partial \mathbf{v}} = \nabla f(\mathbf{x}_0)^T \mathbf{v} < 0, \tag{3.3.5}$$

that is, if the directional derivative of f *at* $\mathbf{x}_0$ *in the direction* $\mathbf{v}$ *is negative.*

Proof. We will apply the multivariate Taylor theorem to prove it. Suppose there is $\mathbf{v} \in \mathbb{R}^d$ such that $\nabla f(\mathbf{x}_0)^T \mathbf{v} = -\eta < 0$. For $\alpha > 0$, the multivariate mean value theorem implies that there is $\xi_\alpha \in (0, 1)$ such that

$$f(\mathbf{x}_0 + \alpha\mathbf{v}) = f(\mathbf{x}_0) + \nabla f(\mathbf{x}_0)^T (\alpha\mathbf{v}) + O(\|\alpha\mathbf{v}\|^2).$$

Hence there is $\alpha^* > 0$ small enough such that

$$\nabla f(\mathbf{x}_0)^T(\alpha\mathbf{v}) + O(\|\alpha\mathbf{v}\|^2) < -\eta/2 < 0, \quad \forall \alpha \in (0, \alpha^*).$$

That implies

$$f(\mathbf{x}_0 + \alpha\mathbf{v}) < f(\mathbf{x}_0) - \alpha\eta/2 < f(\mathbf{x}_0), \quad \forall \alpha \in (0, \alpha^*)$$

and proves the claim. □

Lemma 3.3.5 (Existence of a descent direction). *Let* $f : \mathbb{R}^d \to \mathbb{R}$ *be continuously differentiable at* $\mathbf{x}_0$ *and assume that* $\nabla f(\mathbf{x}_0) \neq 0$. *Then* f *has a descent direction at* $\mathbf{x}_0$.

Proof. Let $\mathbf{v} = -\nabla f(\mathbf{x}_0)$. Then $\nabla f(\mathbf{x}_0)^T\mathbf{v} = -\|\nabla f(\mathbf{x}_0)\|^2 < 0$ since $\nabla f(\mathbf{x}_0) \neq 0$. □

The following theorem extends the result that the derivative of a function is zero at a minimizer.

Theorem 3.3.6 (First-order necessary condition). *Let* $f : \mathbb{R}^d \to \mathbb{R}$ *be continuously differentiable on* $\mathbb{R}^d$. *If* $\mathbf{x}_0$ *is a local minimizer, then* $\nabla f(\mathbf{x}_0) = 0$.

Proof. The result can be easily proved by contradiction. Suppose that $\nabla f(\mathbf{x}_0) \neq 0$. By the existence of a descent direction lemma, there is a descent direction $\mathbf{v} \in \mathbb{R}^d$ at $\mathbf{x}_0$. That implies

$$f(\mathbf{x}_0 + \alpha\mathbf{v}) < f(\mathbf{x}_0), \quad \forall \alpha \in (0, \alpha^*)$$

for some $\alpha^* > 0$. So every open ball around $\mathbf{x}_0$ has a point achieving a smaller value than $f(\mathbf{x}_0)$. Thus $\mathbf{x}_0$ is not a local minimizer, a contradiction. So it must be that $\nabla f(\mathbf{x}_0) = 0$. □

If f is twice continuously differentiable, the Hessian of the function can play an important role.

Definition 3.3.7. A square symmetric $d \times d$ matrix H is positive semidefinite (PSD) if $\mathbf{x}^T H \mathbf{x} \geq 0$ for any $\mathbf{x} \in \mathbb{R}^d$.

Theorem 3.3.8 (Second-order necessary condition). *Let* $f : \mathbb{R}^d \to \mathbb{R}$ *be twice continuously differentiable on* $\mathbb{R}^d$. *If* $\mathbf{x}_0$ *is a local minimizer, then* $\mathbf{H}_f(\mathbf{x}_0)$ *is PSD.*

Proof. This can be proved by contradiction. Suppose that $\mathbf{H}_f(\mathbf{x}_0)$ is not PSD. Since the Hessian is symmetric, $\mathbf{H}_f(\mathbf{x}_0)$ has a spectral decomposition. It follows that $\mathbf{H}_f(\mathbf{x}_0)$ must have at least one negative eigenvalue $-\eta < 0$. Let $\mathbf{v}$ be a corresponding eigenvector. As a result, $\langle \mathbf{v}, \mathbf{H}_f(\mathbf{x}_0)\mathbf{v}\rangle = -\eta < 0$. For $\alpha > 0$, the multivariate Taylor's theorem implies that there is $\xi_\alpha \in (0,1)$ such that

$$
\begin{aligned}
f(\mathbf{x}_0 + \alpha\mathbf{v}) &= f(\mathbf{x}_0) + \nabla f(\mathbf{x}_0)^T(\alpha\mathbf{v}) + (\alpha\mathbf{v})^T \mathbf{H}_f(\mathbf{x}_0)(\alpha\mathbf{v}) + O(\|\alpha\mathbf{v}\|^3) \\
&= f(\mathbf{x}_0) + \alpha^2 \mathbf{v}^T \mathbf{H}_f(\mathbf{x}_0\,\mathbf{v} + O(\|\alpha\mathbf{v}\|^3),
\end{aligned}
$$

where we used $\nabla f(\mathbf{x}_0) = 0$ by the first-order necessary condition. So taking α small enough gives

$$
\mathbf{v}^T \mathbf{H}_f(\mathbf{x}_0)\mathbf{v} < -\eta/2 < 0.
$$

That implies

$$
f(\mathbf{x}_0 + \alpha\mathbf{v}) < f(\mathbf{x}_0) - \alpha^2 \eta/2 < f(\mathbf{x}_0).
$$

Since this holds for all sufficiently small α, every open ball around $\mathbf{x}_0$ has a point achieving a lower value than $f(\mathbf{x}_0)$. Thus $\mathbf{x}_0$ is not a local minimizer, a contradiction. So it must be that $\mathbf{H}_f(\mathbf{x}_0)$ is PSD. $\square$

3.3.1.1 Sufficient conditions for local minimizers

As in the one-dimensional case, the necessary conditions in the previous subsection are not in general sufficient, as the following example shows.

Example 3.3.9. Let $f(x) = x^3$. Then $f'(x) = 3x^2$ and $f''(x) = 6x$ so that $f'(0) = 0$ and $f''(0) \geq 0$. Hence $x = 0$ is a stationary point $(\nabla f(\mathbf{x}_0) = 0)$. But $x = 0$ is not a local minimizer. Indeed, $f(0) = 0$, but for any $\delta > 0$, $f(-\delta) < 0$.

We now state the following theorem, which gives sufficient conditions for local minimizers.

Theorem 3.3.10 (Second-order sufficient condition). *Let $f : \mathbb{R}^d \to \mathbb{R}$ be twice continuously differentiable on $\mathbb{R}^d$. If $\nabla f(\mathbf{x}_0) = 0$ and $\mathbf{H}_f(\mathbf{x}_0)$ is positive definite, then $\mathbf{x}_0$ is a strict local minimizer.*

Proof. Since $\mathbf{H}_f(\mathbf{x}_0)$ is positive definite, all of its eigenvalues are positive. It follows that $\mathbf{v}^T \mathbf{H}_f(\mathbf{x}_0)\mathbf{v} \geq \mu\|\mathbf{v}\|^2$ for all $\mathbf{v} \neq 0$, where μ can be any positive number smaller than the smallest eigenvalue of $\mathbf{H}_f(\mathbf{x}_0)$. By the multivariate Taylor's theorem, for small $\mathbf{v} \neq 0$, we have

$$\begin{aligned} f(\mathbf{x}_0 + \mathbf{v}) &= f(\mathbf{x}_0) + \nabla f(\mathbf{x}_0)^T \mathbf{v} + \mathbf{v}^T \mathbf{H}_f(\mathbf{x}_0) \mathbf{v} + O(\|\mathbf{v}\|^3) \\ &> f(\mathbf{x}_0) + \mu \|\mathbf{v}\|^2 + O(\|\mathbf{v}\|^3) \\ &> f(\mathbf{x}_0). \end{aligned}$$

Therefore $\mathbf{x}_0$ is a strict local minimizer. $\qquad\qquad\qquad\qquad\qquad\square$

3.3.2 Convexity and global minimizers

A real-valued function is called convex if the line segment between any two points on the graph of the function lies above the graph between the two points. Our optimality conditions have only concerned local minimizers. Indeed, in the absence of global structure, local information such as gradients and Hessians can only inform about the immediate neighborhood of points. Here, we consider convexity, under which local minimizers are also global minimizers.

3.3.2.1 Convex sets and functions

We start with convex sets.

Definition 3.3.11 (Convex set). A set $D \subseteq \mathbb{R}^d$ is convex if for all $\mathbf{x}, \mathbf{y} \in D$ and all $\alpha \in [0, 1]$,

$$(1 - \alpha)\mathbf{x} + \alpha\mathbf{y} \in D. \tag{3.3.6}$$

Fig. 3.9(a) is a convex set; Fig. 3.9(b) is not a convex set.

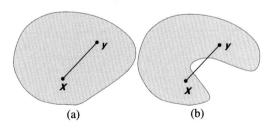

(a)   (b)

Figure 3.9 (a) Convex set (b) Not a convex set.

Example 3.3.12. Any open ball in $\mathbb{R}^d$ is convex. Indeed, let $\delta > 0$ and $\mathbf{x}_0$. For any $\mathbf{x}, \mathbf{y} \in B_\delta(\mathbf{x}_0)$ and any $\alpha \in [0, 1]$, we have

$$
\begin{aligned}
\|[(1-\alpha)\mathbf{x}+\alpha\mathbf{y}] - \mathbf{x}_0\| &= \|(1-\alpha)(\mathbf{x}-\mathbf{x}_0)+\alpha(\mathbf{y}-\mathbf{x}_0)\| \\
&\leq \|(1-\alpha)(\mathbf{x}-\mathbf{x}_0)\| + \|\alpha(\mathbf{y}-\mathbf{x}_0)\| \\
&= (1-\alpha)\|\mathbf{x}-\mathbf{x}_0\| + \alpha\|\mathbf{y}-\mathbf{x}_0\| \\
&\leq (1-\alpha)\delta + \alpha\delta \\
&= \delta,
\end{aligned}
$$

where we used the triangle inequality on the second line. Hence we have established that $(1-\alpha)\mathbf{x}+\alpha\mathbf{y} \in B_\delta(\mathbf{x}_0)$.

Our main interest is in convex functions.

Definition 3.3.13 (Convex function). A function $f : \mathbb{R}^d \to \mathbb{R}$ is convex if, for all $\mathbf{x}, \mathbf{y} \in \mathbb{R}^d$ and all $\alpha \in [0, 1]$,

$$
f((1-\alpha)\mathbf{x}+\alpha\mathbf{y}) \leq (1-\alpha)f(\mathbf{x})+\alpha f(\mathbf{y}). \tag{3.3.7}
$$

More generally, a function $f : D \to \mathbb{R}$ over a convex domains $D \subseteq \mathbb{R}^d$ is convex if the definition above holds over all $\mathbf{x}, \mathbf{y} \in D$.

Fig. 3.10 is a convex function.

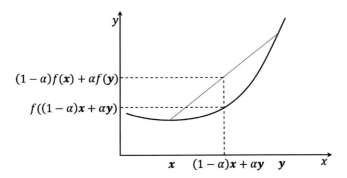

Figure 3.10 Convex function.

Lemma 3.3.14 (Affine functions are convex). *Let $\mathbf{w} \in \mathbb{R}^d$ and $b \in \mathbb{R}$. The function $f(\mathbf{x}) = \mathbf{w}^T \mathbf{x} + b$ is convex.*

Proof. For any $\mathbf{x}, \mathbf{y} \in \mathbb{R}^d$ and $\alpha \in [0, 1]$,

$$
f((1-\alpha)\mathbf{x}+\alpha\mathbf{y}) = \mathbf{w}^T[(1-\alpha)\mathbf{x}+\alpha\mathbf{y}]+b = (1-\alpha)[\mathbf{w}^T\mathbf{x}+b]+\alpha[\mathbf{w}^T\mathbf{y}+b],
$$

which proves the claim.   □

A common way to prove that a function is convex is to look at its Hessian. We start with a first-order condition that will prove useful.

Lemma 3.3.15 (First-order convexity condition). *Let $f : \mathbb{R}^d \to \mathbb{R}$ be continuously differentiable. Then f is convex if and only if for all $\mathbf{x}, \mathbf{y} \in \mathbb{R}^d$,*

$$f(\mathbf{y}) \geq f(\mathbf{x}) + \nabla f(\mathbf{x})^T (\mathbf{y} - \mathbf{x}). \tag{3.3.8}$$

Proof. (First-order convexity condition) Suppose first that $f(\mathbf{z}_2) \geq f(\mathbf{z}_1) + \nabla f(\mathbf{z}_1)^T (\mathbf{z}_2 - \mathbf{z}_1)$ for all $\mathbf{z}_1, \mathbf{z}_2$. For any $\mathbf{x}, \mathbf{y}$ and $\alpha \in [0, 1]$, let $\mathbf{w} = (1 - \alpha)\mathbf{x} + \alpha\mathbf{y}$. Then taking $\mathbf{z}_1 = \mathbf{w}$ and $\mathbf{z}_2 = \mathbf{x}$ gives

$$f(\mathbf{x}) \geq f(\mathbf{w}) + \nabla f(\mathbf{w})^T (\mathbf{x} - \mathbf{w}),$$

and taking $\mathbf{z}_1 = \mathbf{w}$ and $\mathbf{z}_2 = \mathbf{y}$ gives

$$f(\mathbf{y}) \geq f(\mathbf{w}) + \nabla f(\mathbf{w})^T (\mathbf{y} - \mathbf{w}).$$

Multiplying the first inequality by $(1 - \alpha)$ and the second one by α, and adding them up gives

$$(1 - \alpha)f(\mathbf{x}) + \alpha f(\mathbf{y}) \geq f(\mathbf{w}) + \nabla f(\mathbf{w})^T ([(1 - \alpha)\mathbf{x} + \alpha\mathbf{y}] - \mathbf{w}) = f(\mathbf{w}),$$

proving convexity. For the other direction, assume that f is convex. For any $\mathbf{x}, \mathbf{y}$, and $\alpha \in (0, 1)$, by the multivariate mean value theorem, for some $\xi \in (0, 1)$ it holds that

$$f(\mathbf{w}) = f(\mathbf{x} + \alpha(\mathbf{y} - \mathbf{x})) = f(\mathbf{x}) + \alpha(\mathbf{y} - \mathbf{x})^T \nabla f(\mathbf{x} + \xi\alpha(\mathbf{y} - \mathbf{x})),$$

while convexity implies

$$f(\mathbf{w}) \leq (1 - \alpha)f(\mathbf{x}) + \alpha f(\mathbf{y}).$$

Combining, rearranging, and dividing by α gives

$$(\mathbf{y} - \mathbf{x})^T \nabla f(\mathbf{x} + \xi\alpha(\mathbf{y} - \mathbf{x})) \leq f(\mathbf{y}) - f(\mathbf{x}).$$

Taking $\alpha \to 0$ gives the claim.   □

Lemma 3.3.16 (Second-order convexity condition). *Let $f : \mathbb{R}^d \to \mathbb{R}$ be twice continuously differentiable. Then f is convex if and only if, for all $\mathbf{x} \in \mathbb{R}^d$, $\mathbf{H}_f(\mathbf{x})$ is PSD.*

Proof. Suppose first that $\mathbf{H}_f(\mathbf{z}_1)$ is PSD for all $\mathbf{z}_1$. For any $\mathbf{x}, \mathbf{y}$, by the multivariate Taylor theorem, there is $\xi \in (0, 1)$ such that

$$f(\mathbf{y}) = f(\mathbf{x}) + \nabla f(\mathbf{x})^T (\mathbf{y} - \mathbf{x}) + (\mathbf{y} - \mathbf{x})^T \mathbf{H}_f(\mathbf{x} + \xi(\mathbf{y} - \mathbf{x})) (\mathbf{y} - \mathbf{x})$$
$$\geq f(\mathbf{x}) + \nabla f(\mathbf{x})^T (\mathbf{y} - \mathbf{x}),$$

where we used the positive semi-definiteness of the Hessian. By the first-order convexity condition, it implies that f is convex. For the other direction, assume that f is convex. For any $\mathbf{x}, \mathbf{w}$, and $\alpha \in (0, 1)$, by the multivariate Taylor theorem again, for some $\xi_\alpha \in (0, 1)$ it holds that

$$f(\mathbf{x} + \alpha \mathbf{w}) = f(\mathbf{x}) + \alpha \mathbf{w}^T \nabla f(\mathbf{x}) + \alpha^2 \mathbf{w}^T \mathbf{H}_f(\mathbf{x} + \xi_\alpha \alpha \mathbf{w}) \mathbf{w},$$

while the first-order convexity condition implies

$$f(\mathbf{x} + \alpha \mathbf{w}) \geq f(\mathbf{x}) + \alpha \mathbf{w}^T \nabla f(\mathbf{x}).$$

Combining, rearranging, and dividing by α^2 gives

$$\mathbf{w}^T \mathbf{H}_f(\mathbf{x} + \xi_\alpha \alpha \mathbf{w}) \mathbf{w} \geq 0.$$

Taking $\alpha \to 0$ shows that $\mathbf{w}^T \mathbf{H}_f(\mathbf{x}) \mathbf{w} \geq 0$. Since $\mathbf{w}$ is arbitrary, this implies that the Hessian is PSD at $\mathbf{x}$. This holds for any $\mathbf{x}$, which proves the claim. $\square$

Example 3.3.17. Consider the quadratic function

$$f(\mathbf{x}) = \frac{1}{2} \mathbf{x}^T P \mathbf{x} + \mathbf{q}^T \mathbf{x} + r.$$

We showed previously that the Hessian is

$$\mathbf{H}_f(\mathbf{x}) = \frac{1}{2}[P + P^T].$$

So f is convex if and only if the matrix $\frac{1}{2}[P + P^T]$ has only nonnegative eigenvalues.

3.3.2.2 Global minimizers of convex functions

For a convex function, sufficient (and therefore necessary) condition for minimizers is $\nabla f(\mathbf{x}_0) = \mathbf{0}$.

Theorem 3.3.18. *Let $f : \mathbb{R}^d \to \mathbb{R}$ be a continuously differentiable, convex function. If $\nabla f(\mathbf{x}_0) = \mathbf{0}$, then $\mathbf{x}_0$ is a global minimizer.*

Proof. Assume $\nabla f(\mathbf{x}_0) = \mathbf{0}$. By the first-order convexity condition, for any $\mathbf{y}$,

$$f(\mathbf{y}) - f(\mathbf{x}_0) \geq \nabla f(\mathbf{x}_0)^T (\mathbf{y} - \mathbf{x}_0) = 0.$$

That proves the claim. $\square$

In addition, we will show that any local minimizer is global, which is a key property of convex functions.

Theorem 3.3.19 (Global minimizers of convex functions). *Let $f : \mathbb{R}^d \to \mathbb{R}$ be a convex function. Then any local minimizer of f is also a global minimizer.*

Proof. By contradiction, suppose $\mathbf{x}_0$ is a local minimizer, but not a global minimizer. Then there is $\mathbf{y}$ such that

$$f(\mathbf{y}) < f(\mathbf{x}_0).$$

By convexity, for any $\alpha \in (0, 1)$,

$$f(\mathbf{x}_0 + \alpha(\mathbf{y} - \mathbf{x}_0)) \leq (1 - \alpha)f(\mathbf{x}_0) + \alpha f(\mathbf{y}) < f(\mathbf{x}_0).$$

But that implies that every open ball around $\mathbf{x}_0$ contains a point taking a smaller value than $f(\mathbf{x}_0)$, a contradiction. $\square$

Example 3.3.20. Consider the quadratic function

$$f(\mathbf{x}) = \frac{1}{2}\mathbf{x}^T P \mathbf{x} + \mathbf{q}^T \mathbf{x} + r,$$

where P is symmetric and positive definite. The Hessian is then

$$\mathbf{H}_f(\mathbf{x}) = \frac{1}{2}[P + P^T] = P$$

for any $\mathbf{x}$. So f is convex. Further, the gradient is

$$\nabla f(\mathbf{x}) = P\mathbf{x} + \mathbf{q}$$

for all $\mathbf{x}$. Any $\mathbf{x}$ satisfying

$$P\mathbf{x} + \mathbf{q} = \mathbf{0}$$

is a global minimizer. If $P = Q\Lambda Q^T$ is a spectral decomposition of P, where all diagonal entries of Λ are strictly positive, then $P^{-1} = Q\Lambda^{-1}Q^T$ where the diagonal entries of Λ^{-1} are the inverses of those of Λ. This can be seen by checking that

$$Q\Lambda Q^T Q\Lambda^{-1}Q^T = QI_{d\times d}Q^T = I_{d\times d}.$$

So the following is a global minimizer:

$$\mathbf{x}^* = -Q\Lambda^{-1}Q^T\mathbf{q}.$$

3.3.3 Gradient descent

Gradient descent is an iterative optimization algorithm for finding a local minimum of a differentiable function. Once we know a function has a minimizer, we will discuss a class of algorithms known as gradient descent method for solving optimization problems numerically. Let $f : \mathbb{R}^d \to \mathbb{R}$ is continuously differentiable. We restrict ourselves to unconstrained minimization problems of the form

$$\min_{\mathbf{x}\in\mathbb{R}^d} f(\mathbf{x}). \tag{3.3.9}$$

One might evaluate f at a large number of points $\mathbf{x}$ to identify a global minimizer of f. This naive approach seems too expensive. A less naive approach might be to find all stationary points of f, that is, those $\mathbf{x}$'s such that $\nabla f(\mathbf{x}) = \mathbf{0}$. And then choose that $\mathbf{x}$ among them that produces the smallest value of $f(\mathbf{x})$. This indeed works in many problems, like the following example we have encountered previously.

Example 3.3.21. Consider the least–squares problem

$$\min_{\mathbf{x}\in\mathbb{R}^d} \|A\mathbf{x} - \mathbf{b}\|^2,$$

where $A \in \mathbb{R}^{n\times d}$ has full column rank. In particular, $d \leq n$. The objective function is a quadratic function

$$f(\mathbf{x}) = \|A\mathbf{x} - \mathbf{b}\|^2 = (A\mathbf{x} - \mathbf{b})^T(A\mathbf{x} - \mathbf{b}) = \mathbf{x}^T A^T A\mathbf{x} - 2\mathbf{b}^T A\mathbf{x} + \mathbf{b}^T\mathbf{b}.$$

By a previous example,

$$\nabla f(\mathbf{x}) = 2A^T A\mathbf{x} - 2A^T\mathbf{b},$$

where we used that $A^T A$ is symmetric. So the stationary points satisfy

$$A^T A\mathbf{x} = A^T\mathbf{b},$$

which you may recognize as the normal equations for the least-squares problem. We have previously shown that there is a unique solution to this system when A has full column rank. Moreover, this optimization problem is convex. Indeed, by our previous example, the Hessian of f is

$$\mathbf{H}_f(\mathbf{x}) = 2A^T A.$$

This Hessian is clearly PSD, since for any $\mathbf{z} \in \mathbf{R}^d$,

$$\langle \mathbf{z}, 2A^T A\mathbf{z} \rangle = 2(A\mathbf{z})^T (A\mathbf{z}) = 2\|A\mathbf{z}\|^2 \geq 0.$$

So any local minimizer, which is necessarily a stationary point, is also a global minimizer. So we have found all global minimizers.

In general, identifying stationary points often leads to systems of non-linear equations that do not have explicit solutions. Hence, unfortunately, we resort to gradient descent methods.

3.3.3.1 Steepest descent

The steepest descent approach is to find smaller values of f by successively following directions in which f decreases. As we have seen in the proof of the first-order necessary condition, $-\nabla f$ provides such a direction.

Lemma 3.3.22 (Steepest descent). *Let $f : \mathbb{R}^d \to \mathbb{R}$ be continuously differentiable at $\mathbf{x}_0$. For any unit vector $\mathbf{v} \in \mathbb{R}^d$,*

$$\frac{\partial f(\mathbf{x}_0)}{\partial \mathbf{v}} \geq \frac{\partial f(\mathbf{x}_0)}{\partial \mathbf{v}^*}, \tag{3.3.10}$$

where

$$\mathbf{v}^* = -\frac{\nabla f(\mathbf{x}_0)}{\|\nabla f(\mathbf{x}_0)\|}. \tag{3.3.11}$$

Proof. By the chain rule and Cauchy–Schwarz,

$$\begin{aligned}
\frac{\partial f(\mathbf{x}_0)}{\partial \mathbf{v}} &= \nabla f(\mathbf{x}_0)^T \mathbf{v} \\
&\geq -\|\nabla f(\mathbf{x}_0)\| \|\mathbf{v}\| \\
&= -\|\nabla f(\mathbf{x}_0)\| \\
&= \nabla f(\mathbf{x}_0)^T \left(-\frac{\nabla f(\mathbf{x}_0)}{\|\nabla f(\mathbf{x}_0)\|} \right) \\
&= \frac{\partial f(\mathbf{x}_0)}{\partial \mathbf{v}^*}. \quad \square
\end{aligned}$$

At each iteration of steepest descent, we take a step in the direction of the negative of the gradient, that is,

$$\mathbf{x}^{k+1} = \mathbf{x}^k - \alpha_k \nabla f(\mathbf{x}^k), \quad k = 0, 1, 2 \dots$$

for a sequence of step lengths $\alpha_k > 0$. α_k are called step sizes. In general, we will not be able to guarantee that a global minimizer is reached in the limit, even if one exists. We have the following results ([31]).

Theorem 3.3.23. *Suppose that $f : \mathbb{R}^d \to \mathbb{R}$ is twice continuously differentiable. The step size is chosen to minimize*

$$\alpha_k = arg\ min_{\alpha > 0} f(\mathbf{x}^k - \alpha \nabla f(\mathbf{x}^k)).$$

Then steepest descent started from any $\mathbf{x}^0$ produces a sequence $\mathbf{x}^k$, $k = 1, 2, \dots$ such that if $\nabla f(\mathbf{x}^k) \neq 0$, then

$$f(\mathbf{x}^{k+1}) \leq f(\mathbf{x}^k), \quad \forall k \geq 1.$$

3.4 Logistic regression

Logistic regression is a model that in its basic form uses a logistic function to model a binary dependent variable. It can be extended to several classes of events such as the classification of images. In this section, we illustrate the use of gradient descent on binary classification by logistic regression.

Given the input data is of the form $\{(\boldsymbol{\alpha}_i, b_i) : i = 1, \dots, n\}$ where $\boldsymbol{\alpha}_i \in \mathbb{R}^d$ are the features and $b_i \in \{0, 1\}$ is the label. As before, we use a matrix representation: $A \in \mathbb{R}^{n \times d}$ has rows $\boldsymbol{\alpha}_j^T, j = 1, \dots, n$, and $\mathbf{b} = (b_1, \dots, b_n)^T \in \{0, 1\}^n$. We wish to find a function of the features that approximates the probability of the label 1. For this purpose, we model the logit function of the probability of label 1 as a linear function of the features. Fig. 3.11 is the graph of the logit function.

For $\mathbf{x}, \boldsymbol{\alpha} \in \mathbb{R}^d$, let $p(\boldsymbol{\alpha}; \mathbf{x})$ be the probability of the output to be 1. We define

$$\log \frac{p(\boldsymbol{\alpha}; \mathbf{x})}{1 - p(\boldsymbol{\alpha}; \mathbf{x})} = \boldsymbol{\alpha}^T \mathbf{x}.$$

Here, $\boldsymbol{\alpha}^T \mathbf{x} = \sum x_i \alpha_i$ can be viewed as a regression problem, which seeks the best parameters ($\mathbf{x}$) with given data ($\boldsymbol{\alpha}$). Rearranging this expression gives

$$p(\boldsymbol{\alpha}; \mathbf{x}) = \sigma(\boldsymbol{\alpha}^T \mathbf{x}),$$

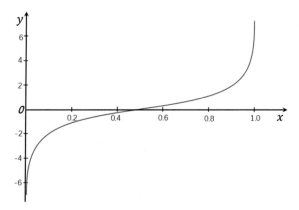

Figure 3.11 Logit function.

where the sigmoid function is

$$\sigma(t) = \frac{1}{1 + e^{-t}}$$

for $t \in \mathbb{R}$. To maximize the likelihood of the data, we assume the labels are independent given the features, which is given by

$$\mathcal{L}(\mathbf{x}; A, \mathbf{b}) = \prod_{i=1}^{n} p(\boldsymbol{\alpha}_i; \mathbf{x})^{b_i} (1 - p(\boldsymbol{\alpha}_i; \mathbf{x}))^{1 - b_i}.$$

Taking a logarithm, multiplying by $-1/n$ and substituting the sigmoid function, we want to minimize the cross-entropy loss:

$$\ell(\mathbf{x}; A, \mathbf{b}) = -\frac{1}{n} \sum_{i=1}^{n} b_i \log(\sigma(\boldsymbol{\alpha}^T \mathbf{x})) - \frac{1}{n} \sum_{i=1}^{n} (1 - b_i) \log(1 - \sigma(\boldsymbol{\alpha}^T \mathbf{x})).$$

That is, we solve

$$\min_{\mathbf{x} \in \mathbb{R}^d} \ell(\mathbf{x}; A, \mathbf{b}).$$

To use gradient descent, we need to compute the gradient of ℓ. We use the chain rule and first compute the derivative of σ, which is

$$\sigma'(t) = \frac{e^{-t}}{(1 + e^{-t})^2} = \frac{1}{1 + e^{-t}} \left(1 - \frac{1}{1 + e^{-t}}\right) = \sigma(t)(1 - \sigma(t)).$$

It follows that $\sigma(t)$ satisfies the logistic differential equation. It arises in a variety of applications, including the modeling of population dynamics.

Here, it will be a convenient way to compute the gradient. Indeed observe that by the chain rule

$$\nabla_{\mathbf{x}} \sigma(\boldsymbol{\alpha}^T \mathbf{x}) = \sigma(\boldsymbol{\alpha}^T \mathbf{x})(1 - \sigma(\boldsymbol{\alpha}^T \mathbf{x})) \boldsymbol{\alpha},$$

where we use a subscript $\mathbf{x}$ to make it clear that the gradient is with respect to $\mathbf{x}$.

With the same approach, we have

$$\nabla_{\mathbf{x}} \ell(\mathbf{x}; A, \mathbf{b}) = -\frac{1}{n} \sum_{i=1}^{n} \frac{b_i}{\sigma(\boldsymbol{\alpha}_i^T \mathbf{x})} \nabla_{\mathbf{x}} \sigma(\boldsymbol{\alpha}_i^T \mathbf{x}) + \frac{1}{n} \sum_{i=1}^{n} \frac{1 - b_i}{1 - \sigma(\boldsymbol{\alpha}_i^T \mathbf{x})} \nabla_{\mathbf{x}} \sigma(\boldsymbol{\alpha}_i^T \mathbf{x})$$

$$= -\frac{1}{n} \sum_{i=1}^{n} \left(\frac{b_i}{\sigma(\boldsymbol{\alpha}_i^T \mathbf{x})} - \frac{1 - b_i}{1 - \sigma(\boldsymbol{\alpha}_i^T \mathbf{x})} \right) \sigma(\boldsymbol{\alpha}_i^T \mathbf{x})(1 - \sigma(\boldsymbol{\alpha}_i^T \mathbf{x})) \boldsymbol{\alpha}_i$$

$$= -\frac{1}{n} \sum_{i=1}^{n} (b_i - \sigma(\boldsymbol{\alpha}_i^T \mathbf{x})) \boldsymbol{\alpha}_i.$$

To compute the Hessian, we note that

$$\nabla_{\mathbf{x}}(\sigma(\boldsymbol{\alpha}^T \mathbf{x}) \alpha_j) = \sigma(\boldsymbol{\alpha}^T \mathbf{x})(1 - \sigma(\boldsymbol{\alpha}^T \mathbf{x})) \boldsymbol{\alpha} \, \alpha_j,$$

so that

$$\nabla_{\mathbf{x}}(\sigma(\boldsymbol{\alpha}^T \mathbf{x}) \boldsymbol{\alpha}) = \sigma(\boldsymbol{\alpha}^T \mathbf{x})(1 - \sigma(\boldsymbol{\alpha}^T \mathbf{x})) \boldsymbol{\alpha}\boldsymbol{\alpha}^T.$$

Thus

$$\nabla_{\mathbf{x}}^2 \ell(\mathbf{x}; A, \mathbf{b}) = \frac{1}{n} \sum_{i=1}^{n} \sigma(\boldsymbol{\alpha}_i^T \mathbf{x})(1 - \sigma(\boldsymbol{\alpha}_i^T \mathbf{x})) \boldsymbol{\alpha}_i\boldsymbol{\alpha}_i^T,$$

where $\nabla_{\mathbf{x}}^2$ indicates the Hessian with respect to the $\mathbf{x}$ variables. Now each $\boldsymbol{\alpha}_i\boldsymbol{\alpha}_i^T$ is a symmetric matrix and PSD. As a result, the function $\ell(\mathbf{x}; A, \mathbf{b})$ is convex as a function of $\mathbf{x} \in \mathbb{R}^d$. We want to comment that convexity is one reason for working with the cross-entropy loss rather than the mean squared error.

To update the iteration formula: for step size β, one step of gradient descent is therefore

$$\mathbf{x}^{k+1} = \mathbf{x}^k + \beta \frac{1}{n} \sum_{i=1}^{n} (b_i - \sigma(\boldsymbol{\alpha}_i^T \mathbf{x}^k)) \boldsymbol{\alpha}_i.$$

In stochastic gradient descent, a variant of gradient descent, we pick a sample I uniformly at random in $\{1, \ldots, n\}$ and update as follows:

$$\mathbf{x}^{k+1} = \mathbf{x}^k + \beta \, (b_I - \sigma(\boldsymbol{\alpha}_I^T \mathbf{x}^k)) \, \boldsymbol{\alpha}_I.$$

3.5 K-means

k-means clustering is a popular method of vector quantization that aims to partition n observations into k clusters in which each observation belongs to the cluster with the nearest mean (cluster centers or cluster centroid), serving as a prototype of the cluster. k-means clustering minimizes within-cluster variances (squared Euclidean distances), but not regular Euclidean distances. While k-means general converge quickly to a local optimum, the problem is computationally difficult (NP-hard). This is shown in Fig. 3.12.

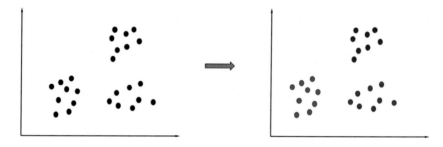

Figure 3.12 k-means clustering.

Given a $(x_1, x_2, ...x_n)$ where each observation is a d-dimensional real vector, k-means clustering aims to partition the n observations into $k(< n)$ sets $S = \{S_1, ...S_k\}$ so as to minimize the within–cluster sum of squares (WCSS) (i.e., variance), the squared distance of each vector from its centroid summed over all vectors:

$$\mathrm{WCSS}_i = \sum_{x \in S_i} ||x - \mu(S_i)||^2,$$

where $\mu(S_i)$ is the mean of points in S_i,

$$\mu(S) = \frac{1}{|S|} \sum_{\mathbf{x} \in S} \mathbf{x}.$$

The objective is to find

$$\arg\min_S \sum_{i=1}^{k} WCSS_i.$$

K-means Clustering Algorithm:
1. Cluster the data into k groups where k is predefined.
2. Select k points at random as cluster centers.
3. Assign objects to their closest cluster center according to the Euclidean distance function.
4. Calculate the centroid or mean of all objects in each cluster.
5. Repeat steps 3 and 4 until the same points are assigned to each cluster in consecutive rounds.

We now show that k-means converge by proving that $\sum_{i=1}^{k} WCSS_i$ monotonically decreases in each iteration. First, $\sum_{i=1}^{k} WCSS_i$ decreases in the reassignment step since each vector is assigned to the closest centroid, so the distance it contributes to $\sum_{i=1}^{k} WCSS_i$ decreases. Second, it decreases in the recomputation step because the new centroid is the vector $\mathbf{v}$ for which $WCSS_i$ reaches its minimum

$$WCSS_i(\mathbf{v}) = \sum_{\mathbf{x}=(x_j) \in S_i} |\mathbf{v} - \mathbf{x}|^2 = \sum_{\mathbf{x}=(x_j) \in S_i} \sum_{j=1}^{d} (v_j - x_j)^2$$

$$\frac{\partial WCSS_i(\mathbf{v})}{\partial v_m} = \sum_{\mathbf{x}=(x_j) \in S_i} 2(v_m - x_m),$$

where x_m and v_m are the mth components of their respective vectors. Setting the partial derivative to zero, we get

$$\mathbf{v} = \frac{1}{|S_i|} \sum_{\mathbf{x}=(x_j) \in S_i} x_j,$$

which is the componentwise definition of the centroid. Thus we minimize $WCSS_i$ when the old centroid is replaced with the new centroid. The sum of the $WCSS_i$ must then also decrease during recomputation.

3.6 Support vector machine

Support–vector machines (SVMs) are supervised learning models in machine learning, which aim to analyze data for classification and regression

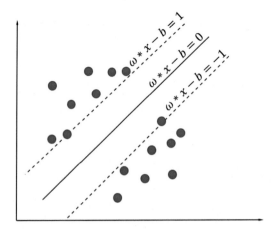

Figure 3.13 Hyperplane and margins for a SVM trained with samples from two classes. Samples on the margin are called the support vectors.

analysis. Given a set of training examples, each marked as belonging to one of two categories, a SVM training algorithm builds a model that assigns new examples to one category or the other. The objective of the support vector machine algorithm is to find a hyperplane in a high-dimensional space of the number of features that distinctly classifies the data points. A SVM maps training examples to points in space so as to maximize the width of the gap between the two categories. Predictions of new data are based on which side of the gap they fall.

As is shown in Fig. 3.13, we are given a training data set of n points of the form

$$(\mathbf{x}_1, y_1), ..., (\mathbf{x}_n, y_n)$$

where the y_i are either 1 or -1, each indicating the class to which the point x_i belongs. Each x_i is a p-dimensional real vector. We want to maximize the margin distance of hyperplanes that divides the group of points x_i for which $y_i = 1$ from the group of points for which $y_i = -1$. Maximizing the margin distance provides some reinforcement so that future data points can be classified with more confidence.

A hyperplane can be written as the set of points $\mathbf{x}$ satisfying

$$\mathbf{w}^T\mathbf{x} - b = 0,$$

where $\mathbf{w}$ is the normal vector to the hyperplane. If the training data is linearly separable, we can select two parallel hyperplanes that separate the two classes of data, so that the distance between them is as large as possible. The region bounded by these two hyperplanes is called the "margin," and the maximum-margin hyperplane is the hyperplane that lies halfway between them as in Fig. 3.13. We are interested in two regions: anything on or above this boundary is of one class, with label 1 and anything on or below this boundary is of the other class, with label -1. The two hyperplanes can be respectively described by the equations:

$$\mathbf{w}^T\mathbf{x} - b = 1$$

and

$$\mathbf{w}^T\mathbf{x} - b = -1.$$

We wish all data points to fall into the margin, which can be expressed as for each i either

$$\mathbf{w}^T\mathbf{x}_i - b \geq 1, \ \text{if } y_i = 1,$$

or

$$\mathbf{w}^T\mathbf{x}_i - b \leq -1, \ \text{if } y_i = -1.$$

Together the two constraints that each data point must lie on the correct side of the margin and can be rewritten as

$$y_i(\mathbf{w}^T\mathbf{x}_i - b) \geq 1, \ \text{for all } 1 \leq i \leq n.$$

We can put this together to get the optimization problem. The goal of the optimization then is to minimize

$$\min_{\mathbf{w},b} \left(\underbrace{\lambda\|\mathbf{w}\|^2}_{regularizer} + \underbrace{\frac{1}{n}\sum_{i=1}^{n} \max\{0, 1 - y_i(\langle \mathbf{w}, \mathbf{x}_i \rangle - b)\}}_{error\ term} \right),$$

which minimizes $\|\mathbf{w}\|$ subject to $y_i(\mathbf{w}^T\mathbf{x}_i - b) \geq 1$, for all $1 \leq i \leq n$. The first term above is called the regularization term which arises directly from the margin. The parameter λ adjusts the trade-off between increasing the margin size and ensuring that $\mathbf{x}_i$ lie on the correct side of the margin while we choose the distance of two hyperplanes to be $2/\|\mathbf{w}\|$.

In principle, the unconstrained optimization problem can be directly solved with gradient descent methods. Because this function is convex in the $\mathbf{w}$, we can easily apply a gradient descent method to find the minimum.

For example. with stochastic gradient descent pick an i at random and update according to

$$\text{New } b = \text{Old } b - \beta \begin{cases} y_i, & \text{if } 1 - y_i(\mathbf{w}^T\mathbf{x}_i - b) > 0, \\ 0, & \text{otherwise,} \end{cases} \tag{3.6.1}$$

and

$$\text{New } \mathbf{w} = \text{Old } \mathbf{w} - \beta \begin{cases} 2\lambda\mathbf{w} - \frac{1}{n}y_i\mathbf{x}_i, & \text{if } 1 - y_i(\mathbf{w}^T\mathbf{x}_i - b) > 0, \\ 2\lambda\mathbf{w}, & \text{otherwise.} \end{cases} \tag{3.6.2}$$

3.7 Neural networks

Artificial neural networks is a collection of connected layers of units or nodes to loosely model the neurons in a biological brain. In this section, we illustrate the use of differentiation for training artificial neural networks to minimize cost functions.

3.7.1 Mathematical formulation

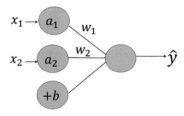

Figure 3.14 A simple neural network with one layer.

Fig. 3.14 shows the simplest network. x_1 and x_2 are inputs from the left, and a forecast output on the right, $\hat{y}$, which is modified by the activation function $\sigma(z)$ chosen in advance:

$$\hat{y} = \sigma(z) = \sigma(w_1 a_1 + w_2 a_2 + b), a_1 = x_1, a_2 = x_2.$$

In neural networks, the weights, the w_i, and the bias, b, will be found numerically in order to best fit our forecast output with our given data.

For a general neural network as in Fig. 3.15 is a neural network. A general network may have hundreds or thousands of nodes. It demonstrates

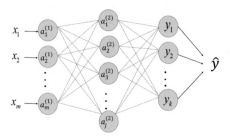

Figure 3.15 A general neural network.

the inputs and outputs of neural networks. The input units receive various forms and structures of information based on an internal weighting system, and the neural network attempts to learn about the information presented to produce one output report. Specifically, it adjusts its weighted associations according to a learning rule and using this error value. Successive adjustments will cause the neural network to produce output, which is increasingly similar to the target output. After a sufficient number of these adjustments the training can be terminated based upon certain criteria. This is known as supervised learning.

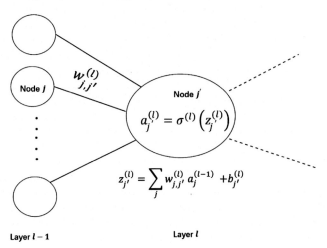

Figure 3.16 A detail of the network and a formula.

Now we formulate mathematical notation for a neural network. In Fig. 3.16, we look at how values of layer l are determined from layer $l-1$, w^l, b^l. We label the two layers as $l-1$ and l. Also notice that the general node in the left-hand layer is labeled j and one in the right-hand layer,

layer l, is labeled j'. We want to calculate what value goes into the j'th node of the lth layer. First, multiply the value $a_j^{(l-1)}$ in the jth node of the previous, $(l-1)^{th}$, layer by the parameter $w_{j,j'}^{(l)}$ and then add another parameter $b_{j'}^{(l)}$. Then we add up all of these for every node in layer $l-1$. Let

$$z_{j'}^{(l)} = \sum_{j=1}^{J_{l-1}} w_{j,j'}^{(l)} a_j^{(l-1)} + b_{j'}^{(l)},$$

where J_l means the number of nodes in layer l. For a given activation function, σ, we end up with the following expression for the values in the next layer:

$$a_{j'}^{(l)} = \sigma(z_{j'}^{(l)}).$$

In matrix form,

$$z^{(l)} = \mathbf{W}^{(l)}\mathbf{a}^{(l-1)} + \mathbf{b}^{(l)},$$

with the matrix $\mathbf{W}^{(l)}$ containing all the multiplicative parameters, that is, the weights $w_{j,j'}^{(l)}$, and $\mathbf{b}^{(l)}$ is the bias. The bias is just the constant in the linear transformation:

$$a^{(l)} = \sigma\left(\mathbf{z}^{(l)}\right) = \sigma\left(\mathbf{W}^{(l)}\mathbf{a}^{(l-1)} + \mathbf{b}^{(l)}\right). \tag{3.7.1}$$

3.7.2 Activation functions

In neural networks, the activation function of a node abstracts the output of that node given an input or set of inputs for specific purposes, for example, classification. In biological neural networks, the activation function may represent an electrical signal whether if the neuron fires. We use σ to represent the activation functions. It will be the same for all nodes in a layer:

$$a^{(l)} = \sigma\left(\mathbf{z}^{(l)}\right) = \sigma\left(\mathbf{W}^{(l)}\mathbf{a}^{(l-1)} + \mathbf{b}^{(l)}\right). \tag{3.7.2}$$

Here, we discuss a number of activation functions.

3.7.2.1 Step function

$$\sigma(x) = \begin{cases} 0, & x < 0, \\ 1, & x \geq 0. \end{cases}$$

This is also called the Heaviside step function, or the unit step function, often represents a signal that switches on at a specified time and stays switched on indefinite. The step function can be use for classification problems.

3.7.2.2 ReLU function

Positive linear/ReLU function is defined as

$$\sigma(x) = \max(0, x).$$

ReLU stands for rectified linear units. It is one of the most commonly used activation function. The signal either passes through untouched or dies completely. It was found to enable better training of deeper networks compared to the widely used activation functions. Rectified linear units, compared to sigmoid function or similar activation functions, allow faster and effective training of deep neural architectures on large and complex data sets.

3.7.2.3 Sigmoid

Sigmoid or logistic function

$$\sigma(x) = \frac{1}{1 + e^{-x}}.$$

The logistic function finds applications in a range of fields, including biomathematics. The logistic sigmoid can be used in the output layer for predicting probability.

3.7.2.4 Softmax function

The softmax function converts a vector of numbers (an array of K values (z)) into a vector of probabilities, where the probabilities of each value are proportional to the relative scale of each value in the vector. It is thus a function that turns several numbers into quantities that can be perhaps interpreted as probabilities:

$$\frac{e^{z_k}}{\sum_{k=1}^{K} e^{z_k}}.$$

It is often used in the final, output layer of a neural network, especially with classification problems.

3.7.3 Cost function

In practice, we can use the least squares for a cost function. Since we will have a set of independent input data y^n (from the training data set) and corresponding output data $\hat{y}^n$ or the forecast output. k is the kth node of the output. We define the cost function as

$$J = \frac{1}{2} \sum_{n=1}^{N} \sum_{K=1}^{K} \left(\hat{y}_k^{(n)} - y_k^{(n)} \right)^2.$$

For classification problems where only one output, the cost function commonly used for such an output is similar to logistic regression. And this is, for a binary classification ($y^{(n)} = 0, 1$), the cost function is

$$J = -\sum_{n=1}^{N} \left(y^{(n)} \ln \left(\hat{y}^{(n)} \right) + (1 - y^{(n)}) \ln \left(1 - \hat{y}^{(n)} \right) \right).$$

This is related to the cross entropy function.

3.7.4 Backpropagation

Backpropagation is the essence of neural network training. It is the practice of fine-tuning the weights of a neural network based on the error rate (i.e., loss) obtained in the previous iteration. Proper tuning of the weights ensures lower error rates, making the model reliable by increasing its generalization. We want to minimize the cost function, J, with respect to the parameters, the components of $\mathbf{W}$ and b. To do that using gradient descent, we are going to need the derivatives of J with respect to each of those parameters. Here, we focus the layer l and node j' and node j from layer $l-1$:

$$\frac{\partial J}{\partial w_{j,j'}^{(l)}} \text{ and } \frac{\partial J}{\partial b_{j'}^{(l)}}.$$

We introduce the quantity

$$\delta_{j'}^{(l)} = \frac{\partial J}{\partial z_{j'}^{(l)}}.$$

From the chain rule again, we have

$$\delta_j^{(l-1)} = \frac{\partial J}{\partial z_j^{(l-1)}} = \sum_{j'} \frac{\partial J}{\partial z_{j'}^{(l)}} \frac{\partial z_{j'}^{(l)}}{\partial z_j^{(l-1)}}.$$

It follows that

$$z_{j'}^{(l)} = \sum_j w_{j,j'}^{(l)} a_j^{(l-1)} + b_{j'}^{(l)} = \sum_j w_{j,j'}^{(l)} \sigma\left(z_j^{(l-1)}\right) + b_{j'}^{(l)}.$$

In addition,

$$\delta_j^{(l-1)} = \left.\frac{d\sigma}{dz}\right|_{z_j^{(l-1)}} \sum_{j'} \frac{\partial J}{\partial z_{j'}^{(l)}} w_{j,j'}^{(l)} = \left.\frac{d\sigma}{dz}\right|_{z_j^{(l-1)}} \sum_{j'} \delta_{j'}^{(l)} w_{j,j'}^{(l)}.$$

As a result, we can find the δs in a layer if we know the δs in all layers to the right. In summary, we have

$$\frac{\partial J}{\partial w_{j,j'}^{(l)}} = \frac{\partial J}{\partial z_{j'}^{(l)}} \frac{\partial z_{j'}^{(l)}}{\partial w_{j,j'}^{(l)}} = \delta_{j'}^{(l)} a_j^{(l-1)}.$$

Now the derivatives of the cost function, J, to the ws can be written in terms of the δs, which in turn are backpropagated from the network layers that are just to the right, one nearer the output. And the derivatives of the cost function to the bias, b is quite simple,

$$\frac{\partial J}{\partial b_{j'}^{(l)}} = \delta_{j'}^{(l)}.$$

It is clear that the derivatives of J is dependent on which activation function we use. If it is ReLU, then the derivative is either zero or one. If we use the logistic function, then we find that $\sigma'(z) = \sigma(1 - \sigma)$.

3.7.5 Backpropagation algorithm

From above analysis, we can easily derive the backpropagation algorithm as follows. First, we initialize weights and biases, typically at random. Then pick input data and input the vector x into the left side of the network, and calculate all the z_s, a_s, etc. And finally calculate the output $\hat{y}$. We now can update the parameters by the (stochastic) gradient descent. Repeat the process until the desired accuracy is reached. For example, if using the quadratic cost function in one dimension, then

$$\delta^{(L)} = \left.\frac{d\sigma}{dz}\right|_{z_j^{(L)}} (\hat{y} - y).$$

Continue to the left,

$$\delta_j^{(l-1)} = \frac{d\sigma}{dz}\bigg|_{z_j^{(l-1)}} \sum_j \delta_{j'}^{(l)} w_{j,j'}^{(l)}.$$

Then update the weights and biases using the following formulas:

$$\text{New } w_{j,j'}^{(l)} = \text{Old } w_{j,j'}^{(l)} - \beta \frac{\partial J}{\partial w_{j,j'}^{(l)}} = \text{Old } w_{j,j'}^{(l)} - \beta \delta_{j'}^{(l)} a_j^{(l-1)},$$

and

$$\text{New } b_{j'}^{(l)} = \text{Old } b_{j'}^{(l)} - \beta \frac{\partial J}{\partial b_{j'}^{(l)}} = \text{Old } b_{j'}^{(l)} - \beta \delta_{j'}^{(l)}.$$

CHAPTER 4

Network analysis

Contents

4.1 Introduction

Network analysis is essential in the analysis of data not only because social networks create a huge amount of data, but also many data are network structured. One of the simple ways to introduce a network structure is to analyze correlations between variables and create correlation networks, which are widely used data mining methods for studying biological networks (e.g., biological networks) based on pairwise correlations between variables.

Networks can be conveniently modeled by graphs, which we often refer to as a social graph. The individuals within a network are the nodes, and an edge connects two nodes if the nodes are related by the relationship that characterizes the network. The explosive growth of social media in recent years has attracted millions of end users, thus creating social graphs with millions of nodes and billions of edges reflecting the interactions and relationship between these nodes.

Networks often exhibit community structure with inherent clusters. Detecting clusters or communities is one of the critical tasks in network analysis because of its broad applications to matters such as friend recommendations, link predictions, and collaborative filtering in online social networks. From the graph theory perspective, clustering and community

Mathematical Methods in Data Science
https://doi.org/10.1016/B978-0-44-318679-0.00010-7

Copyright © 2023 China Science Publishing &
Media Ltd. Published by Elsevier Inc.
All rights reserved.

detection essentially are to discover a group of nodes in a graph that are more connected with each other within the group than those nodes outside the group. Given the size and complexity of today's networks, clustering and community detection in these networks face the inherent challenges.

Communities (clusters) are essential to gain spatio-temporal inside into big data sets from networks. Spatial distances often describe the strength of network connectivity among communities (clusters) rather than individual nodes. As a result, good clustering results will enable us to capture key characteristics of data sets in networks.

In this chapter, we discuss graph models of online social networks and clustering techniques. Although there exist many clustering algorithms such as k-means clustering, in this book we focus on spectral clustering analysis because our data from online social networks are graph structured. Part of the materials in this chapter is based on the authors' papers [67] on design and analysis of influenza-like illness in the US.

4.2 Graph modeling

In this section, we briefly review some of the common notation used in graphs. Any graph consists of both a set of objects, called nodes, and the connections between these nodes, called edges. Mathematically, a graph G is denoted as pair $G(V, E)$, where $V = \{v_1, v_2, ...v_n\}$ represents the set of nodes and $E = \{e_1, e_2, ..., e_m\}$ represents the set of edges and the size of the set is commonly shown as $m = |E|$. Edges are also represented by their endpoints (nodes), so $e(v_1, v_2)$ or (v_1, v_2) defines an edge between nodes v_1 and v_2. Edges can have directions if one node is connected to another, but not vice versa. When edges have directions, $e(v_1, v_2)$ is not the same as $e(v_2, v_1)$. When edges are undirected, nodes are connected both ways and are called *undirected edges* and this kind of graph is called *an undirected graph*. Graphs that only have directed edges are called *directed graphs* and ones that only have undirected edges are called *undirected graphs*. Finally, mixed graphs have both directed and undirected edges.

A sequence of edges where nodes and edges are distinct, $e_1(v_1, v_2)$, $e_2(v_2, v_3)$, $e_3(v_3, v_4)$, ..., $e_i(v_i, v_{i+1})$, is called a path. A closed path is called a cycle. The length of a path or cycle is the number of edges traversed in the path or cycle. In a directed graph, we only count directed paths because traversal of edges is only allowed in the direction of the edges. For a connected graph, multiple paths can exist between any pair of nodes. Often, we are interested in the path that has the shortest length. This path is called the shortest path. We will also use the shortest path as the distance for modeling on networks. The concept of the neighborhood of a node v_i can be generalized using shortest paths. An n-hop neighborhood of node v_i is the set of nodes that are within n hops distance from the node v_i.

The degree of a node in a graph, which is the number of edges connected to the node, plays a significant role in the study of graphs. For a directed graph, there are two types of degrees (1) in-degrees (edges toward the node) and (2) out-degrees (edges away from the node). In a network, nodes with the most connections possess the greatest degree of centrality. Degree centrality measures relative levels of importance. We often regard people with many interpersonal connections to be more important than those with few. In-degree centrality describes the popularity of a node and its prominence or prestige. Out-degree centrality describes the gregariousness of the node. For social media, degree represents the number of friends for each given user. On Facebook, a degree represents the number of friends. For Twitter, in-degree and out-degree show the number of followers and followees, respectively.

A graph with n nodes can be represented by a $n \times n$ adjacency matrix. A value of 1 at row i, column j in the adjacency matrix indicates a connection between nodes v_i and v_j, and a value of 0 denotes no connection between the two nodes. When generalized, any real number can be used to show the strength of connection between two nodes. In directed graphs, we can have two edges between i and j (one from i to j and one from j to i), whereas in undirected graphs only one edge can exist. As a result, the adjacency matrix for directed graphs is not in general symmetric, whereas the adjacency matrix for undirected graphs is symmetric ($A = A^T$). In social media, there are many directed and undirected networks. For instance, Facebook is an undirected network and Twitter is a directed network.

Consider a weighted graph $G = (V, E)$ with n vertices and m edges each with weights $E_{i,j}$ connecting nodes i, j. The adjacency of matrix M of a graph is defined by $M_{ij} = E_{ij}$ if there is an edge $\{i, j\}$ and $M_{ij} = 0$, otherwise. The Laplacian matrix L of G is an n by n symmetric matrix, with one row and column for each vertex, such that

$$L_{ij} = \begin{cases} \sum_k E_{ik}, & i = j, \\ -E_{ij}, & i \neq j, \text{ and } v_i \text{ is adjacent to } v_j, \\ 0, & \text{otherwise.} \end{cases}$$

In addition, a $n \times m$ incidence matrix of G, denoted by I_G has one row per vertex and one column per edge. The column corresponding to edge

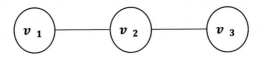

Figure 4.1 A three-node graph.

$\{i, j\}$ of I_G is zero except the ith and jth entries, which are $\sqrt{E_{ij}}$ and $-\sqrt{E_{ij}}$, respectively. The adjacent matrix can effectively describe a graph as demonstrated in the following two examples.

Example 4.2.1. Given a graph in Fig. 4.1, its adjacency matrix is

$$A = \begin{pmatrix} 0 & 1 & 0 \\ 1 & 0 & 1 \\ 0 & 1 & 0 \end{pmatrix}. \qquad (4.2.1)$$

We wish to use a vector $\mathbf{c}$ to describe the significance of each node by multiplying the corresponding degree of each node.

$$\lambda \mathbf{c} = A\mathbf{c},$$

which is

$$(A - \lambda I)\mathbf{c} = 0.$$

Assuming that $\mathbf{c} = [u_1 \ u_2 \ u_3]^T$,

$$\begin{pmatrix} 0 - \lambda & 1 & 0 \\ 1 & 0 - \lambda & 1 \\ 0 & 1 & 0 - \lambda \end{pmatrix} \begin{pmatrix} u_1 \\ u_2 \\ u_3 \end{pmatrix} = \begin{pmatrix} 0 \\ 0 \\ 0 \end{pmatrix}.$$

Because $\mathbf{c} \neq [0\ 0\ 0]^T$, the characteristic equation is

$$det(A - \lambda I) = \begin{vmatrix} 0 - \lambda & 1 & 0 \\ 1 & 0 - \lambda & 1 \\ 0 & 1 & 0 - \lambda \end{vmatrix} = 0,$$

which is the same as

$$-\lambda(\lambda^2 - 1)(-1) - \lambda = 2\lambda - \lambda^3 = \lambda(2 - \lambda^2) = 0.$$

Therefore the eigenvalues are $(-\sqrt{2}, 0, \sqrt{2})$. The largest eigenvalue is $\sqrt{2}$, and that is what we choose to compute. The computed corresponding eigenvector is

$$\begin{pmatrix} 0-\sqrt{2} & 1 & 0 \\ 1 & 0-\sqrt{2} & 1 \\ 0 & 1 & 0-\sqrt{2} \end{pmatrix} \begin{pmatrix} u_1 \\ u_2 \\ u_3 \end{pmatrix} = \begin{pmatrix} 0 \\ 0 \\ 0 \end{pmatrix}.$$

Assuming the **c** vector has norm is 1, the solution for it is

$$\mathbf{C_e} = \begin{bmatrix} u_1 \\ u_2 \\ u_3 \end{bmatrix} = \begin{bmatrix} \frac{1}{2} \\ \frac{\sqrt{2}}{2} \\ \frac{1}{2} \end{bmatrix},$$

which states that node v_2 is the most central node, while nodes v_1 and v_3 possess equal centrality values.

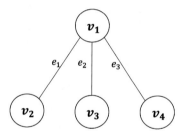

Figure 4.2 A four-node graph.

Example 4.2.2. Given a graph as in Fig. 4.2, its adjacency matrix is

$$A = \begin{pmatrix} 0 & e_1 & e_2 & e_3 \\ e_1 & 0 & 0 & 0 \\ e_2 & 0 & 0 & 0 \\ e_3 & 0 & 0 & 0 \end{pmatrix},$$

and its Laplacian matrix is

$$L = \begin{pmatrix} e_1+e_2+e_3 & -e_1 & -e_2 & -e_3 \\ -e_1 & e_1 & 0 & 0 \\ -e_2 & 0 & e_2 & 0 \\ -e_3 & 0 & 0 & e_3 \end{pmatrix},$$

and its incidence matrix is

$$
I_G = \begin{pmatrix} \sqrt{e_1} & -\sqrt{e_2} & -\sqrt{e_3} \\ -\sqrt{e_1} & 0 & 0 \\ 0 & \sqrt{e_2} & 0 \\ 0 & 0 & \sqrt{e_3} \end{pmatrix}.
$$

A is positive semi-definite can be decomposed into the product of I_G and its transpose:

$$
L = I_G \cdot I_G^T
$$
$$
= \begin{pmatrix} \sqrt{e_1} & -\sqrt{e_2} & -\sqrt{e_3} \\ -\sqrt{e_1} & 0 & 0 \\ 0 & \sqrt{e_2} & 0 \\ 0 & 0 & \sqrt{e_3} \end{pmatrix} \begin{pmatrix} \sqrt{e_1} & -\sqrt{e_1} & 0 & 0 \\ -\sqrt{e_2} & 0 & \sqrt{e_2} & 0 \\ -\sqrt{e_3} & 0 & 0 & \sqrt{e_3} \end{pmatrix}.
$$

Note that

$$
L\mathbf{e} = 0, \text{ if } \mathbf{e} = \begin{pmatrix} 1 \\ 1 \\ 1 \\ 1 \end{pmatrix}.
$$

Given

$$
\mathbf{x} = \begin{pmatrix} x_1 \\ x_2 \\ x_3 \\ x_4 \end{pmatrix},
$$

it is easy to see that

$$
I_G^T \mathbf{x} = \begin{pmatrix} \sqrt{e_1} & -\sqrt{e_1} & 0 & 0 \\ -\sqrt{e_2} & 0 & \sqrt{e_2} & 0 \\ -\sqrt{e_3} & 0 & 0 & \sqrt{e_3} \end{pmatrix} \begin{pmatrix} x_1 \\ x_2 \\ x_3 \\ x_4 \end{pmatrix} = \begin{pmatrix} (x_1 - x_2)\sqrt{e_1} \\ (x_3 - x_1)\sqrt{e_2} \\ (x_4 - x_1)\sqrt{e_3} \end{pmatrix}.
$$

Therefore

$$\mathbf{x}^T L \mathbf{x} = \mathbf{x}^T I_G I_G^T \mathbf{x} = (I_G^T \mathbf{x})^T \cdot (I_G^T \mathbf{x})$$

$$= \left(\ (x_1 - x_2)\sqrt{e_1} \quad (x_3 - x_1)\sqrt{e_2} \quad (x_4 - x_1)\sqrt{e_3} \ \right)$$

$$\times \begin{pmatrix} (x_1 - x_2)\sqrt{e_1} \\ (x_3 - x_1)\sqrt{e_2} \\ (x_4 - x_1)\sqrt{e_3} \end{pmatrix}$$

$$= (x_1 - x_2)^2 e_1 + (x_3 - x_1)^2 e_2 + (x_4 - x_1)^2 e_3$$

$$= \sum_{(i,j)\in E} E_{ij}(x_i - x_j)^2.$$

We can summarize the above example and state the following properties of L ([15,16]).

Theorem 4.2.3. *The Laplacian matrix L of has the following properties:*
1. $L = D - M$, *where M is the adjacency matrix and D is the diagonal degree matrix with $D_{ii} = \sum_k E_{ik}$.*
2. $L = I_G I_G^T$.
3. *L is symmetric positive semi-definite. All eigenvalues of L are real and non-negative, and L has a full set of n real and orthogonal eigenvectors.*
4. *Let $\mathbf{e} = [1, ..., 1]^T$. Then $L\mathbf{e} = 0$. Thus 0 is the smallest eigenvalue and e is the corresponding eigenvector.*
5. *If the graph G has c connected components, then L has c eigenvalues that is 0.*
6. *For any vector $\mathbf{x}$, $\mathbf{x}^T L \mathbf{x} = \sum_{\{i,j\}\in E} E_{ij}(x_i - x_j)^2$.*
7. *For any vector $\mathbf{x}$ and scalars α, β, $(\alpha \mathbf{x} + \beta \mathbf{e})^T L (\alpha \mathbf{x} + \beta \mathbf{e}) = \alpha^2 \mathbf{x}^T L \mathbf{x}$.*
8. *The problem*

$$min_{\mathbf{x} \neq 0} \mathbf{x}^T L \mathbf{x}, \ subject \ to \ , \mathbf{x}^T \mathbf{x} = 1, \ \mathbf{x}^T \mathbf{e} = 0, \qquad (4.2.2)$$

is solved when x is the eigenvector corresponding to the second smallest eigenvalue (the Fiedler vector) λ_2 of the eigenvalue problem

$$L\mathbf{x} = \lambda \mathbf{x}. \qquad (4.2.3)$$

The first 6 statements can be easily verified by computation as in Example 4.2.2. In particular, the statement 5 comes from the fact, if a graph has more than one connected components, L can be rearranged into a few blocks, each of them has a Laplacian matrix whose first eigenvalue is zero. The statement 7 is a direct consequent of the statement 4. Here, we use an example to demonstrate the computation in the first 6 statements. The last statement of Theorem 4.2.3 results from the following result, which is also useful for many optimization problem.

Theorem 4.2.4 (Courant–Fischer theorem). *Let A be $n \times n$ symmetric matrix A with the an orthogonal diagonalization $A = PDP^{-1}$. The columns of P are orthonormal eigenvectors $\mathbf{v}_1, ..., \mathbf{v}_n$ of A. Assume that the diagonal of D are arranged so that $\lambda_1 \le \lambda_2, ... \le \lambda_n$. Let S_k be the span of $\mathbf{v}_1, ..., \mathbf{v}_k$ and $S_k^{\perp}$ denote the orthogonal complement of S_k. Then*

$$min_{\mathbf{x} \neq 0,\, \mathbf{x} \in S_{k-1}^{\perp}} \frac{\mathbf{x}^T A \mathbf{x}}{\mathbf{x}^T \mathbf{x}} = \lambda_k.$$

When $k = 2$, $S_1^{\perp}$ is all $\mathbf{x}$ such that

$$\mathbf{x} \perp \mathbf{v_1}, \text{ or } \mathbf{v_1}^T \cdot \mathbf{x} = 0,$$

which implies the following result.

Corollary 4.2.5. *Let A be $n \times n$ symmetric matrix A with the orthogonal diagonalization t $A = PDP^{-1}$. The columns of P are orthonormal eigenvectors $\mathbf{v}_1, ..., \mathbf{v}_n$ of A. Assume that the diagonal of D are arranged so that $\lambda_1 \le \lambda_2, ... \le \lambda_n$. Then*

$$min_{\mathbf{x} \neq 0,\, \mathbf{x}^T \mathbf{v_1} = 0} \frac{\mathbf{x}^T A \mathbf{x}}{\mathbf{x}^T \mathbf{x}} = \lambda_2.$$

Proof. From the assumption, we have

$$A = P \begin{pmatrix} \lambda_1 & & \\ & \ddots & \\ & & \lambda_n \end{pmatrix} P^T,$$

and

$$P = \begin{bmatrix} \mathbf{v_1} & \cdots & \mathbf{v_n} \end{bmatrix}.$$

Rearranging the terms gives

$$P^T A P = \begin{pmatrix} \lambda_1 & & \\ & \ddots & \\ & & \lambda_n \end{pmatrix}.$$

In addition, note that

$$A \mathbf{v_i} = \lambda_i \mathbf{v_i},$$

$$\mathbf{x} = P\mathbf{y},$$

and

$$\sum x_i^2 = \sum y_i^2.$$

Now take any $\mathbf{x}$ such that $\mathbf{x} \in S_{k-1}^{\perp}$ and $\mathbf{v_i}^T \cdot \mathbf{x} = 0$ for $i = 1, \dots k-1$,

$$\mathbf{y} = P^T \mathbf{x} = \begin{bmatrix} \mathbf{v_1}^T \\ \vdots \\ \mathbf{v_n}^T \end{bmatrix} \mathbf{x} = \begin{bmatrix} \mathbf{v_1}^T \cdot \mathbf{x} \\ \vdots \\ \mathbf{v_n}^T \cdot \mathbf{x} \end{bmatrix},$$

and

$$\frac{\mathbf{x}^T A \mathbf{x}}{\sum x_i^2} = \frac{\lambda_k y_k^2 + \cdots + \lambda_n y_n^2}{\sum y_i^2} \geq \lambda_k.$$

In particular, when $y_1 = 0, \dots, y_{k-1} = 0, y_k = 1, y_{k+1} = 0, \dots, y_n = 0$, $\frac{\mathbf{x}^T A \mathbf{x}}{\sum x_i^2} = \lambda_k$. $\square$

4.3 Spectral graph bipartitioning

Graph partition aims to find out a partition such that the cut (the total number of edges between two disjoint sets of nodes) is minimized. For a weighted graph $G = (V, E)$, given a bipartition of V into disjoint V_1 and V_2 ($V_1 \cup V_2 = V$), the cut between them can be defined as

$$cut(V_1, V_2) = \sum_{i \in V_1, j \in V_2} M_{ij}. \tag{4.3.1}$$

The definition of cut is easily extended to k vertex subsets

$$cut(V_1 V_2, \dots V_k) = \sum_{i<j} cut(V_i, V_j). \tag{4.3.2}$$

The classical graph bipartitioning problem is to find nearly equally-sized vertex subset V_i, V_2 of V such that $cut(V_1^*, V_2^*) = \min_{V_1, V_2} cut(V_1, V_2)$. For this purpose, let us define the partition vector $\mathbf{p}$ that captures this division:

$$p_i = \begin{cases} +1, & i \in V_1, \\ -1, & i \in V_2. \end{cases} \tag{4.3.3}$$

The cut can be characterized by the Rayleigh quotient as follows.

Lemma 4.3.1. *Given the Laplacian matrix L of G and a partition vector* **p**, *the Rayleigh quotient*

$$\frac{\mathbf{p}^T L \mathbf{p}}{\mathbf{p}^T \mathbf{p}} = \frac{1}{n} \cdot 4cut(V_1, V_2). \qquad (4.3.4)$$

Proof. The result can be simply proved by the properties of the Laplacian matrix. In particular, from Theorem 4.2.3(6),

$$\mathbf{p}^T L \mathbf{p} = \sum_{\substack{\{i,j\} \text{ in the same set}}} E_{ij}(p_i - p_j)^2 + \sum_{\substack{\{i,j\} \text{ not in the same set}}} E_{ij}(p_i - p_j)^2,$$

and

$$\mathbf{p}^T L \mathbf{p} = 0 + \sum_{\substack{\{i,j\} \text{ in the same set}}} E_{ij}(p_i - p_j)^2 = 4cut(V_1, V_2).$$

Note $\mathbf{p}^T \mathbf{p} = n$ and we arrive at the conclusion. The result indicates that the minimization of the cut can be represented by the Rayleigh quotient with some partition vector (p_i) whose values is either -1 or 1. $\qquad \square$

In practical applications, we also need an objective function to balance cuts. Such an objective function can be formulated as follows. Let us define a diagonal matrix with W where w_{ii} is a weight for each vertex i. For a subset of vertices V_l, define its weight to be weight $W_{V_l} = \sum_{i \in V_l} w_{ii}$. Now we try to balance subsets V_1 and V_2 in such a way that the following objective function, $Q(V_1, V_2)$, is minimized:

$$Q(V_1, V_2) = \frac{cut(V_1, V_2)}{W_{V_1}} + \frac{cut(V_1, V_2)}{W_{V_2}}. \qquad (4.3.5)$$

The minimization of $Q(V_1, V_2)$ favors partitions that have a small cut value and are balanced because for two different partitions with the same cut value, the above objective function value is smaller for the more balanced partitioning.

The objective function can be characterized by the Rayleigh quotient of the following generalized partition vector q. Recall that all eigenvalues of L are real and non-negative, and 0 is the smallest eigenvalue of L. For a given graph G, let L and W be its Laplacian and vertex weight matrices, respectively. Let $e = [1, ..., 1]^T$, $v_1 = W_{V_1}$, and $v_2 = W_{V_2}$, then the following result holds.

Theorem 4.3.2. *The serialized partition vector* $\mathbf{q} = (q_i)$,

$$q_i = \begin{cases} +\sqrt{\frac{v_2}{v_1}}, & i \in V_1, \\[2mm] -\sqrt{\frac{v_1}{v_2}}, & i \in V_2, \end{cases} \qquad (4.3.6)$$

satisfies

1.

$$\mathbf{q}^T W \mathbf{e} = 0, \quad \mathbf{q}^T W \mathbf{q} = v_1 + v_2.$$

2.

$$\frac{\mathbf{q}^T L \mathbf{q}}{\mathbf{q}^T W \mathbf{q}} = \frac{cut(V_1, V_2)}{v_1} + \frac{cut(V_1, V_2)}{v_2}. \qquad (4.3.7)$$

3. *The problem*

$$min_{q \neq 0} \frac{\mathbf{q}^T L \mathbf{q}}{\mathbf{q}^T W \mathbf{q}}, \ \text{subject to } \mathbf{q}^T W \mathbf{e} = 0, \qquad (4.3.8)$$

is solved when $\mathbf{q}$ *is the eigenvector corresponding to the second smallest eigenvalue* λ_2 *of the generalized eigenvalue problem,*

$$L\mathbf{x} = \lambda W \mathbf{x}. \qquad (4.3.9)$$

The proof of Theorem 4.3.2 can be achieved through the following observations.

Proof. Let $\mathbf{y} = W\mathbf{e}$, $y_i = w_{ii}$,

$$\mathbf{q}^T W \mathbf{e} = \sqrt{\frac{v_2}{v_1}} \sum_{i \in V_1} weight(i) - \sqrt{\frac{v_1}{v_2}} \sum_{i \in V_2} weight(i)$$

$$= \sqrt{\frac{v_2}{v_1}} v_1 - \sqrt{\frac{v_1}{v_2}} v_2$$

$$= \sqrt{v_1 v_2} - \sqrt{v_1 v_2}$$

$$= 0,$$

$$\mathbf{q}^T W \mathbf{q} = \sum_{i=1}^{n} w_{ii} q_i^2$$

$$= \sum_{i \in V_1} w_{ii} \left(\sqrt{\frac{v_2}{v_1}} \right)^2 + \sum_{i \in V_2} w_{ii} \left(\sqrt{\frac{v_1}{v_2}} \right)^2$$

$$= \frac{v_2}{v_1} \cdot v_1 + \frac{v_1}{v_2} v_2$$

$$= v_2 + v_1$$

$$= weight(V).$$

If we can examine each component of $\mathbf{q}$ and $\mathbf{e}$, it is easy to verify that

$$\mathbf{q} = \frac{v_1 + v_2}{2\sqrt{v_1 v_2}} \mathbf{p} + \frac{v_2 - v_1}{2\sqrt{v_1 v_2}} \mathbf{e}.$$

The second statement of this theorem can be derived from Theorem 4.2.3(7),

$$\mathbf{q}^T L \mathbf{q} = \frac{(v_1 + v_2)^2}{4 v_1 v_2} \mathbf{p}^T L \mathbf{p}$$

$$= \frac{(v_1 + v_2)^2}{4 v_1 v_2} \cdot 4 Cut(V_1, V_2).$$

Therefore

$$\frac{\mathbf{q}^T L \mathbf{q}}{\mathbf{q}^T W \mathbf{q}} = \frac{1}{v_1 + v_2} \frac{(v_1 + v_2)^2}{4 v_1 v_2} \cdot 4 Cut(V_1, V_2)$$

$$= \frac{v_1 + v_2}{v_1 v_2} \cdot Cut(V_1, V_2).$$

We now turn to the last statement of this theorem. Since

$$L\mathbf{x} = \lambda W \mathbf{x},$$

we make the following transformations:

$$W^{-\frac{1}{2}} L \mathbf{x} = \lambda W^{\frac{1}{2}} \mathbf{x},$$

$$W^{-\frac{1}{2}} L W^{-\frac{1}{2}} W^{\frac{1}{2}} \mathbf{x} = \lambda W^{\frac{1}{2}} \mathbf{x}.$$

Let $\tilde{L} = W^{-\frac{1}{2}} L W^{-\frac{1}{2}}$ and $\mathbf{u} = W^{\frac{1}{2}} \mathbf{x}$. The new equation is

$$\tilde{L} \mathbf{u} = \lambda \mathbf{u}.$$

Note that $W^{\frac{1}{2}}\mathbf{q} = V$. It follows that

$$\frac{\mathbf{q}^T L \mathbf{q}}{\mathbf{q}^T W \mathbf{q}} = \frac{\mathbf{q}^T W^{\frac{1}{2}} \tilde{L} W^{\frac{1}{2}} \mathbf{q}}{\mathbf{q}^T W^{\frac{1}{2}} W^{\frac{1}{2}} \mathbf{q}} = \frac{V^T \tilde{L} V}{V^T \dot{V}},$$

and

$$\mathbf{q}^T W \mathbf{e} = (W^{\frac{1}{2}} \mathbf{q})^T W^{\frac{1}{2}} \mathbf{e} = V^T W^{\frac{1}{2}} \mathbf{e} = 0.$$

In addition,

$$L\mathbf{e} = 0 \Rightarrow L W^{-\frac{1}{2}} W^{\frac{1}{2}} \mathbf{e} = 0 \Rightarrow W^{-\frac{1}{2}} L W^{-\frac{1}{2}} W^{\frac{1}{2}} \mathbf{e} = 0.$$

$$\tilde{L} W^{\frac{1}{2}} \mathbf{e} = 0.$$

This indicates that 0 is an eigenvalue of $\tilde{L}$ and corresponding eigenvector is $W^{\frac{1}{2}}\mathbf{e}$. Now we can use Corollary 4.2.5 to show the third statement of this theorem.   □

Now we choose a weight(i) $= 1$ for all vertices i. This leads to the ratio-cut objective,

$$\text{Ratio-cut}(V_1, V_2) = \frac{\text{cut}(V_1, V_2)}{|V_1|} + \frac{\text{cut}(V_1, V_2)}{|V_2|}. \tag{4.3.10}$$

One commonly used $W = \text{diag}(w_{ii})$ is to choose w_{ii} to be the sum of the weights of edges incident on the node i, that is, $w_{ii} = \sum_k E_{ik}$. This leads to the normalized cut criterion that was for image segmentation. Note that for this choice of vertex weights, the vertex weight matrix W equals the degree matrix D, and weight

$$\sum_{j \in V_i} w_{ij} = \text{cut}(V_1, V_2) + \text{within}(V_i)$$

for $i = 1, 2$, where within (V_i) is the sum of the weights of edges with both end-points in V_i. Then the normalized-cut objective function may be expressed as

$$\text{Normalized-cut}(V_1, V_2) = \frac{\text{cut}(V_1, V_2)}{\sum_{i \in V_1} w_{ii}} + \frac{\text{cut}(V_1, V_2)}{\sum_{i \in V_2} w_{ii}} = 2 - S(V_1, V_2), \tag{4.3.11}$$

where $S(V_1, V_2) = \frac{\text{within}(V_1)}{\sum_{i \in V_1} w_{ii}} + \frac{\text{within}(V_2)}{\sum_{i \in V_2} w_{ii}}$. Note that $S(V_1, V_2)$ describes the strengths of associations within each partition. As a result, minimizing the normalized-cut is to maximize the proportion of edge weights that lie within each partition while balancing the cut.

To demonstrate the two cuts, we examine the two examples.

Example 4.3.3. Two commonly used variants are *ratio cut* and *normalized cut*. Let $\pi = (C_1, C_2, \cdots, C_k)$ be a graph partition such that $C_i \cap C_j = \varnothing$ and $\cup_{i=1}^{k} C_i = V$. The ratio cut and the normalized cut are defined as

$$Ratio\ Cut(\pi) = \sum_{i=1}^{k} \frac{cut(C_i, \bar{C_i})}{|C_i|}, \tag{4.3.12}$$

$$Normalized\ Cut(\pi) = \sum_{i=1}^{k} \frac{cut(C_i, \bar{C_i})}{vol(C_i)}, \tag{4.3.13}$$

where $\bar{C_i}$ is the complement of C_i, and $vol(C_i) = \sum_{j \in C_i} d_j$, where d_j is the degree of node j. Both objectives attempt to minimize the number of edges between communities, yet avoid the bias of trivial-size communities like singletons.

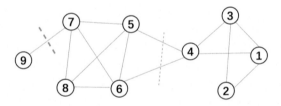

Figure 4.3 Two different cuts of a graph.

Given a graph in Fig. 4.3, the green cut (thick dashed line) between two sets of nodes 1, 2, 3, 4, and 5, 6, 7, 8, 9 with $C_1 = \{9\}$ and $C_2 = \{1, 2, 3, 4, 5, 6, 7, 8\}$. Let this partition be denoted as π_1. It follows that $cut(C_i, \bar{C_i}) = 1$, $|C_1| = 1$, $|C_2| = 8$, $vol(C_1) = 1$, and $vol(C_2) = 27$. Consequently,

$$Ratio\ Cut(\pi_1) = \frac{1}{1} + \frac{1}{8} = 1.12,$$

$$Normalized\ Cut(\pi_1) = \frac{1}{1} + \frac{1}{27} = 1.04.$$

Now for another more balanced partition π_2 (thin dashed lines) with $C_1 = 1, 2, 3, 4$ and $C_2 = 5, 6, 7, 8, 9$, we have

$$Ratio\ Cut(\pi_2) = \frac{2}{4} + \frac{2}{5} = 0.9 < Ratio\ Cut(\pi_1),$$

$$Normalized\ Cut(\pi_2) = \frac{2}{12} + \frac{2}{16} = 0.3 < Normalized\ Cut(\pi_1).$$

Though the cut of partition π_1 is smaller, partition π_2 is preferable based on the ratio cut or the normalized cut.

4.4 Network embedding

In order to use partial differential equations to model information diffusion in online social network, it is essential to embed the corresponding graph into Euclidean spaces. For a given graph $G(V, E)$, Theorem 4.2.3(6) includes the following relation:

$$x^T L x = \sum_{\{i,j\}\in E} E_{ij}(x_i - x_j)^2,$$

where x is a vector, L is the Laplacian matrix, and E_{ij} is the weights connecting nodes i, j. If we interpret $x = (x_i)$ as positions in a line, then Theorem 4.2.3(7) indicates that the Fiedler vector (the eigenvector corresponding to the second largest eigenvalue), which is a particular (x_i) could be used to map a weighted graph onto a line such that connected nodes stay as close as possible [12]. For a small graph, embedding of nodes of a graph may be acceptable. However, for a graph with a larger number of nodes, we need to apply clustering algorithms to find meaningful communities/clusters. In this situation, we can treat clusters as a node in a new graph where the strength of edges are the summation of all weights between two clusters, then this approach can be used for embedding clusters into Euclidean spaces as illustrated in Fig. 4.4.

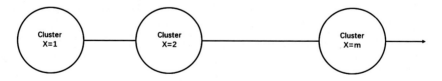

Figure 4.4 Embedding of clusters into the x-axis.

In addition, we could choose other meaningful methods relevant to a specific clustering technique. Assume that we breakdown the user population U into a set of groups, that is, $U = \{U_1, U_2, ...U_i, ..., U_m\}$. If the clustering is based on the shortest friendship hops from the source, the group U_x consists of users who share the same distance of x to the source and m is the maximum distance from the users to the source s. For the friendship hop partition, as a result, there is a natural spatial arrangement of these clusters. We arrange U_i by the distance from the source. For partition based on shared interest, we arrange U_i by their shared interests. For general clustering partitions, the spatial arrangement of U_i can be based on specific modeling goals and social or geographical characteristics of the underlying network. In [21,22], we use the level of democracy, diaspora size, international economic relations, or geographical proximity to order U_i. Here, we choose the increment between each cluster to be 1, but it can be adjusted according to specific cases. Following [29], we use the x-axis as the social distance and embed the density U_x at location x.

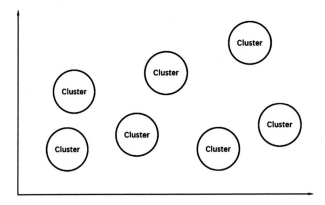

Figure 4.5 Embedding in high-dimensional Euclidean space with respect to two communication channels A and B.

If we intend to examine a diffusion process along multiple factors or communication channels, we may embed the graph into a high-dimensional space R^n, as illustrated in Fig. 4.5. For higher-dimensional mapping, we use more eigenvectors of the Laplacian matrix to minimize $x^T L x$ to make sure that connected nodes stay as close as possible.

4.5 Network based influenza prediction

Influenza poses a significant risk to public health, as evidenced by the 2009 H1N1 pandemic, which caused up to 203,000 deaths worldwide. Predicting the spatio-temporal information of disease in the incubation period is crucial because the prime aim of it is to provide guidance on preparing a response and avoid presumably adverse impact caused by a pandemic. In this section, we design and analyze a prediction system about Influenza-Like

Illness (ILI) from the latent temporal and spatial information. In this system, (1) multivariate polynomial regression is employed to investigate the spatial distribution of ILI data; (2) the phase space reconstructed by delay-coordinate embedding is used to explore the dynamical evolution behavior of the 1-D ILI series; (3) a Dynamical Radial Basis Function Neural Network (DRBFNN) method, which is the kernel of the system, is proposed to predict the ILI values based on the correlations between the observations space and reconstructed phase space. The performance analysis of our system shows that the regression equations coupling with spatial distribution information can be used to supplement the missing data, and the proposed DRBFNN method can predict the trends of ILI for the following one year. This section is based on the authors' paper [67] on design and analysis of Influenza-Like Illness in the US.

4.5.1 Introduction

Influenza is a highly contagious respiratory illness, and there have been about 10 influenza pandemics worldwide during the last 300 years [68]. The first influenza pandemic agreed by all authors occurred in 1580. The largest influenza pandemic, the famous "Spanish flu," occurred between 1918 and 1919, caused 20–40 million deaths, more than the number of deaths in the First World War, ranked first in all infectious diseases [69,70]. Not only can influenza cause a large number of population morbidity and mortality, especially in vulnerable populations [71], but also substantial economic losses and social burdens to a country. The annual financial damages caused by the influenza pandemic risk in the United States alone were expected to be about 500 billion US dollars [72]. Thus studying the trend of influenza can be of great significance. Influenza-like illness (ILI), known as acute respiratory infection and flu-like syndrome/symptoms, is a medical diagnosis of possible influenza or other illness causing a set of common symptoms. US Centers for Disease Control and Prevention (CDC) defined ILI as "fever (temperature of 100°F [37.8°C] or greater) and a cough and/or a sore throat without a known cause other than influenza" [73].

The CDC continuously monitors the level of ILI circulation in the US population by gathering information from physicians' reports, which record the percentage of patients who seek medical attention exhibiting ILI symptoms. It shows that adults with underlying health conditions were more likely to report ILI, but the majority did not seek care promptly, missing opportunities for early influenza antiviral treatment [74]. What is more, by accurately forecasting the outbreak of influenza and taking preventative measures, such as school closures [75], the impact of influenza could be minimized. However, the CDC fails to reflect the latest development and process since there is a delay (least 7 to 14 days) caused by manual data collection and complicated reporting processes.

In the past decade, many attempts have been made to estimate the ILI activity in the US ahead of the release of the CDC reports. Polgreen et al. used the frequency of internet searches for influenza surveillance, which could provide 1–3 weeks in advance of the influenza occurrence [76]. Google Flu Trends (GFT), a widely accepted digital disease detection system, achieved an impressive accuracy of 97% in its early stage [77], but its inaccuracies in multiple time periods of high ILI (in the interval of 2011–2013) have led to doubts about the utility of these data [78,79]. This promoted the use of other online search engines such as Twitter [80–82], Wikipedia [83,84], and social media streams [85–87] to provide information regarding ILI activity. Furthermore, the mathematical SIR, SEIR models, and discrete-time SEIR [88–90] are proposed to analyze and predict the ILI in recent years.

For early detection of disease outbreaks, researchers have used different mathematical methods and machine learning algorithms on different sources of data. Ginsberg et al. [77] applied the Google Flu Trends (GFT) system to estimate current flu activity, and successfully predicted the spread of H1N1 in a very timely manner. The working principle of GFT is that if a person is suffering from the flu, he or she is likely to search the Internet for information related to the disease. By extracting search-engine keywords associated with the flu, such as "cold," "sore throat," "fever," and other symptoms of the disease, and analyzing the data, regional influenza epidemic situations can be estimated. Google has indeed become a more efficient and well-timed indicator than the official health organizations. However, the *Nature* article titled "When Google got flu wrong" [78] reported GFT's over-estimation of the peak of US flu activity. The number of ILI clinic visits predicted by GFT was up to two times higher than that predicted by the CDC. The *Science* paper [79] asserted that the over-estimation was caused by big data hubris and algorithm dynamics. Big data have substantial potential in regard to improving public health, but the numbers are misleading if background information is insufficient.

GFT team no longer published current estimates because of its drop in accuracy in the interval of 2011–2013. This promotes the use of other online search engines, the designing of machine learning algorithms. McIver and Brownstein [83] developed a Wikipedia-derived Poisson model that accurately estimates the level of ILI activity in the American population, up to 2 weeks ahead of the CDC. Lee et al. [85] presented a model with flu-related Twitter data as features, and predicted a weekly percentage of the US population with ILI by a multi-layer perceptron back- propagation algorithm. The proposed model predicts current and future influenza activities with high accuracy 2–3 weeks faster than the traditional flu surveillance system. Santillana et al. [86] used an autoregressive model based on multiple data sources, including Google searches, Twitter microblogs, nearly real-time hospital visit records, and data from a participatory surveillance system to boost the influenza surveillance. They exploited the information in each data source and produced accurate weekly ILI predictions for up to 4 weeks ahead of the release of the CDC's ILI reports. Wang et al. [81] developed a prototype system to automatically collect, analyze, and model flu trends via Twitter data streams. They also proposed a dynamic spatial-temporal mathematical model to predict future Twitter indicative flu cases:

$$\frac{\partial u}{\partial t} = \frac{\partial (ae^{-bx}\frac{\partial u}{\partial x})}{\partial x} + r(t)u\left[h(x) - \frac{u}{K}\right],$$

where $u = u(x, t)$ is the flu cases density in region x at time t, $\partial u/\partial t$ corresponds to the rate of change of u as time progresses, $\partial u/\partial x$ corresponds to the rate of change of u across regions, $\partial(ae^{-bx}\frac{\partial u}{\partial x})/\partial x$ indicates the flu spreading within a certain region, and $r(t)u[h(x) - u/K]$ represents flu spreading across regions. This PDE model is meaningful as it can give prediction in both spatial and temporal dimensions. However, detail comparisons with the CDC data and analysis on the properties of the PDE model are absent. Xue et al. [87] established five kinds of regression models with the GFT data and the CDC data to predict and assess the influenza activity across 10 regions of the United States. The GFT regression model (model a), weighted GFT regression model (model b), the CDC regression model (model c) weighted CDC regression model (model d), and GFT–CDC regression model (model e) were established in that paper:

$$a: ILI_{i,t} = \sum_{k=1}^{P} \chi_k X_{i,t-k} + \tau_t,$$

$$b: ILI_{i,t} = \beta_1 X_{i,t} + \sum_{j \neq i, j=1}^{N} \lambda_j \omega_{i,j} X_{j,t} + v_t,$$

$$c: ILI_{i,t} = \sum_{k=1}^{P} \alpha_k ILI_{i,t-k} + \varepsilon_t,$$

$$d: ILI_{i,t} = \sum_{k=1}^{P} \beta_k ILI_{i,t-k} + \sum_{j \neq i, j=1}^{N} \lambda_j \omega_{i,j} ILI_{j,t} + \theta_t,$$

$$e: ILI_{i,t} = \sum_{k=1}^{P} \mu_k ILI_{i,t-k} + \sum_{m=1}^{P} \delta_m X_{i,t-m} + \sigma_t.$$

Here, $ILI_{i,t}$ is the number of the CDC ILIs in the ith region in week t; $X_{i,t}$ is the number of GFT ILIs in the ith region in week t; P is the lagged order of the dependent variable $X_{i,t-k}$; N is the number of regions; $\omega_{i,j}$ is the weight of the relationship between region i and region j; χ_k, α_k, β_k, μ_k, δ_m, and λ_j are the coefficients of models; τ_t, ν_t, ε_t, θ_t, and σ_t are the residual of the model for week t. Those models introduced lagged variables and applied multiple regression methods in prediction. The least squares and artificial neural network including BP and BP-GA algorithms were used to fit the model parameters, and the accuracy of each model was compared. Results showed that 16 weeks of future value could be predicted accurately with the seasonal GFT+CDC regression model.

In the theoretical analysis, researchers employed the transmission dynamic models, such as Susceptible Infected Recovered (SIR) model [88], Susceptible Exposed Infectious Recovered (SEIR) model [89], and discrete-time SEIR [90] model, to characterize the disease spread. The parameters and variables in the above model were iteratively optimized using real-time observations and the ensemble adjustment Kalman filter. The pivot epidemiological parameters, including population susceptibility, the basic reproductive number, attack rate, and infectious period were simultaneously estimated. Meanwhile, the asymptotic stability of the dynamic system was also analyzed. These decisive epidemiological parameters and the stability of the system are critical for characterizing disease spread and devising prevention and containment measures.

According to our previous work [91], the prediction of low-dimensional time series can be achieved by the correlation function, Φ, defined on the multiple observations space, X, to the dynamical evolution phase space, $Y = \Phi(X)$. The unknown values, with respect to the target variable can be predicted when the function Φ is established.

Inspired by the design and analysis of anomaly detection systems in industrial process [92,93], we aim to design a prediction system based on multivariate observations and dynamical evolution behavior. The ANN method is proposed to establish the correlation function, Φ. This system not only forecasts future influenza activities in advance only using aggregated ILI data by the CDC, but also explores the relevance among different variables (the ILI data in different regions) by multi-variable regression analysis.

4.5.2 Data analysis with spatial networks

In this subsection, we first state the weighted ILI data collected by the CDC and give some definitions corresponding to the prediction system. Then we analyze the spatial distribution information of these data by multivariate regression. The regression equations coupling with spatial distribution information can be used to supplement the missing data in the target region. The sensitivity of regression coefficients and correlation analyses are also included to reveal the hidden relations among different regions.

4.5.2.1 Collection of data

In the United States, the CDC records the number of people seeking medical attention with ILI symptoms. The agency's web site http://gis.cdc.gov/grasp/fluview/fluportaldashboard.html provides both new and historical data, where the national, regional, and state level ILI are available through ILInet. From this web site, we obtained the weekly data set that ranged from 2010 to 2018 on weighted ILI of ten regions (defined by Health and Human Services). Fig. 4.6(a) shows the 10 regions defined by Health and Human Services in America. In addition, we draw the contour map of weighted ILI data set distributing in temporal and spatial dimensions; see Fig. 4.6(b).

From the contour map, we can simply observe the outbreaks of ILI are approximately periodic, that is, seasonal in the temporal dimension. The ILI reaches peak prevalence in winter each year. However, there are differences among the various regions on the magnitude of ILI, and the data collected in Region 6 are relatively higher than those in other regions. On the other hand, the information about dynamical evolution and diffusion of ILI extracted from temporal and spatial levels can contribute to the accurately predicting of its outbreak.

To accurately predict the outbreak of ILI, the statistical analysis of the temporal and spatial distribution of ILI is of crucial importance. As we collected weekly data from 1st week 2010 to 52nd week 2018 (469 weeks in total), the week can be defined as the time variable. That is to say, the time variable is varied from 1 to 469. Besides, the ILI reaches its peak prevalence in winter each year. For convenience of extracting the information of temporal distribution, we set the 30th week in a year as an initial point of a segment, and the 29th week in the next year as an end point.

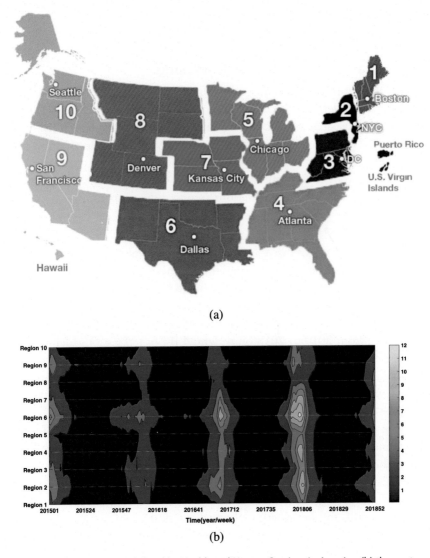

(a)

(b)

Figure 4.6 (a) Ten regions defined by Health and Human Services in America; (b) the contour map of weighted ILI data set distributing in temporal and spatial dimensions.

4.5.2.2 Regression models for spatial network

For the spatial distribution information of the weighted ILI, we aim to find the interrelationship between one region and the other regions, then build up the regression equation. According to the regression equation, researchers can supplement the lack of data in the target region. Moreover, the regression equation can help us investigating the spread and diffusion of ILI among different regions. Here, we simply consider the regression equation of ith region as a linear one,

$$\hat{x}_i = c_0 + c_t * week + \sum_{j=1, j \neq i}^{10} c_j * x_j, \tag{4.5.1}$$

where, $week$ is time variable, x_i is the weighted ILI in ith region, c_0, c_t, and c_i are the corresponding regression coefficients, respectively. Then the performance of regression is measured by Pearson correlation coefficient. The Pearson correlation coefficient between the variable x_i and $\hat{x}_i$ is defined as

$$Cor(x_i, \hat{x}_i) = \frac{Cov(x_i, \hat{x}_i)}{\sqrt{Var(x_i) \, Var(\hat{x}_i)}}, \tag{4.5.2}$$

where $Cov(x_i, \hat{x}_i)$ is the covariance between x_i and $\hat{x}_i$, $Var(x_i)$ is the variance of x_i, and $Var(\hat{x}_i)$ is the variance of $\hat{x}_i$. The regression coefficients of each region are listed in Table 4.1.

A positive value of the regression coefficient means that the corresponding region is positively related to the appointed region, and the negative value represents a negative relation. The magnitude of coefficient value reflects the intensity of the correlation. Take Region 6 as an example, the Cor value equals to 0.952, which means the original values in Region 6 can be well approximated by the regression equation (see Fig. 4.7(a)). However, some coefficients such as $week$, c_1 and c_2 are not significant, which means that the time variable, Region 1 and Region 2 have a relatively small influence on Region 6 (see Table 4.1).

Besides, parametric sensitivity analyses are proposed to investigate the effect of parameter changes on the model outputs. Mathematically, the sensitivity coefficients are the first-order derivatives of model outputs with respect to the model parameters.

$$S_i = \frac{\partial y_i}{\partial p} = \lim_{\Delta p \to 0} \frac{y_i(p + \Delta p) - y_i(p)}{\Delta p}, \tag{4.5.3}$$

where y_i is the ith model output and p is the model input parameter. In this paper, we use sensitivity index (SI), computed by taking the mean value of finite difference approximation of the partial derivative,

$$SI = \frac{1}{N} \sum_{i=1}^{N} \frac{y_i(p + \Delta p) - y_i(p)}{\Delta p}. \tag{4.5.4}$$

Table 4.1 The regression coefficients of weighted ILI in each region ("Rg" means Region), where the regression equation is defined in form of $\hat{x}_i = c_0 + c_t * week + \sum_{j=1, j \neq i}^{10} c_j * x_j$:

$$\hat{x}_i = c_0 + c_t * week + \sum_{j=1, j \neq i}^{10} c_j * x_j$$

	Rg 1	Rg 2	Rg 3	Rg 4	Rg 5	Rg 6	Rg 7	Rg 8	Rg 9	Rg 10
c_0	−0.35	0.07	0.40	0.15	0.02	−0.23	−0.51	−0.03	1.41	−0.46
c_t	8E−4	2E−3	−7E−4	−8E−4	6E−4	2E−3	−8E−4	−2E−4	−2E−3	3E−4
c_1		0.89	0.36	−0.18	−0.01	0.09	0.18	0.02	0.25	−0.12
c_2	0.26		0.06	0.14	−0.03	−0.08	0.09	−0.04	−4.E−3	0.10
c_3	0.26	0.16		0.36	0.19	−0.20	−0.09	0.27	−0.13	−0.11
c_4	−0.10	0.28	0.28		0.22	0.66	0.16	−0.26	−0.03	0.07
c_5	−0.02	−0.16	0.39	0.58		0.41	0.45	0.27	−0.04	0.01
c_6	0.02	−0.06	−0.05	0.23	0.05		0.14	0.06	0.08	−0.03
c_7	0.10	0.17	−0.06	0.16	0.16	0.39		0.09	−4.E−3	0.15
c_8	0.03	−0.20	0.55	−0.68	0.26	0.45	0.26		0.36	0.30
c_9	0.14	−0.01	−0.10	−0.03	−0.02	0.24	−5.E−3	0.14		0.42
c_{10}	−0.11	0.31	−0.12	0.11	0.01	−0.12	0.24	0.17	0.65	
Cor	0.933	0.928	0.955	0.959	0.972	0.952	0.965	0.949	0.921	0.932

Recalling that our regression model is $y_i = c_0 + c_t * week + \sum_j c_j * x_j^i$. If we vary the variable x_k (the weighted ILI of kth region), then

$$SI^k(c) = \frac{1}{N} \sum_{i=1}^{N} \frac{y_i(x + \Delta x_k^i) - y_i(x)}{\Delta x_k^i}$$

$$= \frac{1}{N} \sum_{i=1}^{N} \frac{\sum_j c_j * (x_j^i + \Delta x_k^i) - \sum_j c_j * x_j^i}{\Delta x_k^i}$$

$$= \frac{1}{N} \sum_{i=1}^{N} c_k = \bar{c}_k.$$

The sensitivity index $SI^k(c)$ is a posteriori estimation of regression coefficient c_k, and the posteriori error is defined as $c_k - SI^k(c)$. The regression coefficient and its posteriori error of the regression model about Region 6 are shown in Fig. 4.7(b). If we vary the regression coefficient c_k, then

$$SI^k(x) = \frac{1}{N} \sum_{i=1}^{N} \frac{y_i(c + \Delta c_k^i) - y_i(c)}{\Delta c_k^i}$$

$$= \frac{1}{N} \sum_{i=1}^{N} \frac{\sum_j (c_j^i + \Delta c_k^i) * x_j - \sum_j c_j * x_j^i}{\Delta c_k^i}$$

$$= \frac{1}{N} \sum_{i=1}^{N} x_k = \bar{x}_k.$$

The $SI^k(x)$ reflects the mean amplitude of the weighted ILI in Region x_k. That is to say, the sensitivity index of y_i with respect to c_k indicates the proportion of x_k majoring in the regression. The SI values of the regression model about Region 6 with respect to various regions are shown in Fig. 4.7(c).

Furthermore, the correlation between parameters is studied by computing the correlation between the dynamic sensitivities. The correlation matrix (see Fig. 4.7(d)) corresponding to the regression model of Region 6 gives two clusters, one is constituted by Region 2, Region 3, and Region 10, another cluster is constituted by Region 1, Region 4, Region 5, Region 7, Region 8, and Region 9. It shows a strong positive correlation internal of clusters, but a strong negative correlation between the two clusters. There should be different ways of the spread and diffusion of ILI with respect to Region 6 in different clusters. The negative correlations between clusters indicate a competition during the diffusion. To some extent,

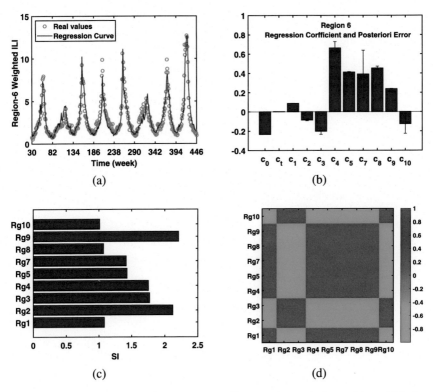

Figure 4.7 (a) regression curve; (b) regression coefficient and posteriori error; (c) sensitivity indices; (d) correlation matrix.

we believe that the structure and the correlation of the cluster could help us explore the spatial information among the different regions in further works.

From the obtained regression coefficients shown in Table 4.1, we choose the first two dominant regions related to each target region to build the network. Taking Region 6 as an example, the first two dominant regions relate to "Rg 6" are Region 4 and Region 8, and the weight of corresponding relation between "Rg 6" and Region 4, Region 8 equals to 0.66, 0.45, respectively. The selected dominant regions of each target region and the constructed network are shown in Fig. 4.8.

In the network, each region is treated as a point, and the related regions are connected by the weighted edge (see details in Fig. 4.8). The network cluster is selected according to the contribution of different regions to the target area in the regression equation. Thus the obtained network reflects

Rg1	Rg2	Rg3	Rg4	Rg5	Rg6	Rg7	Rg8	Rg9	Rg10
2	1	5	5	4	4	5	3	8	8
3	10	8	8	8	8	8	5	10	9

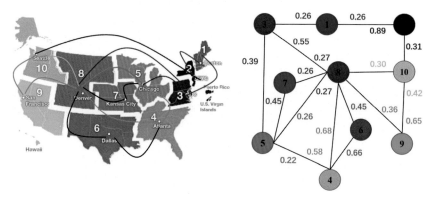

Figure 4.8 The network obtained by regression analysis. Two related regions corresponding to the target region are selected to build the network.

Rg1	Rg2	Rg3	Rg4	Rg5	Rg6	Rg7	Rg8	Rg9	Rg10
2	1	1	3	3	4	5	3	1	7
3	4	5	5	4	5	8	4	8	8
9	10	8	8	8	8	10	5	10	9

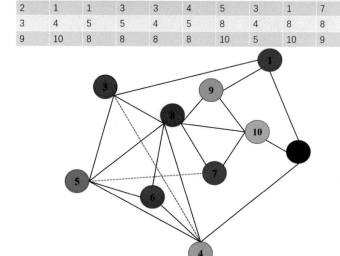

Figure 4.9 The network obtained by regression analysis. Three related regions corresponding to the target region are selected to build the network.

the spatial distribution information extracted by regression equation, to some extent. In addition, Fig. 4.9 shows the constructed network if we choose the first three dominant regions related to the target region.

4.5.3 ANN method for prediction

From the temporal and spatial distribution information, we find that the temporal-spatial complexity of the system is quite crucial. We should add a detailed analysis of the dynamical complexity [94–96]. In this section, we first analyze the dynamical complexity of ILI data in each region by the largest Lyapunov exponent (λ) and Approximate Entropy (ApEn). Then we use the DRBFNN method to establish the correlation function Φ between observations phase space (constituted by the variables in the cluster of network) and dynamical evolution phase space. The established Φ can be used to forecast the future influenza activities in advance.

4.5.3.1 Dynamical complexity of ILI

According to the Takens embedding theory [97], the dynamical behavior of time series $\{x_i\}$ can be described by the reconstruction phase space. Trajectory in reconstructed phase space is diffeomorphic to the track in the original system (where the time series $\{x_i\}$ is observed). The reconstructed phase space with respect to x_i is defined by the delay-coordinate technique,

$$
Y_i = \begin{pmatrix}
x_i(1) & x_i(2) & \cdots & x_i(N-(m-1)\tau) \\
x_i(1+\tau) & x_i(2+\tau) & \cdots & x_i(N-(m-2)\tau) \\
\vdots & \vdots & \vdots & \vdots \\
x_i(1+(m-1)\tau) & x_i(2+(m-1)\tau) & \cdots & x_i(N)
\end{pmatrix}. \tag{4.5.5}
$$

Here, N is the length of time series x_i, m is the embedding dimension, and τ is the time delay, which can be calculated by mutual information technique [98]. The embedding dimension m is fixed to 10 in this dynamical complexity analysis.

The m-dimensional phase space can be reconstructed by the optimal time delay and embedding dimension. Then the largest Lyapunov exponent, which is a significant parameter for characterizing the dynamic behaviors of the trajectories in phase space, is calculated by the Wolf's method [99]. Take an initial point, $Y(t_0)$, and its nearest neighbor point, $Y^*(t_0)$, in the reconstructed phase space, and denote the distance between these two points by $L_0 = |Y(t_0) - Y^*(t_0)|$. Tracking the evolution of these two points till time, t_1, the two points evolve to $Y(t_1)$ and $Ye^*(t_1)$, and the distance, L_0, changes to be $D_0 = |Y(t_1) - Ye^*(t_1)|$. At the time, t_1, $Ye^*(t_1)$ may not be the nearest neighbor point of $Y(t_1)$. Thus we need to find another point, $Y^*(t_1)$, which is the nearest neighbor point of $Y(t_1)$. The distance between $Y(t_1)$ and $Y^*(t_1)$ is $L_1 = |Y(t_1) - Y^*(t_1)|$. We set the angle between D_0 and L_1 as small as possible to ensure that the influence on orbit evolution is small. Then tracking the evolution to obtain D_1 and repeat the above process until the end of the time series. Assume the number of these iterations is K. Here, we have $L_k = |Y(t_k) - Y^*(t_k)|$, and $D_k = |Y(t_{k+1}) - Ye^*(t_{k+1})|$, $k = 0, 1, \cdots, K - 1$. The largest Lyapunov exponent is

$$\lambda = \frac{1}{t_{K-1} - t_0} \sum_{k=0}^{K-1} ln\frac{D_k}{L_k}. \tag{4.5.6}$$

The Approximate Entropy (ApEn) [100–102] is introduced to further characterize the complexity of the system. In the reconstructed phase space, the number of points whose distance to ith point, $Y(t_i)$, less than r, is defined as P^i. Here, r is a positive real number and specifies a filtering level. For smaller r values, the numerically conditional probability is usually unstable, while for larger r values, too much detailed system information is lost due to filter coarseness. Generally, r ranges from 0.1 to 0.25 standard deviations of the time series. Moreover, to avoid a significant contribution from noise in an ApEn calculation, one must choose r larger than most of the noise. Thus we select $r = 0.25S$, S is the standard deviation of time series $\{x_i\}$. Then the correlation integral is defined as $C_i^m = \frac{P^i}{N-m+1}$, where N is the total number of time series. The approximate entropy is

$$ApEn = \Phi^m - \Phi^{m+1}, \tag{4.5.7}$$

where $\Phi^m = \frac{1}{N-m+1} \sum_{i=1}^{N-m+1} lnC_i^m$ reflects the average relevance of the system.

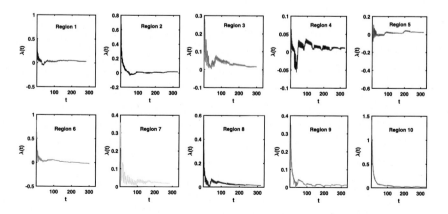

Figure 4.10 The evolution of largest Lyapunov exponent with respect to ILI in each region.

The largest Lyapunov exponent and approximate entropy of each reconstructed phase space with respect to ILI is calculated. The largest Lyapunov
exponent quantifies the rate of the divergence of the trajectories in phase
space, a larger positive value reflects more chaotic of system. The approximate entropy is the probability of time series generating new patterns when
the dimension changes, a larger probability value indicates less regularity
and more perplexity of system. In a word, a larger positive value of largest
Lyapunov exponent and approximate entropy indicates more complexity
of the time series and more difficulty in predicting the future values. The
evolution of largest Lyapunov exponent with respect to ILI in each region
is shown in Fig. 4.10. Note that λ in Table 4.2 is the mean value of $\lambda(t)$
in each region. The values of λ in Table 4.2 are all positive, which indicate
that the dynamical evolution of ILI is unstable. Moreover, the values of λ
and $ApEn$ in Region 1, Region 3, Region 7, and Region 10 are larger than
that of other regions. These larger values reflect the corresponding regions
have more complex dynamics, and are more difficult to be predicted.

Table 4.2 The time delay, τ, largest Lyapunov exponent, λ, and Approximate Entropy (ApEn) of ILI time series in each regions.

	Time delay (τ)	Largest Lyapunov exponent (λ)	Approximate Entropy (ApEn)
Region 1	9	0.0409	1.4729
Region 2	4	0.0219	1.2468
Region 3	7	0.0375	1.4589
Region 4	4	0.0125	1.0849
Region 5	5	0.0174	1.2128
Region 6	7	0.0298	1.3824
Region 7	9	0.0363	1.4503
Region 8	5	0.0345	1.2327
Region 9	3	0.0246	1.2120
Region 10	3	0.0694	1.5212

4.5.3.2 DRBFNN method for prediction

In light of the generalized embedding theorems [103], there exists a correlation function between the reconstructed phase space and the observations.
In this paper, the DRBFNN method is applied to build the correlation
function, and make a prediction for the ILI time series.

Radial basis function neural network (RBFNN) is an artificial neural
network that uses radial basis functions as its activation functions [104]. It

has been proven that the RBFNN is superior in approximating continuous functions [105]. Moreover, RBFNN can avoid falling into local minimum when the training is in progress [106]. In our method, the dynamical evolution phase space, that is, the reconstructed phase space, Y_i corresponding to time series x_i is designed as the output of RBFNN for prediction. The dynamical evolution of x_i may only relate to some regions, so the input of RBFNN can be defined as

$$X_k^i = W_k^i * \begin{pmatrix} x_1(1) & x_1(2) & \cdots & x_1(N) \\ x_2(1) & x_2(2) & \cdots & x_2(N) \\ \vdots & \vdots & \vdots & \vdots \\ x_n(1) & x_n(2) & \cdots & x_n(N) \end{pmatrix}. \tag{4.5.8}$$

Here, W_k^i means to select all the k interrelated regions corresponding to the ith region in the network. X_k^i consist of k variables selected from the 10 regions.

Recalling that the output Y_i has M $(M = N - (m-1)\tau)$ columns. That is to say, the dynamical phase space has M m-dimensional points. So we need to take M points from X_k^i to train the network, that is, establish the correlation function, Φ:

$$Y_i = \begin{pmatrix} x_i(1) & x_i(2) & \cdots & x_i(M) \\ x_i(1+\tau) & x_i(2+\tau) & \cdots & x_i(M+\tau) \\ \vdots & \vdots & \vdots & \vdots \\ x_i(1+(m-1)\tau) & x_i(2+(m-1)\tau) & \cdots & x_i(M+(m-1)\tau) \end{pmatrix}$$

$$= \Phi \left(W_k^i * \begin{pmatrix} x_1(1) & x_1(2) & \cdots & x_1(M) \\ x_2(1) & x_2(2) & \cdots & x_2(M) \\ \vdots & \vdots & \vdots & \vdots \\ x_{10}(1) & x_{10}(2) & \cdots & x_{10}(M) \end{pmatrix} \right). \tag{4.5.9}$$

Then the $M+1$ to N columns of X_k are used for prediction by the established Φ:

$$\begin{pmatrix} x_i(M+1) & x_i(M+2) & \cdots & x_i(N) \\ x_i(M+1+\tau) & x_i(M+2+\tau) & \cdots & x_i(N+\tau) \\ \vdots & \vdots & \vdots & \vdots \\ x_i(N+1) & x_i(N+2) & \cdots & x_i(N+(m-1)\tau) \end{pmatrix}$$

$$= \Phi \left(W_k^i * \begin{pmatrix} x_1(M+1) & x_1(M+2) & \cdots & x_1(N) \\ x_2(M+1) & x_2(M+2) & \cdots & x_2(N) \\ \vdots & \vdots & \vdots & \vdots \\ x_{10}(M+1) & x_{10}(M+2) & \cdots & x_{10}(N) \end{pmatrix} \right). \tag{4.5.10}$$

Here, the W_k is selected by the network shown in Fig. 4.8.

It should be noted that there are two crucial parameters in the phase space reconstruction, the embedding dimension m and the time delay τ. The embedding dimension corresponds to the number of independent quantities needed to specify the state of the system at any given instant. If m is too small, the attractor cannot be completely expanded, yet a large m will increase the redundancy. Define a kth-order conditional probability distribution of a coordinate x, $P(x|x_1, x_2, \ldots; \tau)$, as the probability of observing the value x given that x_1 was observed time τ before, x_2 was observed time 2τ before, and so on. If we take τ to be small, the k conditions are nearly equivalent to the specification of the value of x at some time along with values of all its derivatives up to order $k - 1$. The points $X(t)$ and $X(t + \tau)$ in the reconstructed phase space cannot be separated. If τ is too large, $X(t)$ and $X(t + \tau)$ will be less correlated, and the information generated from the flow properties would randomize the samples with respect to each other. The reconstructed phase space cannot accurately reflect the evolution rules about the attractor unless the time delay and embedding dimension are chosen appropriately. So, the traversal algorithm and Particle Swarm Optimization (PSO) algorithm are used to find the optimal embedding dimension, m, and time delay, τ, to minimize the prediction error. The correlation function, Φ, is trained by RBFNN through the MATLAB® program.

The Relative Squared Error (RSE), Mean Squared Error (MSE), and Relative Mean Squared Error (RMSE) are applied to characterize the prediction error,

$$RSE(j) = \left(\frac{x_i'(j) - x_i(j)}{x_i(j)} \right)^2, \tag{4.5.11}$$

$$MSE = \frac{1}{N - M} \sum_{j=M+1}^{N} \left(x_i'(j) - x_i(j) \right)^2, \tag{4.5.12}$$

$$RMSE = \frac{1}{N - M} \sum_{j=M+1}^{N} \left(\frac{x_i'(j) - x_i(j)}{x_i(j)} \right)^2, \tag{4.5.13}$$

where $x_i'(j)$ is the predicted value, $x_i(j)$ is the real value, and n is the number of predicted values. The schematic diagram for prediction by this DRBFNN is shown in Fig. 4.11, and the pseudo-code of the program is shown in Algorithm 1.

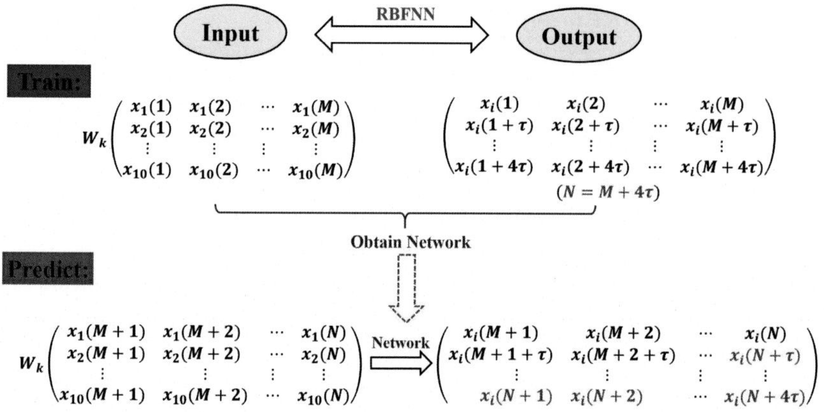

Figure 4.11 The schematic diagram for prediction by DRBFNN: the first M columns of X_k are used for training the network; then, the $M+1$ to N columns of X_k are used for prediction by the network.

Algorithm 1 DRBFNN.

Input: $X = (x_1, x_2, \cdots, x_{10})^T$, $Y_i = (x_i(j), x_i(j+\tau), \cdots, x_i(j+(m-1)\tau))^T$, $i = 1, 2, \cdots, 10$.

Output: $\{x_i(N+1), x_i(N+2), \cdots\}$,

1: Built the observations phase space X_k of the target variable according to the network;

2: Apply the traversal algorithm or PSO algorithm to select the optimal parameters, and use the MATLAB command 'newrb' for RBFNN;

3: **for** each m, and τ **do**

4:     Training the network between, $X_k^i = W_k^i * X$ and Y_i, compute the prediction error, Error, at step t;

5:     **if** Error(t)<Error(t-1) **then**

6:         Record the corresponding parameter values;

7:     **else**

8:         Run the next loop;

9:     **end if**

10: **end for**

11: Predict the unknown data with respect to x_i by the obtained network;

12: **return** Predicted values corresponding to minimum prediction error.

4.5.3.3 Performance analysis

Form the contour map of weighted ILI data (Fig. 4.6(a)), we find that the high prevalence and incidence of weighted ILI occur in winter each year, and Region 6 divided by US Health and Human Services is more severe than other regions. The possible influence factors are as follows. In winter, the air circulation in the household is reduced because of the cold weather, and people do less outdoor activities, such that the body is susceptible to be infected. Furthermore, the considerable number of passenger flow in big cities such as Dallas (Region 6), San Francisco (Region 9), Washington, D.C. (Region 3), etc. increase the probability of contact with patients.

We use the multivariate polynomial regression to extract the spatial distribution information. The regression equation can be used to fill up the

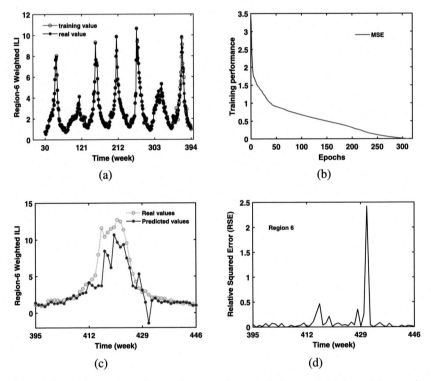

Figure 4.12 Training and prediction of weighted ILI data in Region 6; (a) the training results and real values from 30 to 394 weeks (30th week 2010 to 29th week 2017); (b) the training performance characterized by Mean Squared Error (MSE); (c) the predicted results and real values from the 395th to the 446th week (30th week 2017 to 29th week 2018); (d) predicted error characterized by Relative Squared Error (RSE).

missing data in the target region by the data in some other regions. The correlation analysis of the regression equation indicates that some coastal regions are highly related, such as Region 4 and Region 9. This may be owing to the similar local climate environment, which is favorable for the growth of pathogens. The cluster extracted by the correlation matrix, for example, the cluster Region 1-4-5-7-8-9 and Region 2-3-10 in regressing the ILI data of Region 6, helps us establish recommendation scheme based on diffusion features [107].

In this section, the dynamical evolution information of ILI is considered, and radial basis function neural network is employed to build the correlation between observations and dynamic phase space. Prediction achieved by the obtained network can capture the peak value of weighted ILI to some extent. Take the prediction performance of Region 6 as an example (see Fig. 4.12 (prediction of weighted ILI in other regions by DRBFNN are shown in Fig. 4.13)); the trend in the following 52 weeks is well predicted by the DRBFNN. The training performance characterized by Mean Squared Error (MSE) is shown in Fig. 4.12(a) and Fig. 4.12(b). The fluctuation of MES over epochs reflects the convergence, stability of

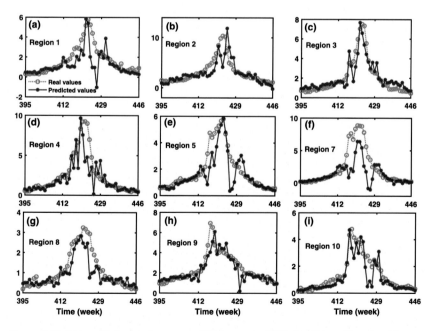

Figure 4.13 The prediction performance of 8th segment (2017–2018) in each region (the performance of Region 6 is shown in Fig. 4.12) by the DRBFNN method.

Table 4.3 The Relative Mean Squared Error (RMSE) of the DRBFNN method compared with the BPNN method used in [82].

MSE & RMSE	DRBFNN		BPNN in Ref. [15]	
	20 points	52 points	5 points	20 points
Region 1	0.0518 & 0.1735	1.1669 & 0.2131	0.0241 & 0.0475	*no predict*
Region 2	0.2628 & 0.0995	2.5080 & 0.1369	0.0100 & 0.0041	*no predict*
Region 3	0.0918 & 0.1582	0.4975 & 0.1984	0.0919 & 0.1075	*no predict*
Region 4	0.1286 & 0.0897	2.0598 & 0.1406	0.0466 & 0.0165	*no predict*
Region 5	0.0464 & 0.0373	0.7519 & 0.0977	0.0673 & 0.0509	*no predict*
Region 6	0.3290 & 0.0360	3.5881 & 0.1073	0.0445 & 0.0103	*no predict*
Region 7	0.1145 & 0.2773	4.4230 & 0.3346	0.1007 & 0.1155	*no predict*
Region 8	0.0493 & 0.2415	0.2450 & 0.1955	0.0549 & 0.1043	*no predict*
Region 9	0.1473 & 0.0610	0.5379 & 0.0625	0.2831 & 0.1016	*no predict*
Region 10	0.0561 & 0.2854	0.3951 & 0.1817	0.8188 & 0.8519	*no predict*

our algorithm. And the repeatability of our approach can be verified by the predictions of weighted ILI among different regions (see Fig. 4.13), and also can be verified by the following application on the American Stock Market. The prediction error characterized by Relative Squared Error (RSE) is shown in Fig. 4.12(d). Moreover, MSE and RMSE are also calculated to compare the prediction performance of the DRBFNN method with the Back Propagation Neural Network (BPNN) method (see Table 4.3). The DRBFNN can predict the next following 52 points, while the BPNN used in [82] only predicts the next following 5 points. The MSE & RMSE for the next 20 points prediction by the DRBFNN approach are close to that 5 points prediction by the BPNN method. From this table, we can see the prediction errors of Region 5, Region 9, and Region 10 are smaller by our DRBFNN method than these of the BPNN method. Note that the RMSE for Region 1, Region 3, Region 7, Region 8 are relatively larger than those of other regions, because these regions have more complex dynamics indicated by a higher largest Lyapunov exponent (see Table 4.3).

From the above prediction performance, we conclude that the DRB-FNN is an efficient approach to predict the weighted ILI data. Our proposed system can effectively predict the activities of ILI based on the temporal and spatial information.

CHAPTER 5

Ordinary differential equations

Contents

5.1 Introduction

Ordinary differential equation models play an increasingly important role in data science. For example, ordinary differential equation models, in particular, SIR (Susceptible-Infected-Recovered) models, have been extensively used for infectious disease modeling and prediction. With the availability of an unprecedented amount of clinical, epidemiological, and social COVID-

Mathematical Methods in Data Science
https://doi.org/10.1016/B978-0-44-318679-0.00011-9

Copyright © 2023 China Science Publishing &
Media Ltd. Published by Elsevier Inc.
All rights reserved.

19 data, data-driven differential equation models have revealed new insights into the spread and control of COVID-19. Another example is information diffusion over social networks. Information diffusion over online social networks has become a fast growing research domain encompassing techniques from a plethora of sciences, among them mathematics, computer science, communications, and marketing, etc. Diffusion of innovations is a theory that seeks to explain how new ideas and technologies spread through cultures. Rogers [27] defined an innovation as an idea, practice, or object if it is perceived as novel by an individual or other unit of adoption. A piece of news being reposted many times in online social networks is a typical example of innovations diffusing across online social networks. The rise of social media has provided a new platform to study diffusion of innovation. Diffusion research centers on identifying the conditions to facilitate the increase or decrease of the likelihood that a new idea, product, or practice will be adopted by members of a given culture. More importantly, it is of great interest to predict how fast innovations spread and how media as well as interpersonal contacts influence opinion and judgment. Mathematical models based on the logistic adoption curve and five categories of adopters may provide guidance for taking appropriate actions to promote or control information spreading in online social networks. Part of the materials in this chapter is based on the authors' papers [108] on Prediction of daily PM2.5 concentration in China, [181] on modeling COVID-19 with difference equations, and [231] on modeling the spread of COVID-19 in Arizona with a simple SIR model.

5.2 Basic differential equation models

5.2.1 Logistic differential equations

Logistic differential equations are capable of representing the level or spread of an infectious disease, innovation among a given set of prospective population in a social or biological system with respective to time. The advantage of differential equation models is to give the successive increase in the number of infected or adopting units over time. Thus differential equation models permit prediction of the continued development of the diffusion process over time within a fixed population and further facilitates a theoretical insight of the dynamics of a spreading process. Extensive research has been attempted to expand the logistic differential equations models to analyze growth in environments with limited resource in various fields as an extension of the logistic models in population dynamics [24].

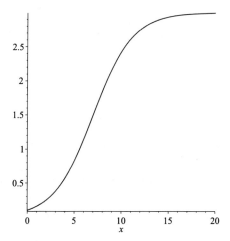

Figure 5.1 Diffusion growth curve.

The model takes the following form:

$$\frac{dN(t)}{dt} = \beta N(t)[\bar{N} - N(t)] \tag{5.2.1}$$

with the initial condition $N(0) = N_0$. Here, $N(t)$ is the cumulative number of infected at time t in a network. $\bar{N}$ denotes the total number of potential adopters or susceptibles. It states that the rate of diffusion of infection at any time t is directly proportional to the gap or difference between the total number of potential adopters or susceptibles and the number of previous adopters or susceptibles at that time. The peak of the solution is also called the carrying capacity. The fundamental diffusion model is called the *internal-influence diffusion model*. This is a more realistic model. For the internal-influence diffusion model, by solving (5.2.1), we have

$$N(t) = \frac{\bar{N}}{1 + \frac{\bar{N} - N_0}{N_0} e^{-\beta \bar{N} t}}.$$

Fig. 5.1 is the graph of $N(t)$ for the logistic equations.

5.2.2 Epidemical model

Epidemics of infectious disease have frequently affected our lives. The spread of infectious diseases among a population has been studied for centuries in an effort to understand spreading patterns, such as trends and ratios of people getting infected and, therefore, to implement effective prevention strategies. Compartmental epidemic models describing the transmission of communicable diseases have been extensively studied, and have many applications to emerging fields such as socio-biological systems and social media. Epidemic models have inspired many unsolved mathematical questions and re-energized novel mathematical research [13]. Conclusions and methods of mathematical modeling of infectious diseases have been accepted as a matter of general interest. More information can be found in [14,18,19,23,24].

In the present century, deterministic epidemic models have been increasingly adopted to describe and predict computer virus infections and information propagation. For ordinary differential equation models, epidemic models assume an implicit network and unknown connections among individuals. Similar to diffusion of innovations models, ordinary differential models are more suitable for studying global patterns, such as trends and ratios of people getting infected, and not interested in who infects whom. Partial differential equation models have spatial factors involved. Here, we review two basic epidemic models and one SIR model with standard incidence. In particular, we will discuss some extensions of the models in information diffusion over online social networks.

The spread of infectious diseases often involves a complex phenomenon with many interacting factors, and consists of a pathogen being spread, a population of hosts such as humans among others, and a spreading mechanism. The same components are required for news or rumors to spread. Compartmental epidemic models abstract the population into compartments under certain assumptions. These compartments represent their health status with respect to the pathogen in the system. Let N define the size of this population. Any member of the population can be in either one of three states: (1) Susceptible ($S(t)$), the number of the susceptibles at time t as $S(t)$; (2) Infected ($I(t)$), the number of infected individuals at time t; (3) Recovered (or Removed) ($R(t)$), the size of this set at time t. When an individual is in the susceptible state, he or she can potentially get infected by the disease. An infected individual has the chance of infecting susceptible parties. Individuals can only get infected by infected people in the population. The recovered are individuals who have either recovered from the disease, and hence have complete or partial immunity against the infection or were killed by the infection. The simple Kermack–McKendrick model [20] is the starting point for many epidemic models. In a closed population, which consists of susceptible individuals ($S(t)$), infected individuals ($I(t)$) and removed individuals ($R(t)$), the simple deterministic susceptible-infected-removed (SIR) is

$$S' = -\beta SI \tag{5.2.2}$$

$$I' = \beta SI - \gamma I \tag{5.2.3}$$

$$R' = \gamma I \tag{5.2.4}$$

where β is the transmission coefficient and γ is the recovery rate. It is clear that total population $N = S + I + R$ is constant. The underlying assumptions are that the system has a high level of uncertainty, and individuals usually do not decide whether to get infected or not. In addition, it is assumed that no contact network information is available and the process by which hosts get infected is unknown. In general, a complete understanding of the epidemic process requires substantial knowledge of the biological process within each host. Various extensions of SIR models have been extensively studied on general networks (see, e.g., [26,32]) and online social networks as well [33].

It is reasonable to assume that the population is closed and fixed when modeling epidemics where the disease spreads quickly in the population and dies out within a short time. In reality, infections can come from outside the population where the disease is being spread (e.g., by genetic mutation, contact with an animal, etc.). Further, if the human or animal population growth or decrease is significant or the disease causes enough deaths to influence the population size, then it is not reasonable to assume that the population size is constant (Mena-Lorca and Hethcote [23]). To account for variable population sizes, many researchers have proposed epidemic models with the transmission coefficient taking the following form:

$$\tilde{\beta}(N) = \frac{C(N)}{N}, \tag{5.2.5}$$

where $N = S + I + R$ is the total population size and $C(N)$ is the adequate contact rate. Then mass-action incidence corresponds to the choice $C(N) = \beta N$ and standard incidence corresponds to $C(N) = \beta$, where β is a positive constant. In general, $C(N)$ is a non-decreasing function with respect to N. For example,

$$C(N) = \frac{aN}{1 + bN + \sqrt{1 + 2bN}}$$

(Heesterbeek and Metz [18]),

$$C(N) = \lambda N^\alpha, \alpha = 0.05$$

(Mena-Lorca and Hethcote [23]). Other types of $C(N)$ can be found in [13] and references therein.

In Wang et al. [28], a general diffusive Kermack–McKendrick SIR model was studied with the assumption that some of the infective individuals will be removed from the population by disease-induced death or quarantine, but the recovered individuals will return to the community. The total population is $N = S + I + R$ and is not fixed. In this case, we have the following Kermack–McKendrick SIR model with standard incidence

$$\frac{dS}{dt} = -\frac{\beta SI}{N}, \tag{5.2.6}$$

$$\frac{dI}{dt} = \frac{\beta SI}{N} - \gamma I - \delta I, \tag{5.2.7}$$

$$\frac{dR}{dt} = \gamma I. \tag{5.2.8}$$

SIR models with standard incidence may be more suitable for studying information diffusion in online social networks because of rapid changes of online user dynamics.

5.3 Prediction of daily PM2.5 concentration

5.3.1 Introduction

This section is based on the authors' work on prediction of PM2.5 Concentration in China [108]. Air pollution has became one of the most challenging environmental problems. PM2.5 (particulate matter smaller than 2.5 μm) has been found to play a significant role for decreasing visibility, negative effects on human health, and influence on air pollution. In addition, the spread of pollution causes the spread of the epidemic [109,110]. Accurate and timely forecasting of PM2.5 concentration is essential for improving public health and economic conditions. Because PM2.5 concentrations are dynamic and exhibit wide variation for different cities in China, accurate description and prediction in China have become a highly challenging task for scientists.

There is a host of studies on PM2.5 prediction. Each approach addresses the problem from different perspectives. Physico-chemical methods and satellite remote sensing techniques are widely used in meteorological science. For example, 3-D chemistry transport models (CTMs) [37,38] mainly address the formation mechanism of PM2.5 from the view of physico-chemical and meteorological processes through the temporal dynamics of the emission quantities of various pollutants. This approach needs a large number of various meteorological data and perfect representation of the physico-chemical processes; therefore, it is difficult to guarantee real-time forecast. Satellite remote sensing techniques [43] have the advantages of spatially seamless and long-term coverage; as s result, in recent years they have been widely employed to predict PM2.5 by considering satellite-derived aerosol optical depth empirically correlated with PM2.5. However, the equipment expense for this type of research is relatively high.

Statistical approach is a very popular empirical prediction method. It aims to detect certain correlated patterns between air quality data and various selected predictors, thereby predicting the pollutant concentrations in future. Common statistical approaches, such as linear regression models [39,40], neural networks [41], nonlinear regression models [42], and neurofuzzy models are easier to implement but limited to specific geographical locations. In our previous work [111,112], a PDE model, specifically a linear diffusive equation and a advection equation, were applied to describe the spatial-temporal characteristics of PM2.5 for short-term prediction separately. In [111], the average prediction accuracy of the PDE model over all-city regions is 93% or 83% with different accuracy definitions. We use a simple logistic growth PDE model with reasonable assumptions based on meteorological knowledge and applied mathematics knowledge. In this section, we present a data-driven method to improve the simple PDE for predicting $PM_{2.5}$ in China.

A large amount of available data has sprung up in our lives. Nowadays, monitoring stations in a city can provide real-time air quality. The evolutionary modeling method, as a data-driven identification algorithm, is used to help build ODE models for $PM_{2.5}$ prediction. Genetic programming (GP) is an important EM method, which mimics the mechanisms of natural selection and genetic variation. Based on some suitable coding, GP uses genetic operators and the principle of "survival of the fittest" to search for the optimal solutions. An evolutionary modeling method of ODEs with GP is proposed in [113] and [114], in which a genetic algorithm is applied to optimize the parameters of a model. Compared with the genetic algorithm for parameter optimization, the least square method can analytically calculate the linear-in-parameter models. Therefore, in [115] a GP method with least square method for identification of linear-in-parameter models is proposed.

In this section, we extend the work of [113] and [115] to develop an algorithm for constructing ODEs, which combines the GP algorithm and orthogonal least square (OLS) algorithm. Specifically, the ODE model will involve the concentrations y of PM2.5 varying with time t and its change rate $y'(t)$ and $y''(t)$, which are related to the current concentration y and the current time t. Therefore, the dynamic process of PM2.5 concentration is naturally described by an ordinary differential equation,

$$\frac{dy}{dt} = f_1(y, t) \qquad (5.3.1)$$

or

$$\frac{d^2y}{dt^2} = f_2(y, \frac{dy}{dt}, t), \qquad (5.3.2)$$

but the exact mathematical formulas of $f_1(y, t)$ and $f_2(y, \frac{dy}{dt}, t)$ will be determined by PM2.5 data. We may make some reasonable preassumptions about the model structure. But it is almost impossible to develop a model to include all factors that affect the PM2.5, which needs more knowledge of the specific atmosphere details. The aim of this section is to apply genetic algorithm to identify the model structure from real data of PM2.5 concentrations, thus to further make prediction for PM2.5 in the future.

5.3.2 Genetic programming for ODE

In this section, we develop a genetic programming algorithm to construct ODEs for PM2.5 prediction. The higher-order ODE (5.3.2) can be converted into an ODE system with the form of

$$\begin{cases} \frac{dy_1}{dt} = y_2, \\ \frac{dy_2}{dt} = f_2(y_1, y_2, t) \end{cases} \qquad (5.3.3)$$

If we know the construction of $f_2(y_1, y_2, t)$, we just replace y_1 and y_2 by y and $\frac{dy}{dt}$, respectively; then we can easily obtain the structure of (5.3.2). Therefore, the construction of (5.3.2) equals the construction of the following:

$$\frac{dy_2}{dt} = f_2(y_1, y_2, t), \qquad (5.3.4)$$

where y_1 satisfies $\frac{dy_1}{dt} = y_2$. As a result, the construction of (5.3.1) and (5.3.2) is essentially the same problem as the construction of one-order ODEs (5.3.1) and (5.3.4). In the following, we discuss only problem (5.3.1). Problem (5.3.2) can be discussed in the same way.

The ODE construction of (5.3.1) contains the structure construction of the function $f(y, t; p)$ and parameter identification of vector p from

$$
\begin{cases}
\frac{dy}{dt} = f(y, t; p), \\
y(t_0) = y_0 \in \mathfrak{R}^1,
\end{cases}
\tag{5.3.5}
$$

using additional measurements of the following type:

$$
y(t_k) = Y_k, \ k = 0, 1, 2, \ldots, n.
\tag{5.3.6}
$$

We reduce problems (5.3.5) and (5.3.6) to an optimization problem, which consists in minimizing of the functional

$$
J(f, p) = \frac{1}{n} \left\{ \sum_{k=2}^{n-1} \left(f(Y_k, t_k; p) - \frac{Y_{k+1} - Y_{k-1}}{2\Delta t} \right)^2 \right.
$$
$$
+ \left(f(Y_1, t_1; p) - \frac{-Y_3 + 4Y_2 - 3Y_1}{2\Delta t} \right)^2
$$
$$
\left. + \left(f(Y_n, t_n; p) - \frac{3Y_n - 4Y_{n-1} + Y_{n-2}}{2\Delta t} \right)^2 \right\},
\tag{5.3.7}
$$

where Δt is the time interval.

The construction of the ODEs contains structure selection and parameter selection. GP is an evolutionary computation technique, which transforms the structure selection problem to a symbolic optimization problem, in which the search space consists of possible compositions of predefined symbols from the symbol set. Specifically, the construction of the ODE models is concluded as follows:

1) Defining initial function set and operator set.

Denote the function set as I_1, containing the predefined elementary functions in f; Denote the operator set as I_0, including the basic arithmetic operations existing between the elementary functions in f.

2) Generating an initial population.

Each ODE model can be uniquely represented by a tree [113,114]. Under the condition that the maximum tree depth does not exceed predefined constant D, based on the function set I_1 and operator set I_0, the algorithm randomly generates a lot of potential structures of f in the form of tree structure. Every f is regarded as an individual of the population in GP. This is the first generation of the genetic system and the optimal ODE structure is evolved from the first generation.

3) Structure selection.

We define the fitness function as (5.3.7) and it measures which of the current ODE structure is better suited to the PM2.5 concentration. Calculate the fitness value of every tree in the current generation, and operate mutation and crossover on the ODE trees with lower fitness in the current generation (they are parents of the next generation). Measure the fitness of the newly-generated offsprings. Select predefined number of individuals from all the parents and offsprings by the rule of higher fitness value, which has most wins to form the next generation.

Specifically, mark T^a and T^b are two ODE-trees of the current generation:

• **Crossing.** As the predefined crossover rate, perform crossover on the trees with the lower fitness. Tree-level crossover performs the following operations on parent T^a and T^b. Randomly, select a node in each tree as crossover point, exchange the subtree rooted at the crossover points and generate two new ODE trees T^c and T^d.

• **Mutating.** According to a predetermined mutation rate, perform mutation on the trees with lower fitness. For example parent T^a, randomly select a node within the tree as the mutation point with a randomly generated tree, thus an offspring T^e is generated.

• **Selecting.** Compute the fitness value of all the parents and the newly-produced offsprings and delete the trees who have lower fitness as the number of the new generation we predefined.

4) Parameter identification.

At some interval of the generations, select the better structures to optimize parameter by OLS methods.

5) Forming new generations recursively.

Combining Step 3 and Step 4, the algorithm forms the new generation.

6) Checking the exit conditions.

Step 3 and Step 4 are repeated in each generation until a predefined number of generations has reached or the best ODE structure is found.

More specific ODE construction, for the prediction of PM2.5, will be described in the next section.

5.3.2.1 Construction of ODEs for prediction of PM2.5 concentration

As described in (5.3.5) above, PM2.5 concentrations can be described by a dynamical system. As the right part of the ODE model, $f(y, t; p)$ should consist of multiple elementary functions. In this section, we develop an ODE-construction algorithm by combining the genetic algorithm and the

OLS method. Our goal is to construct $f(y, t; p)$ by identifying the elementary functions in $f(y, t; p)$ and associated parameters p.

5.3.2.2 Genetic programming for ODE structure

We will explain the genetic programming for constructing ODE in this subsection. For convenience, in this subsection we use specific sets of elementary functions and operations, but it can easily be expand to other sets of elementary functions and operations. Suppose that $f(y, t; p)$ can be described by four correlated functions $y(t)$, t, $sin(t)$, e^t and the basic arithmetic operations between these functions are "plus," "minus," and "multiply"; therefore we denote $I_0 = \{+, \times\}$ and $I_1 = \{y(t), t, sin(t), e^t\}$. The reason we choose these two sets is that the varying rate of PM2.5 concentration is related to the existing concentration $y(t)$ and the time t. And it behaves periodically (therefore we select $sin(t)$) or shows rapid growth (therefore we select e^t) in certain weather conditions. Now suppose that a series of observed values of $y(t_i)$ are collected at the time $t_i = t_0 + i \times \Delta t$, $(i = 1, 2, \ldots, n)$; thus $X(t) = [y(t), t, sin(t), e^t]$ can be written as

$$X = \begin{pmatrix} y(t_1) & t_1 & sin(t_1) & e^{t_1} \\ y(t_2) & t_2 & sin(t_2) & e^{t_2} \\ \vdots & \vdots & \vdots & \vdots \\ y(t_n) & t_n & sin(t_n) & e^{t_n} \end{pmatrix}. \tag{5.3.8}$$

$dY(t) = \frac{dy}{dt}$ at time t_i, $i = 1, 2, \ldots, n$ can be approximated by its second-order difference format as

$$dY(t_i) = \frac{dy}{dt}(t_i) = \begin{cases} \frac{-Y_{i+2}+4Y_{i+1}-3Y_i}{2\Delta t}, & i = 1 \\ \frac{Y_{i+1}-Y_{i-1}}{2\Delta t}, & i = 2, 3, \ldots, n-1 \\ \frac{3Y_i-4Y_{i-1}+Y_{i-2}}{2\Delta t}, & i = n \end{cases}$$

thus $dY(t) = \frac{dy}{dt}$ can be expressed as

$$dY = \begin{pmatrix} \frac{dy}{dt}(t_1) \\ \frac{dy}{dt}(t_2) \\ \vdots \\ \frac{dy}{dt}(t_n) \end{pmatrix}. \tag{5.3.9}$$

Denote $f(X) = [f(X(1, :)), f(X(2, :)), \ldots, f(X(n, :))]^T$, where

$$f(X(i, :)) = f(y(t_i), t_i, sin(t_i), e^{t_i})$$

is the composite function of the elementary functions involving variables $y(t)$, t, $sin(t)$, e^t and the function space defined by those functions can be denoted by F. Then the optimal problem is to find the model, having the form of

$$dY^* = f(X^*)$$

such that

$$min\{||dY^* - dY||, \forall f \in F\}, \tag{5.3.10}$$

where

$$||dY^* - dY|| = \frac{1}{n} \sum_{i=1}^{n} \left(dY(t_i) - f(X(i, :)) \right)^2.$$

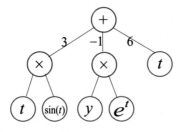

Figure 5.2 The representation of a ODE model.

With a predefined function set F, for any function $f \in F$, it is easy to see that an ODE can be uniquely represented by a tree [113,114]. As is the case with $f(t, sin(t), e^t, y)$, an ODE model with the form of

$$f(t, sin(t), e^t, y) = 3t\, sin(t) - ye^t + 6t, \tag{5.3.11}$$

can be uniquely represented by a tree as Fig. 5.2.

Therefore when we perform crossover, mutation, and selection on the ODE tree model, the ODE structure f in (5.3.5) will update till satisfying (5.3.10). And if the genetic programming is confined around a local minimum, the mutation step will help to get out of it. As practice shows, a global minimum of (5.3.10) should be obtained.

5.3.2.3 Fitness function

To construct the structure of the ODE model, we discuss f having the form of

$$f(t_k) = \sum_{i=1}^{M} p_i F_i(X(k,:)), k = 1, 2, \ldots, n, \qquad (5.3.12)$$

where $F_1, F_2, \ldots, F_M$ contain all the non-linear parts of function f, and the parts are composed of the values of the predefined function set at t_k. As is the case with (5.3.11), they are composed of t_k, $sint_k$, e^{t_k}, $y(t_k)$ based on the operation "minus" and "plus." Eq. (5.3.12) is essentially a linear-in-parameters model. We make this assumption because an overly complex model is not conducive to describing the nature of the problem and we have put all the potential nonlinear form in the function set I_1, which is included in F_i, $i = 1, 2, \ldots, M$.

In this section, we define the fitness function as

$$
\begin{aligned}
Fitness &= \frac{1}{n} \sum_{k=1}^{n} \left(\frac{dy}{dt}(t_k) - \sum_{i=1}^{M} p_i F_i\left(X(k,:)\right) \right)^2 \\
&= \frac{1}{n} \left\{ \sum_{k=2}^{n-1} \left(\frac{Y_{k+1} - Y_{k-1}}{2\Delta t} - \sum_{i=1}^{M} p_i F_i\left(X(k,:)\right) \right)^2 \right. \\
&\quad + \left(\frac{-Y_3 + 4Y_2 - 3Y_1}{2\Delta t} - \sum_{i=1}^{M} p_i F_i\left(X(1,:)\right) \right)^2 \\
&\quad + \left. \left(\frac{3Y_n - 4Y_{n-1} + Y_{n-2}}{2\Delta t} - \sum_{i=1}^{M} p_i F_i\left(X(n,:)\right) \right)^2 \right\},
\end{aligned}
$$

and ODE models whose fitness values are too low will be eliminated in the process of genetic programming.

5.3.2.4 Parameter identification

Once the ODE-structure is obtained, there are three groups of methods [116] for solving the minimization problem (5.3.7): local, global, and hybrid optimization methods. Orthogonal least square algorithm, as a global method, can analytically determine parameters for linear-in parameter models. In this article, we use this method to obtain the optimal model parameters. The idea of OLS algorithm is as follows:

Mark F and P as

$$F = \begin{pmatrix} F_1(X(t_1)) & \cdots & F_M(X(t_1)) \\ \vdots & \ddots & \vdots \\ F_1(X(t_N)) & \cdots & F_M(X(t_N)) \end{pmatrix}, P = \begin{pmatrix} p_1 \\ \vdots \\ p_M \end{pmatrix}.$$

Then the parameter identification equals solving vector P, which meets $dY = FP$. Here, dY is the measured output vector, defined as in Eq. (5.3.9); F is the regression matrix, where M is the number of regressors describing the basic unit of f, and N is the length of vector dY.

As illustrated in [115], the OLS assumes that F can be factorized as

$$F = QR,$$

where Q is an $N \times M$ orthogonal matrix and the columns of Q are orthogonal satisfying $Q^T Q = D$, and R is an $M \times M$ upper triangular matrix. Therefore

$$Q^T dY = Q^T FP = Q^T QRP = DRP,$$

the OLS auxiliary parameter vector is $g = D^{-1} Q^T dY$, and the parameters in vector P are readily computed from

$$RP = g.$$

In practice, although some elements of P exist, an overly small value of the element contributes little to the performance of the model. Therefore, we calculate the contribution of every function item corresponding to p_i. Denote

$$dY = FP + e, \tag{5.3.13}$$

where e is the error vector. After inserting $FP = QRP = Qg$ in to (5.3.13), it is easy to get

$$(dY)^T dY = \sum_{i=1}^{M} g_i^2 q_i^T q_i + e^T e,$$

where q_i is the column vector of Q, g_i is the element of vector $g = D^{-1} O^T dY$. Define $Del_i = g_i^2 q_i^T q_i / dY^T dY$. If Del_i is less than the value 0.05 we predefined, we regard the corresponding p_i as zero.

5.3.3 Experimental results and prediction analysis

The research data used in this study cover 120 days from January 21, 2016, to May 19, 2016, in Wuhan, China. The training set contains the former 100 days from January 21, 2016, to April 29, 2016. And the data from April 30, 2016, to June 13, 2016, is the test set. To validate the ODE models proposed in this section, we compare the prediction results with the typical statistical model in the view of in-sample prediction and out-of-sample prediction.

5.3.3.1 Statistical model

Consider the PM2.5 concentration from January 21, 2016, to April 29, 2016, as the training data. By applying unit root test, the time series is stationary; therefore, we use a typical $AR(p)$ model for the data. We apply the well-known Akaike information criterion (AIC) [117] and obtain the order $p = 1$. Therefore, the $AR(1)$ model can describe the time series. We perform out-of-sample one-step-ahead prediction for April 30, 2016, and the real concentration of PM2.5 is 47.1. The statistical model $AR(1)$ obtained through EViews 8 is

$$y_{k+1} = 0.660439 y_k + 23.49820,$$

whose statistical results of out-of-sample one-step-ahead prediction are shown in Table 5.1.

Table 5.1 Out-of-sample one-step-ahead prediction of statistical model for April 30, 2016.

Prediction results	54.7198
Root Mean Squared Error	0.225989
Mean Absolute Error	0.225989
Mean Abs. Percent Error	0.475767

5.3.3.2 ODE models obtained by our data-driven method

Meanwhile, we use data from January 21, 2016, to April 29, 2016, to train our ODE models and make a prediction for April 30, 2016. The experiment parameters are shown in Table 5.2. Generation gap equals 0.8, which means individuals with the top 20% fitness value are selected as the parents of the next generation. When the number of generations reaches 20th, the evolution terminates.

Because the ODE-construction method that we proposed in this section is stochastic, each performing maybe to get different ODEs. We perform

Table 5.2 Experiment parameters for ODE-construction.

Initial population size	30
Initial max tree depth	5
Max generation	20
Crossover rate	0.7
Generation gap	0.8
Mutation rate	0.3

the experiment 1,000 times and all the models and prediction results are as follows:

$$ODE_1 : \frac{dy}{dt} = -0.152040, Pre = 47.3480, Ape = 0.005265393, \quad (5.3.14)$$

$$ODE_2 : \frac{dy}{dt} = -0.113800, Pre = 47.3862, Ape = 0.006076433, \quad (5.3.15)$$

$$ODE_3 : \frac{dy}{dt} = 5.537091 * sin(t) - 0.409219,$$
$$Pre = 50.3057, Ape = 0.068061571,$$

$$ODE_4 : \frac{dy}{dt} = 0.091441 * y * sin^3(t) - 0.292838,$$
$$Pre = 48.0573, Ape = 0.020324841,$$

$$ODE_5 : \frac{dy}{dt} = 0.000846 * y^2 * sin^3(t) - 0.270239,$$
$$Pre = 47.6034, Ape = 0.010687898,$$

$$ODE_6 : \frac{dy}{dt} = 0.000006 * y^3 * sin^3(t) - 0.265039,$$
$$Pre = 47.3608, Ape = 0.005537155,$$

where *Pre* stands for the prediction results; *Ape* is the absolute percent error, namely the absolute relative error. The specific prediction process is as follows: after we use 100 days of data from January 21, 2016, to April 29, 2016, to obtain the models above, we apply the concentration of PM2.5 on April 29, 2016, as the initial value and predict the concentration of PM2.5 on April 30, 2016, just as the predicted y value corresponding to time 101 of x-axis in Fig. 5.3. Also, we can see that (5.3.14) and (5.3.15) are essentially two linear polynomial models and their discrete forms are AR(1) models. As each preforming generates different ODE models, we compute the expectation for the prediction results of one thousand times of performing and compare it with the real date as shown in Table 5.3.

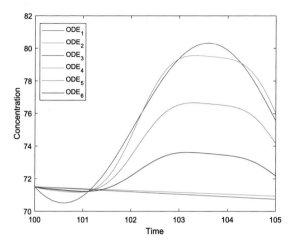

Figure 5.3 Plots of ODE models for April 30, 2016, as shown the value y corresponding 101 of the x-axis.

Table 5.3 Out-of-sample one-step-ahead prediction of ODE model for April 30, 2016.

Expectation (prediction results)	47.88686
Root Mean Squared Error	0.764535
Mean Absolute Error	0.786863
Mean Abs. Percent Error	0.017034

In this part, we list only the ODE models for predicting the concentration of PM2.5 on April 30, 2016. It can be seen that although genetic programming is a stochastic optimization method, the ODE models are different when performing programs each time. In this section, we only select several simple models from this procedure for prediction. We will derive a systematic procedure to determine the best model for prediction in the future.

5.3.3.3 Prediction comparison between statistical model and the ODE models

As seen from Tables 5.2 and 5.3, the ODE prediction models for April 30, 2016, are slight better than AR(1) model in the view of mean absolute percent error, but are worse in the view of root mean squared error and mean absolute error.

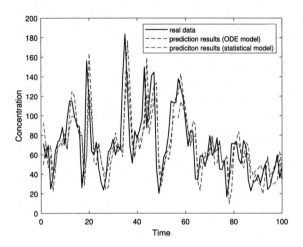

Figure 5.4 In-Sample one-step-ahead for January 21, 2016, to April 29, 2016.

In the statistical field, in-sample and out-of-sample predictions are two points of view from which to measure the models for prediction. Therefore below we will compare our ODE models with the traditional statistical model. Here, in-sample prediction is done to estimate the model with all the observations, and then we use the obtained model to predict some of the observations. For out-of-sample prediction, we divide the total observation into two parts. One part is to build the model and then to predict the other part of the data with the obtained model.

Fig. 5.4 shows the in-sample prediction results. Specifically, we use the data of 100 days from January 21, 2016, to April 29, 2016, to train models, and then we use the obtained model to make one-step ahead prediction for the same time period. It is clear that there is a consistent trend between predicted data (represented by red lines and green lines) and real observations (presented by black lines). In particular, compared with the typical statistical model, the prediction results obtained by the proposed ODE models are fairly good.

Fig. 5.5 shows the out-of-sample one-step-ahead prediction results through the ODE models proposed in this section. Specifically, we use the data from January 21 to April 29, 2016, to train models and then use the obtained models to make one-step-ahead prediction from April 30 to June 13, 2016. It is clear that there is a consistent trend between predicted data (represented by red lines) and real observations (represented by black lines).

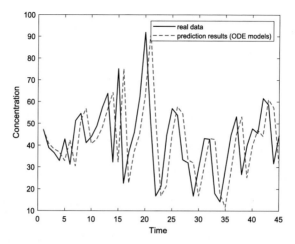

Figure 5.5 Out-of-sample one-step-ahead prediction from April 30, 2016, to June 13, 2016, by ODE-construction genetic program.

As a result, the experiments show that the real-time ODE models are effective in approaching the real-time modeling and predicting tasks of series.

5.3.3.4 Remarks

In this section, ODE models are proposed to predict the daily PM2.5 concentration. Tree-based genetic programming and the least square method are employed to evolve the structure and model parameters of ODEs. The proposed method is based on observed real data and needs almost no meteorological assumptions; therefore it can easily be applied to other problems. The experiment results clearly illustrate that the ODE model can effectively predict the daily concentration of PM2.5.

However, some issues need further discussion in our future work, that includes:

1) In practical application, although our ODE construction algorithm does not need meteorological knowledge or the specific mathematical formulation of the ODE model, some control parameters are predefined before making ODE construction, such as the function set, the operator set, the maximum tree depth, the mutation rate, the crossover rate and so on. We will develop a rule to choose control parameters in future research.

2) The data-driven ODE model obtained in the current work is not unique, as the procedure involves a stochastic input. We will develop a systematic approach to determine the best model for the data.

3) Compared with ODE, a partial differential equation (PDE) involves a spatial dimension to describe the interplay between individuals, thus better describing the dynamic system in the spatial–temporal dimensions. Therefore, a PDE model may better describe the transboundary pollution of PM2.5. A PDE construction method should be developed in our future work.

5.4 Analysis of COVID-19

5.4.1 Introduction

This section is based the authors' paper [181] on the work on analysis of COVID-19 with a SEIR difference equation, which can be viewed a computational version of a SEIR model. At the beginning of 2020, the outbreak of pneumonia caused by novel coronavirus (Coronavirus DISEA SE 2019, COVID-19) occurred around the world. As of April 21, 2020, the total number of confirmed cases worldwide has exceeded 2.45 million, and the total number of deaths has exceeded 170,000 [182]. At present, the epidemic has seriously threatened the safety of human lives and caused huge economic losses. Therefore it is a major problem to be solved to effectively extract the spread characteristics of the epidemic, analyze the effect of prevention and control measures on the epidemic intervention, and accurately forecast the development trend and key nodes of the epidemic. As a result, robust and portable models are needed to apply the experience of the first outbreak countries to the control of the subsequent outbreak countries.

The modeling and analysis of COVID-19 has attracted the attention of many researchers. At the earliest stage, Tang et al. established a network analysis model for infectious diseases using the limited data in the early stage, providing early reference for epidemic prevention and control [183]. Subsequently, they added some updated data and established a discrete dynamic analysis model with the help of data mining [184]. On this basis, Yan et al. introduced the time delay term and established the time-delay dynamics model [185]. Huang et al. further analyzed the epidemic trend and basic parameters based on the transmission dynamics method [186]. Cui et al. established a nonlinear regression model based on the data of the middle and late period of the epidemic in China [187]. Tian and his team quantitatively assessed the effectiveness of China's transmission control measures during the first 50 days of the COVID-19 outbreak [188]. Lau and his team found that COVID-19 patients were most infectious before the onset of symptoms [189]. Xiao et al. established a dynamic infection model of COVID-19 based on cybernetics to simulate the development trend and infection mechanism of COVID-19 in a city and calculated the theoretical number of infected people in closed cities [190]. Existing studies have analyzed the development of the epidemic from various perspectives and predicted the trend of the epidemic, providing important reference information for actual prevention and control. This epidemic situation can be established and analyzed by classical infectious disease dynamics models such as SIR (susceptible-infected-recovered) model [191,192], SIRS (susceptible-infected-recovered-susceptible) model [193–195], SEIR (susceptible-exposed-infectiousness-removed) model [196–198] and other classical infectious disease dynamics model for modeling and analysis. The main idea is to divide the population into susceptible person S, latent person E, infectious person I, confirmed person J, and recovered person R, and establish differential equations through the communication mechanism of transferring one group to another group, so as to reveal the law of epidemic transmission.

Because novel coronavirus has an incubation period, and there is a time-lag relationship between the latent infected, the confirmed infected and the cured. Classic infectious disease models cannot reflect the time delay and also cannot reflect the factors such as policy and medical resources influence on China's epidemic, so development of effective methods to integrate intervention measures, medical conditions, and time–delay relationship into classical epidemic models, can accurately predict the popular trend of COVID, China-19, peak time, and end time.

Based on the current research situation, this section takes into account the development characteristics of the epidemic, the impact of intervention, medical conditions, experience transfer, and other factors, combined with the development process of the epidemic in China, improves the classical epidemiological dynamics model, and establishes a discrete time multi-stage dynamic time-delay dynamics model.

The model divides the development of COVID-19 (so far) into six stages, the early outbreak (no intervention, protective, and medical resources), rapid outbreak period (infections exponential growth, isolating gradually strengthen, medical resources are running short), emergency defense period (infections index growth, government intervention, prohibited cross-regional population flow, major public health emergency response), strong interference, and control period (comprehensive intervention, strict protection, good protection within the region to reduce flow), the turnaround period (the number of new infections per day has obviously started to decline, and the disease control has shown initial results, the prevention and control measures are still strict), the stagnating period (the number of new infections per day has been reduced to hundreds of orders of magnitude, the epidemic has been basically under control, the response to prevention and control has been reduced, the flow of people is partially open, but individuals still adhere to isolation and protection). In the future, as the epidemic is completely controlled or a vaccine is successfully developed, humanity will win this battle and enter a period of full return to normal, and human life will return to the normal state as before the outbreak of the epidemic. Novel coronavirus has an incubation period, and the patient still needs hospitalization and observation from diagnosis to cure, and there is a time-lag relationship between the latent infected person, the confirmed infected person and the cured person [185]. In this section, different models and parameters were used to express different stages, as shown in Table 5.4. Based on the official WHO data (China), the model parameters (which contain the prevention and control isolation effect) were retrieved, and the discrete-time multi-stage time-delay dynamic model was obtained by partial calibration with reference to the conclusions of existing literatures [187].

At the early stage of COVID-19 outbreak in foreign countries, the public did not realize the seriousness of the COVID-19 epidemic, and did not pay enough attention to it. Meanwhile, the confirmations and tests were not timely, resulting in the great difference between the recorded data and the actual number of infected people, which made it difficult to analyze the epidemic situation [199,200]. Aiming at this problem, this section combines the foreign epidemic data record (the data may be distorted after sealing city). The multi-stage dynamic model established based on the real epidemic data of China was transplanted to the analysis of foreign epidemics, we then have COVID-19 trends for Italy, the United States, Germany, and Spain, as well as their current stage and likely future direction of the epidemic. The results showed that the first-stage model in China could well fit the number of infected people in Italy, Spain, and Germany before the city was sealed and the number of infected people in the United States officially announced by WHO. Further, according to the measures and effects of China's epidemic prevention and control, we discussed the situation of Italy, Germany, and Spain under three different prevention and control measures. We discussed the possible trend of the number of confirmed cases in the future, as well as the time interval and number interval of the peak number

Table 5.4 All the parameters.

Parameter	Definition	Value	Source
δ	Recovery rate	0.95	Literature [5]
t_1	Latency time lag	7	Literature [4]
t_2	The time lag of treatment observation period	14	Literature [20]
r_1	Stage II exponential decline rate (confirmed infected person)	0.96	parameter estimation
r_2	Stage III exponential decline rate (confirmed infected person)	1.86	parameter estimation
r_3	Stage II exponential decline rate (Latent period infection)	1.61	parameter estimation
r_4	Stage III exponential decline rate (Latent period infection)	1.89	parameter estimation
$c_0(\theta_{11})$	The number of susceptible people exposed to the confirmed infected person in one day in stage I	5.29	parameter estimation
c_1	The minimum number of susceptible persons exposed to a confirmed infected person in one day in stage II	1.91	parameter estimation
c_2	The minimum number of susceptible persons exposed to a confirmed infected person in one day after stage II	0.47	parameter estimation
$c_3(\theta_{21})$	The number of susceptible people exposed to the latent period infection in one day in stage I	8.11	parameter estimation
c_4	The minimum number of susceptible persons exposed to a latent period infection in one day in stage II	1.88	parameter estimation
c_5	The minimum number of susceptible persons exposed to a latent period infection in one day after stage II	0.96	parameter estimation
β_{11}	Probability of a susceptible person getting sick after contact with a confirmed infection when medical protection materials are scarce	0.09	parameter estimation
β_{21}	Probability of a susceptible person getting sick after contact with a latent period infection when medical protection materials are scarce	0.055	parameter estimation

continued on next page

Table 5.4 (*continued*)

Parameter	Definition	Value	Source
β_{12}	Probability of a susceptible person getting sick after contact with a confirmed infection when medical protection materials are sufficient	0.015	parameter estimation
β_{22}	Probability of a susceptible person getting sick after contact with a latent period infection when medical protection materials are sufficient	0.022	parameter estimation
θ_{12}	The number of susceptible persons exposed to infected persons within one day after the implementation of the isolation strategy	[1.92,5.29]	Eq. (5.4.1)
θ_{22}	The number of susceptible persons exposed to latent period infection persons within one day after the implementation of the isolation strategy	[0.48,1.92]	Eq. (5.4.2)
θ_{13}	The number of susceptible persons exposed to infected persons within one day after the implementation of the compulsory isolation strategy	[1.89,8.11]	Eq. (5.4.1)
θ_{23}	The number of susceptible persons exposed to latent period infection persons within one day after the implementation of the compulsory isolation strategy	[0.97,1.89]	Eq. (5.4.2)

of confirmed cases. Fully excavate the valuable experience accumulated in the process of epidemic prevention and control, correct local data records that may be distorted, and provide more accurate epidemic development forecasts and recommendations for countries that are in a critical period of outbreaks.

5.4.2 Modeling and parameter estimation

5.4.2.1 Model hypothesis

Combined with the transmission characteristics of COVID–19, the model hypothesis is as follows:

1. Both the exposed and the confirmed infected can infect the susceptible, and the confirmed infected are more infectious than the exposed.
2. Although there is a risk of reinfection among the recovered, this examples are so rare that they are not considered in the model.

3. All the exposed can go to the hospital for testing after symptoms appear and become confirmed infected people, and they can be hospitalized immediately after diagnosis.

4. At the isolation stage, everyone accepts isolation.

5. The confirmed infected person was converted to cure when the body temperature was normal and negative within three days after discharge.

5.4.2.2 Model establishment

1. $S(t)$: The number of susceptible persons present at time t.

2. $E(t)$: The existing number of the exposed at time t.

3. $I(t)$: The existing number of confirmed infected persons at time t. Since the official published data does not include the exposed persons, it is assumed in this section that the existing number of infected persons is equivalent to the existing number of confirmed persons.

4. $R(t)$: Accumulated number of recovered persons at time t. Although there is a risk of reinfection in recovered persons, there are few cases and they are not considered in the model.

The infected person has the incubation period of t_1 days before the symptoms appear, after the diagnosis becomes the confirmed infected person, after t_2 days of treatment observation period becomes the recovered, that is, the infected person diagnosed at time t becomes incubation period of infection at time $t - t_1$, The infected person who is cured at the t time becomes the latent infection at the $t - t_1 - t_2$ time and the confirmed infection at the $t - t_2$ time. The process of infection to recovery can be summarized as Fig. 5.6.

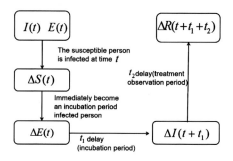

Figure 5.6 Infection-recovery process.

The number of people exposed to the virus has been affected by measures such as the centralized treatment of patients isolated at home by all residents after the outbreak. Assuming the number of susceptible people that a confirmed infected person comes into contact with is θ_1, and the number of susceptible persons that the latent infected person comes into contact with is θ_2. It is assumed that θ_1 and θ_2 are decreasing functions of time t, with exponential form. The coefficient of influence of medical resources on infection is β. Table 5.4 shows the definitions of all the parameters in this article.

$$\theta_1(t) = \begin{cases} c_0, & \text{phase one,} \quad \text{noted as } \theta_{11}, \\ (c_0 - c_1) e^{-r_1(t)-15} + c_1, & \text{phase two,} \quad \text{noted as } \theta_{12}, \\ (c_1 - c_2) e^{-r_2(t)-22} + c_2, & \text{else,} \quad \text{noted as } \theta_{13}. \end{cases} \quad (5.4.1)$$

$$\theta_2(t) = \begin{cases} c_3, & \text{phase one,} \quad \theta_{21} \\ (c_3 - c_4) e^{-r_3(t)-15} + c_4 & \text{phase two,} \quad \theta_{22} \\ (c_4 - c_5) e^{-r_4(t)-22} + c_5 & \text{else,} \quad \theta_{23} \end{cases} \quad (5.4.2)$$

The first stage (2020-01-14 to 2020-01-27, the initial outbreak): the whole country was in the peak period of Spring Festival travel, and no comprehensive quarantine was implemented. Meanwhile, Wuhan was closed on January 22, 2020, banning the movement of people inside and outside the city. Taking both aspects into consideration, the infection coefficient of confirmed infected persons was set as β_{11}, the number of effective contacts was set as θ_{11}, and the infection coefficient of latent infected persons was set as β_{21}, and the number of effective contacts was set as θ_{21} to establish the first stage time-delay discrete dynamic model (unit d):

$$S(t+1) - S(t) = -\beta_{11}\theta_{11}I(t) - \beta_{21}\theta_{21}E(t) \quad (5.4.3)$$

$$E(t+1) - E(t) = \beta_{11}\theta_{11}I(t) + \beta_{21}\theta_{21}E(t) - \beta_{11}\theta_{11}I(t - t_1) - \beta_{21}\theta_{21}E(t - t_1) \quad (5.4.4)$$

$$I(t+1) - I(t) = \beta_{11}\theta_{11}I(t - t_1) + \beta_{21}\theta_{21}E(t - t_1) - \theta\beta_{11}\theta_{11}I(t - t_1 - t_2) \\ - \beta_{21}\theta_{21}E(t - t_1 - t_2) \quad (5.4.5)$$

$$R(t+1) - R(t) = \theta\beta_{11}\theta_{11}I(t - t_1 - t_2) - \beta_{21}\theta_{21}E(t - t_1 - t_2) \quad (5.4.6)$$

Eq. (5.4.1) represents the change of susceptible persons at time t: the number of infected persons in the incubation period and confirmed infected persons at time t; (5.4.2) indicates the change of infection in the incubation period at t time. That is, the number of people infected and diagnosed in the incubation period at t moment minus the number of people who become infected in the incubation period at the time of $t - t_1$ and become confirmed infection after the incubation period. (5.4.3) represents the change of confirmed infected persons at time t: the number of infected persons who become latent at time $t - t_1$ and become confirmed infected after the incubation period minus the number of infected persons who become latent at time $t - t_1 - t_2$ and become cured after the incubation period and treatment period.

The second stage (2020-01-29 to 2020-02-04, rapid outbreak period): the state took compulsory quarantine measures and stopped all gathering activities. The effective contact number of infected people decreased to θ_{12} and θ_{22}, but there was a shortage of medical supplies, and the infection coefficient remained unchanged. The evolution model of $S(t)$, $E(t)$ becomes

$$S(t+1) - S(t) = -\beta_{11}\theta_{12}I(t) - \beta_{21}\theta_{22}E(t) \qquad (5.4.7)$$

$$E(t+1) - E(t) = \beta_{11}\theta_{12}I(t) + \beta_{21}\theta_{22}E(t) - \beta_{11}\theta_{11}I(t - t_1)$$
$$- \beta_{21}\theta_{21}E(t - t_1) \qquad (5.4.8)$$

The third stage (2020-02-05 to 2020-02-11, emergency defense period): the country increases the isolation, the effective contact number of infected people decreases to θ_{13} and θ_{23}, the square capsule hospitals of Mount Thor and Mount Vulcan are built and put into use, the shortage of medical supplies becomes better, and a large number of latent infected people show symptoms, and the transmission coefficients decreased to β_{12} and β_{22}. The evolution model of S, E, I is

$$S(t+1) - S(t) = -\beta_{12}\theta_{13}I(t) - \beta_{22}\theta_{23}E(t) \qquad (5.4.9)$$

$$E(t+1) - E(t) = \beta_{12}\theta_{13}I(t) + \beta_{22}\theta_{23}E(t) - \beta_{11}\theta_{12}I(t - t_1)$$
$$- \beta_{21}\theta_{22}E(t - t_1) \qquad (5.4.10)$$

$$I(t+1) - I(t) = \beta_{11}\theta_{12}I(t - t_1) + \beta_{21}\theta_{22}E(t - t_1) - \theta\beta_{11}\theta_{11}I(t - t_1 - t_2)$$
$$- \beta_{21}\theta_{21}E(t - t_1 - t_2) \qquad (5.4.11)$$

The fourth stage (2020-02-12 to 2020-02-18, intensive intervention and control period): the epidemic peaked, the number of infected people in the incubation period decreased sharply, the isolation intensity remained unchanged, the effective contact number of infected people remained unchanged, and the infection coefficient remained unchanged. The model is as follows:

$$E(t+1) - E(t) = \beta_{12}\theta_{13}I(t) + \beta_{22}\theta_{23}E(t) - \beta_{12}\theta_{13}I(t-t_1)$$
$$- \beta_{22}\theta_{23}E(t-t_1) \tag{5.4.12}$$

$$I(t+1) - I(t) = \beta_{12}\theta_{13}I(t-t_1) - \beta_{22}\theta_{23}E(t-t_1) - \theta\beta_{11}\theta_{11}I(t-t_1-t_2)$$
$$- \beta_{21}\theta_{21}E(t-t_1-t_2) \tag{5.4.13}$$

The fifth stage (2020-02-19 to 2020-02-25, transition period): the medical resources are relatively sufficient, the isolation intensity remains unchanged, the number of existing infected people begins to decline, the number of infected people in the incubation period remains low. The number of new infections per day has dropped to hundreds of orders of magnitude, and the epidemic has basically been brought under control:

$$I(t+1) - I(t) = \beta_{12}\theta_{13}I(t-t_1) + \beta_{22}\theta_{23}E(t-t_1) - \theta\beta_{12}\theta_{12}I(t-t_1-t_2)$$
$$- \beta_{22}\theta_{22}E(t-t_1-t_2) \tag{5.4.14}$$

$$R(t+1) - R(t) = \theta\beta_{12}\theta_{12}I(t-t_1-t_2) - \beta_{22}\theta_{22}E(t-t_1-t_2) \tag{5.4.15}$$

The sixth stage (2020-02-26 to 2020-03-26, stalemate): The number of pneumonia infections decreases rapidly while maintaining the current isolation strength and ensuring adequate medical resources. The difference between this stage and the model of the previous stage are

$$I(t+1) - I(t) = \beta_{12}\theta_{13}I(t-t_1) + \beta_{22}\theta_{23}E(t-t_1) - \theta\beta_{12}\theta_{13}I(t-t_1-t_2)$$
$$- \beta_{22}\theta_{23}E(t-t_1-t_2) \tag{5.4.16}$$

$$R(t+1) - R(t) = \theta\beta_{12}\theta_{13}I(t-t_1-t_2) - \beta_{22}\theta_{23}E(t-t_1-t_2) \tag{5.4.17}$$

The difference between the six models is that the coefficients are different. Different policies and actual conditions determine the coefficient of infection and the number of effective contacts, which also correspond to models at different stages. The development of the epidemic in Italy, Spain, and Germany was analyzed by using the established discrete multi-stage time-delay dynamics model. We are here to discuss the different outcomes of doing nothing, adopting the same prevention and control measures as China, and adopting measures in between.

1. No action was taken:
   The COVID-19 transmission model and coefficients in Italy, Germany, and Spain were the same as those in China during the first phase. The incubation period and treatment period are assumed to be the same as in China, but the cure rate in Italy is 89.8%, Spain is 90.3%, the United States is 94.62%, and Germany has a cure rate of 99.5% [1].

2. Adopting the same prevention and control measures as China:
   Before the city closure, the transmission model and coefficient of COVID-19 in the first phase of the three countries were the same as those in China. After the city closure, the models and coefficients of the second, third, fourth, and fifth stages in the three countries were the same as those in China. In other words, the city was sealed off as strictly as China, with self-isolation and concentrated treatment, and the shortage of medical supplies was improved within 2 weeks of the closure.

3. Adopting measures in between:
   Before the city closure, the first phase transmission model and coefficient of COVID-19 in the three countries were the same as that in China. After city closure, residents' self-isolation effect is poor, the city closure measures are not as strict as China's, and the shortage of medical supplies cannot be effectively improved. The contagion coefficient and contact number of the Italian model in the second, third, fourth, and fifth stages are higher than the corresponding Chinese model, but lower than the Chinese model in the first stage.

The COVID-19 epidemic in the United States is very serious. As of March 25, 2020, the United States does not have strict quarantine measures in place nationwide, and medical supplies are in short supply, with more COVID-19 patients not being tested. This paper analyzes only the officially published COVID-19 data, and uses the first-stage model and parameters in China to fit the development trend of the number of infected people in the United States.

5.4.2.3 Parameter estimation

Accurate and detailed data is essential to enhance the prediction and evaluation ability of the model. However, the detection of COVID-19 this time was greatly limited by the number of kits, especially after Wuhan was closed for a week. Many patients could not be effectively diagnosed due to lack of timely detection, leading to the fact that the confirmed cases lagged behind the actual number of cases, so there was a large underestimate in the data. Since February 12, 2020, the government has changed the method of nucleic acid testing using kits to clinical testing (including CT), resulting in a sudden increase in the cumulative number of confirmed cases, but also resulting in large fluctuations in the existing confirmed cases. Literature [187] analyzed this problem through nonlinear regression, and presented the cumulative number of diagnosed patients after calibration from February 5, 2020, to February 11, 2020, as Table 5.5 and Fig. 5.7 show. In this section, the calibration data were used to obtain the number of confirmed cases from February 5th to February 11th, and used as the accurate data in the third stage for parameter estimation.

Table 5.5 Partial calibration data.

Date	Actual data	Calibration data
02-05	26210	29975
02-06	28874	33890
02-07	31574	37909
02-08	33576	41602
02-09	35802	45247
02-10	37688	48560
02-11	38583	51813

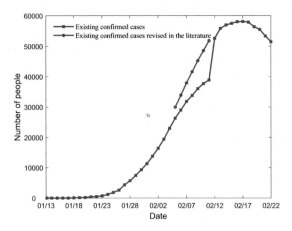

Figure 5.7 Partial calibration data.

The cure rate of COVID-19 was 95% (see [186]). The average incubation period was 5 days (see [185]). The time from the onset of COVID-19 to the diagnosis of COVID-19 patients decreased with the development of the epidemic. After comprehensive consideration, it was set as 2 days.

For the convenience of modeling and calculation, the combination of the incubation period and the time from onset to diagnosis is the latency, that is, t_1 is 7 days. The average treatment period was 11 days [201], plus the observation period of 3 days, so the time lag of treatment observation t_2 was 14 days.

Due to the special significance of infection rate β and contact number θ in this model environment and the lack of experimental data, the parameter inversion method [185] was used in this section to determine the values of β and θ in various cases.

- The value range of infection rate is [0,1], and the value range of contact number is [0,10]. Through the heuristic algorithm, we randomly sampled the value ranges of various parameters with a sampling interval of 0.01 to determine the sampling values of β_{11}, β_{21}, c_0, c_3, respectively. The sampling value was brought into the first-stage model to obtain the estimated value of the number of infected people in each day of the first stage. The number of infected people in each day officially published in the first stage was taken as the actual value, and the optimal parameter was obtained with the goal of minimizing the mean-square error (MSE). The problem of obtaining β_{11}, β_{21}, c_0, c_3 by inversion is transformed into

$$min \sum_{t_1=1}^{N_1} \frac{1}{N_1} (I_{data1} - I(t_1, \beta_{11}, \beta_{21}, c_0, c_3))^2,$$

where t_1 represents the date of the first stage, we default that the first day is January 15, 2020, N_1 is the total number of days of the first stage, I_{data1} is the official published data of the existing infection of the first stage, and $I(t_1, \beta_{11}, \beta_{21}, c_0, c_3)$ is the estimated existing infection data.

- The range of exponential decline rate is [0,2], and parameter c_1, c_4, r_1, r_3 can be obtained by the same method through the number of existing infected persons in the second stage. The problem of obtaining c_1, c_4, r_1, r_3 by inversion is transformed into

$$min \sum_{t_2=15}^{N_2} \frac{1}{N_2 - 15} (I_{data2} - I(t_2, c_1, c_4, r_1, r_3))^2,$$

where t_2 represents the date of the first stage, N_2 is the total number of days of the second stage. The second phase will start on the 15th day. I_{data2} is the official published data of the existing infection of the second stage, and $I(t_2, c_1, c_4, r_1, r_3)$ is the estimated existing infection data.

• β_{12}, β_{22}, c_2, c_5, r_2, r_4 can be obtained from the inversion of the number of existing infected persons in the third stage. The problem of obtaining β_{12}, β_{22}, c_2, c_5, r_2, r_4 by inversion is transformed into

$$min \sum_{t_3=22}^{N_3} \frac{1}{N_3 - 22} (I_{data3} - I(t_3, \beta_{12}, \beta_{22}, c_2, c_5, r_2, r_4))^2,$$

where t_3 represents the date of the third stage, N_3 is the total number of days of the third stage. The third phase will start on the 22nd day. I_{data3} is the official published data of the existing infection of the third stage, and $I(t_3, \beta_{12}, \beta_{22}, c_2, c_5, r_2, r_4)$ is the estimated existing infection data.

5.4.3 Model simulations

The parameter estimation results are shown in Table 5.4. The above parameter values are brought into the six models to obtain the model fitting results, which include the existing number of infected people in China, the number of infected people in the incubation period, and the cumulative number of cured people. Their trend over time is shown in Fig. 5.8.

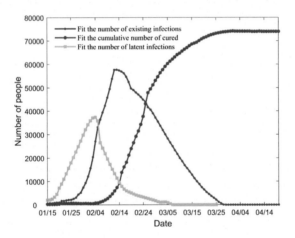

Figure 5.8 Three kinds of population data.

The calculated results of the model show that the latent infections has risen sharply in the first phase, and reached its peak in the second stage. Compulsory quarantine measures, which have been implemented since the second phase, have effectively reduced the number of infected people who are susceptible to infection. As a large number of latent infected persons

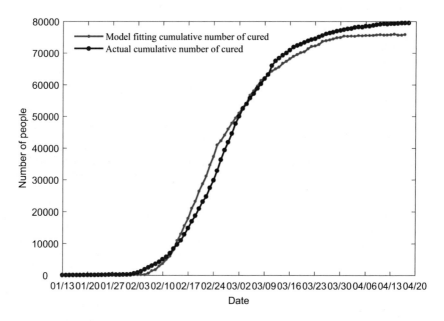

Figure 5.9 The number of people cured.

pass the latent period and become confirmed infected persons, the number of latent infected persons begins to decrease rapidly in the third stage, and decreases to zero in the fifth and sixth stages. The number of infected people has increased exponentially in the first three stages, especially in the second and third stages, when a large number of latent infected people show symptoms and go to hospital, resulting in a severe shortage of medical supplies. The model predicts that the inflection point will occur on February 14, 2020, which is only 3 days away from the actual inflection point. Since the fourth stage, the shortage of medical supplies has been alleviated, the number of latent and confirmed infected people has been decreasing, and the number of cured people has been increasing at a faster rate. The model predicts that the number of existing infections will drop to a lower level around March 26, 2020. According to the conclusion that the zero increase in the number of pneumonia infections plus two 14-day incubation periods is the end time of the epidemic, the model predicts the end time of the epidemic is in late April. By comparing the number of infected people and the number of cured people calculated by the model with the actual data, the fitting results of the model is shown in Fig. 5.9 and Fig. 5.10. The fitting results of the model show that the number of confirmed infected people reached the peak of 57,798 people on February

14, 2020, which was only 243 people short of the actual peak of 58,041 people. The number of people cured reached 68,857 on March 24, 2020. The results of model fitting are consistent with the reality both in terms of quantity and trend, so this model can be used to simulate the development process of the epidemic in China.

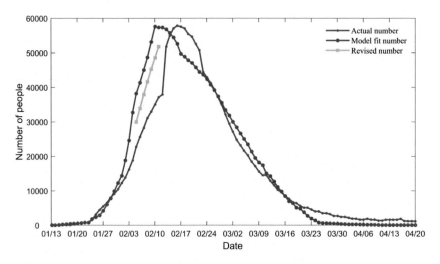

Figure 5.10 The number of people infected.

For COVID-19 outbreaks in Italy, Germany, Spain, and the United States, this section discussed the different results of taking no measures, adopting the same prevention and control measures as China's, and adopting measures in between, respectively, as shown in Fig. 5.12. The results of the model show that the first-stage model and parameters in China can better fit the changing trend of the number of confirmed cases in Italy, Spain, and Germany before the closure, indicating that the development trend of the epidemic in the three countries before the closure is the same as that in China, as shown in the figure. If no action is taken in the three countries, 600,000 people will be infected in Italy on March 24, 2020, 440,000 in Spain on March 29, 2020, and 150,000 in Germany on March 27, 2020. If the three countries had adopted quarantine measures as strict as China's and continued to improve health care, the outbreak in Italy would have peaked on March 25, with a maximum number of 103,761 existing cases. The Spanish outbreak will peak on March 28, 2020, with the maximum number of existing cases being 61,011; The epidemic in Germany will peak on March 31, 2020, and the maximum number of existing infected people will be 95,864. If the three countries take intermediate measures, that is, the isolation and prevention efforts are weaker than that in China, and the phenomenon of lack of medical resources cannot be effectively alleviated, this section presents the results of one of the situations in each country, so as to form a reference with other curves.

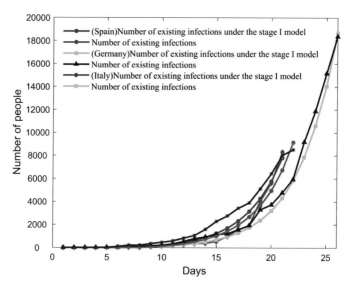

Figure 5.11 The number of people infected.

Before the closure of the city, the number of existing infections fitted by the first-stage model in the three countries was very close to the officially announced number, as Fig. 5.11 displays, but after the closure of the city, the number of existing infections under the three different measures was significantly different from the official announcement. The reason was the closure of the city and there have been a large number of people infected during the incubation period. After the city closure, the three countries did not adopt the same strict quarantine measures as China, and medical resources are in short supply. It is not possible to test all the residents with symptoms, which is contrary to our model assumptions. So there is a big gap between the number of people infected and the actual figure, especially in two countries, Italy and Spain. From the range of the number of existing infected persons under the three different measures in the three countries, it can be seen that Italy is currently in a period of strong intervention and control in the six-stage model. As of April 17, 2020, it is conservatively estimated that there are 230,000 symptomatic patients. The peak of the number of existing infections first appeared on April 14, 2020, and the peak number was about 240,000. The model predicts that around April 21, there will still be about 210,000 symptomatic infections in Italy, but the number of existing infections presents a downward trend.

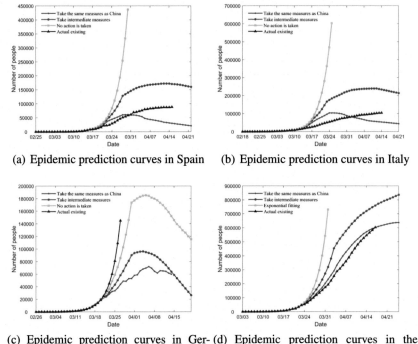

(a) Epidemic prediction curves in Spain   (b) Epidemic prediction curves in Italy

(c) Epidemic prediction curves in Ger-   (d) Epidemic prediction curves in the
many   United States

Figure 5.12 Prediction curve.

This section uses the Chinese multi-stage model and an exponential function to fit the number of confirmed diagnoses officially announced by the United States. The fitting results are shown in Fig. 5.9 (the figure shows the data after March 4, 2020). If the epidemic begins to spread on February 20, 2020, both the exponential function and the China's first stage model will have a better fit to the data of the United States before March 23, 2020 (Fig. 5.12(d)). Since the United States did not take effective measures in the early stage of the epidemic, the current epidemic is still in an emergency defense period. If the same stringent measures as China are adopted from March 20, 2020, and the state of medical resources continues to improve, the peak of the epidemic will appear around April 25, 2020, with a approximately peak number 640,000. If the United States takes intermediate measures from March 20, 2020, the model predicts that the number of existing infections in the United States will reach 840,000 on April 25, 2020, and still growing at a relatively rapid rate. Due to the exponential increase in the number of pre-infections, the United States has not tested all people with symptoms. The interim data is distorted to a certain extent, and the start time of the spread of the epidemic in the United States cannot be completely determined. There is a big difference between the officially announced number of confirmed cases and the actual number of infections.

5.4.4 Conclusion and perspective

In this section, an improved discrete time multi-stage time-delay dynamic model was proposed. Based on the data from China, the correlation between the prevention and control measures and the trend of the epidemic was extracted through parameter inversion, as well as the development characteristics of the epidemic itself, and a dynamic analysis method of COVID-2019 based on experience transmission was established.

An analysis of COVID-19 in Italy, the United States, Germany, and Spain using the proposed model shows that the United States is still in a phase III emergency preparedness period, with the number of infections increasing exponentially. If the United States continues its current approach to control the epidemic, there will be a large-scale outbreak. But if the United States intervenes more intensively, the epidemic will enter phase four—a period of intensive intervention and control—by April 20, 2020. The outbreak will gradually be contained, but the number of infected people could still exceed one million. In Italy and Spain, the epidemic situation is similar. Both countries are in the phase of intensive intervention and control (phase IV) and are about to reach the peak. The current prevention and control methods will continue, and the number of existing infections will decrease in the future. Germany is currently in a transition period, but the peak has passed (mid to late phase 5), and the number of infections will decline relatively rapidly.

To sum up, it is suggested that the United States should strengthen prevention and control intervention to bring the epidemic to the stage of prevention and control as soon as possible. Italy, Spain, and Germany can continue with the current approach until the epidemic reaches phase six or is completely dissipated. All countries around the world need to raise awareness and strengthen personal protection to prevent a second outbreak from asymptomatic people until the epidemic is completely eliminated or a vaccine is developed.

In this section, a multi–stage dynamic system model was used to analyze the epidemic, and the prediction was based on statistical theory, without considering the influence of spatial and temporal distribution on the epidemic. Epidemic modeling needs to consider many factors, especially for the modeling of mega cities. Li et al. proposed a prevention and control system based on spatio-temporal big data [202]. Modeling and prediction combined with spatio-temporal location services will be further considered in subsequent studies.

5.5 Analysis of COVID-19 in Arizona

5.5.1 Introduction

In June 2020, Arizona, US, emerged as one of the world's worst coronavirus disease 2019 (COVID-19) spots with an alarming resurgence of COVID-19 after the stay-at-home order was lifted in the middle of May [203,204]. On June 29, Arizona reported 5,484 new COVID-19 cases, an all-time high record, averaged 3,680 daily new cases reported at the 27th week of 2020. However, with the decisions to reimpose restrictions such as closing bars, gyms, and some businesses, that average has been monotonically declining week-over-week, and on August 20, the average number of new cases in the past 7 days reached 779. While many other states in the US are still experiencing the increase of new cases in October, Arizona is considered to be a suitable model in slowing the epidemic [205]. In the absence of pharmaceutical control measures, mobility restriction is one of the few known interventions to mitigate the disease spread effectively [144,206,207]. However, level and type of restrictions have been questioned, and there is debate over when restrictions should be imposed or lifted [208,209]. The studies used to inform decision-makers are mainly based on parameter values obtained from other scenarios or countries, and it may not be suitable for the specific region. While there are a tremendous number of researches focusing on the specific regions, there are only handful of modeling studies focusing on Arizona [210,211]. To aid in assessing the effect of mobility restrictions in Arizona, the use of daily aggregated real-world data on human mobility can be a helpful tool [212–215]. Google Community Mobility Reports (GCMR) publishes the data on human mobility change, and there have been numerous mathematical modeling studies using the data [216–220]. In the present paper, we aimed to examine the COVID-19 situation in Arizona and assess the impact of change in human mobility. Combining the metapopulation susceptible-infected-removed (SIR) model of COVID-19 transmission with a data set for COVID-19 cases and Google Community Mobility Reports (GCMR), we estimated how transmission differed in three regions in Arizona. Using estimated epidemiological parameters, we simulated how human mobility affects the epidemic of COVID-19. Our findings may provide useful insight when implementing a policy to mitigate the epidemic in Arizona.

5.5.2 Data sources and collection

There are 15 counties in the US state of Arizona. In general, Arizona is divided into Northern, Central, and Southern Arizona. Although the boundaries of the regions are not well-defined, as we aim to assess human mobility during the COVID-19 epidemic in Arizona, we group the counties of Arizona into the three regions in Fig. 5.13. The three regions represent different geographical and social characteristics in terms of the spread of COVID-19. Much of the Northern region is National Forest Service land, parkland, and includes Navajo reservations. Central Arizona (Maricopa County), where the city of Phoenix is located, has about 60% of the population in Arizona, and more than half of COVID-19 cases are reported in this region. Southern Arizona includes Tucson and several other small cities close to the border of the US and Mexico. In the following, we will use NAZ, CAZ, and SAZ to denote the clusters of the Arizona counties.

To estimate the COVID-19 transmission dynamics in Arizona, we fitted the mobility integrated metapopulation SIR model to publicly available data sets on Arizona cases between March 1, 2020, and October 17, 2020. We compute the COVID-19 prevalence of each region by adding the cases of all counties belonging to a region. We use the COVID-19 data from the New York Times at the state and the county level over time. The New York Times compiles the time series data from state and local governments and health departments to provide a complete record of the ongoing outbreak. Daily epicurve stratified by the data, and the timing of policy implementations are shown in Fig. 5.13. Besides, we incorporate the GCMR to model the inter-region human movement. These reports provide insights into how people's social behaviors have been changing in response to policies aimed at combating COVID-19. The reports provide the changes in movement trends compared to baselines overtime at the US county level, across different categories of activities: retail and recreation, groceries and

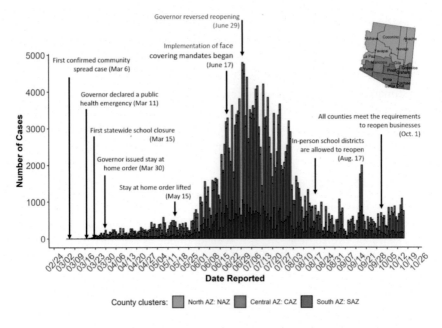

Figure 5.13 Geographical distribution and temporal dynamics of confirmed COVID-19 cases.

pharmacies, parks, transit stations, workplaces, and residential [221]. Then we compute each region's daily changes by adding the changes of all counties belonging to a region. We create two time series from the GCMR. We accumulate the data for retail recreation, groceries, pharmacies, parks, transit stations, and workplaces as activities outside of the home, which are believed to increase the number of COVID-19 cases. The data for residential activities describes stay-at-home activities that are believed to slow down COVID-19 epidemics.

5.5.3 Model simulations

We divided the population according to the infection status into susceptible (S), infected (I), and removed (R) individuals, and according to three sub-populations. Susceptible individuals get infected at a given rate when they come in effective contact with an infectious individual, acquire infectiousness, and later either recover or die. We assumed Arizona to be a closed system with a constant population size of 7.3 million (i.e., $S + I + R = 7.3$ million) throughout this epidemic. Additionally, we incorporated the effect of human mobility change based on GCMR.

For a given region i, the evolution of the population in each status over time can be described by

$$\frac{dS_i}{dt} = -\left(\sum_{j=1}^{3} \beta_j \frac{I_j}{N_j} p_{ij} \phi_j(t)\right) S_i \qquad (5.5.1)$$

$$\frac{dI_i}{dt} = \left(\sum_{j=1}^{3} \beta_j \frac{I_j}{N_j} p_{ij} \phi_j(t)\right) S_i - \gamma_i \hat{\phi}_l(t) I_i \qquad (5.5.2)$$

$$\frac{dR_i}{dt} = \gamma_i \hat{\phi}_l(t) I_i \qquad (5.5.3)$$

where β_i is the transmission rate, γ_i is the recovery rate, p_{ij} describe the intra-region relative contact rate between region i and region j (i.e., $p_{ij} = 1$ for $i = j$). $\phi_i(t)$ is a function, which describes activities outside of the home and $\hat{\phi}_l(t)$ describes stay-at-home activities and it is written in a form

$$\phi_i(t) = \begin{cases} \frac{1}{1+\exp(-m_i(t-10))}, & i = j \\ 1, & \text{otherwise} \end{cases} \qquad (5.5.4)$$

where $m_i(t - 10)$ and $\hat{m}_l(t - 10)$ are empirical data for human mobility outside of the home and stay-at-home activities, respectively ($\hat{\phi}_l(t)$ takes the same function as $\phi_i(t)$). We assume that time lags between mobility and COVID-19 cases are 10 days based on our analysis. The parameters for SIR were found using least-squares analysis and a quasi-Newton method. Models were fit to empirical infected cases per day.

To assess the applicability of the model (i.e., determine whether the algorithm converge), we varied the starting date and the final date of the data and simulated for 460 different time period separately (i.e., for one set of simulation, we set the end date as October 17, 2020, and varied the starting date from March 1, 2020, to October 16, 2020, and ran the simulation for each 230 time-period separately. For the other set of simulation, we set the start as March 1, 2020, and varied the end date from March 2, 2020, to October 17, 2020, and ran the simulation for each 230 time-period separately.) To validate that the model has better ability to estimate the parameters for each time period than the simple metapopulation SIR model without mobility data, we calculated Akaike Information Criterion (AIC) and compared with the AIC for the model without GCMR data. The code of the simulation is available at https://github.com/madonnaojorin/COVID19.

Table 5.6 Parameter values used for SIR model for three regions.

Region	Population	$p_{i,j}$: From NAZ to	$p_{i,j}$: From CAZ to	$p_{i,j}$: From SAZ to
NAZ	848,693	1	0.0012	0.0018
CAZ	4,485,414	0.013	1	0.049
SAZ	1,944,610	0.0025	0.005	1

Table 5.7 Estimated parameter values for the metapopulation SIR model.

Parameters	β_1	β_2	β_3	γ_1	γ_2	γ_3
Values	0.263	0.850	0.943	0.209	0.500	0.620

For the intra-region movement (which are described as relative contact rate between region and region (i.e., for), we used Census commuting flows [222] and adjusted by the proportion of the population working from home estimated at 50% [223].

For the COVID-19 epidemic in three Arizona regions, we estimated the model parameters summarized in Tables 5.6 and 5.7 based on data from March 1, 2020, to October 17, 2020. This period includes the recent restrictions enforced since June 29, 2020, which have slowed down the epidemic's spread. Fig. 5.14 illustrates our estimates of COVID-19 cases in 3 regions during the above mentioned period. The red dotted lines represent the prevalence based on the observed COVID-19 cases, and blue lines represent the predicted COVID-19 cases. Our estimations underestimate the number of cases before the exponential growth phase; however, it captures the trend well after the phase.

5.5.4 Remarks

Strict control measures, such as stay-at-home orders (i.e., mobility restrictions), have been implemented to contain the COVID-19 outbreak in many countries, and it has been shown to be effective [152,224–226]. To evaluate the effect of policy implementation and its issued timing on the dynamics of COVID-19 spread, we incorporated empirical human mobility data in our metapopulation SIR model. We estimated parameter values, simulated outbreaks using the parameters, and assessed the impacts of mobility restrictions. Our findings suggest that rapid and effective policy implementation might have successfully slowed down the COVID-19 outbreak in Arizona.

Applications of digital technologies in public health have caught attention in the past few years [227] and it has been applied to assess this current

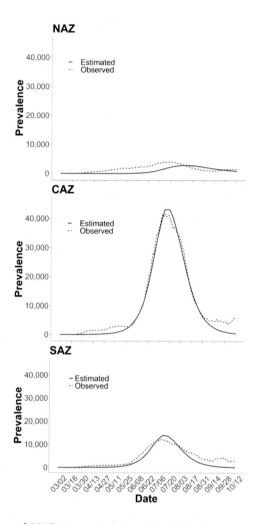

Figure 5.14 Estimate of COVID-19 cases in three regions in Arizona.

COVID-19 pandemic in Arizona [211,212]. Because mobility restrictions are known to have a significant role in mitigating the COVID-19 epidemic, several mathematical modeling studies incorporated human mobility data [211–220]. However, evidence of the direct effect of policy implementations on behavioral changes, which leads to mitigation of COVID-19 outbreaks, are scarce. Because our analysis is based on real-time data and estimated parameters using the data (i.e., our analyses did not depend on the parameter values obtained from literature), we captured the effects of policy implementation directly without relying on assumed characteristics of COVID-19 and interventions' effectiveness.

The effect of mobility restrictions is known to be perceptible after few weeks because of the incubation period of severe acute respiratory syndrome coronavirus 2 and reporting delay [228]. To estimate the parameter, which describes the current COVID-19 epidemic in Arizona, we first estimated the time lag using Pearson's correlation analysis. Our analysis revealed that the impact of mobility changes on COVID-19 cases is observed 10 days after the policy shift, which agrees with what Badr et al. [212] estimated. Unlike other studies, we were able to analyze not only the decrease in COVID-19 cases due to policy implementation but also the increase in cases due to a lifting of stay-at-home order followed by another decrease. Our study focuses on Arizona, because Arizona was previously recorded as one of the worst hot spots of the COVID-19 epidemic in the world because of the early reopening of the economy, and started to decline significantly in cases after the state reimposed restrictions.

Geographic heterogeneity in Arizona should also be mentioned. We divided Arizona into NAZ, CAZ, and SAZ because they represent different geographical and social characteristics regarding the spread of COVID-19. NAZ is considered to be rural; it is sufficient to prevent the cluster of cases in places like a gym or bar. CAZ is the metro city where more than 60% of the COVID-19 cases are reported. Because the population size and epidemic size are large, it is not enough to target only retail and recreation, but it is vital to reduce mobility overall. Since the epidemic size can quickly blow up, the policy implementation's timing is also crucial. SAZ includes the city of Tucson and several other small cities close to the border of the US and Mexico, containing the disease is more complex despite their population size. Therefore, we have simulated three regions separately to capture the actual dynamics.

In the basic scenario with empirical data, the epidemic peak time in NAZ was predicted in late September, and CAZ and SAZ have already peaked in early July. While mobility restrictions are crucial to containing the virus, there is severe debate over the level of restrictions considering economic impacts and other possible harms attributed to school closure [229,230]. In this regard, we have conducted another Pearson correlation analysis and discovered that retail and recreation have the strongest correlation with the COVID-19 growth rate.

CHAPTER 6

Partial differential equations

Contents

6.1 Introduction

The partial differential equation models provide a new efficient approach of studying social phenomena and predicting spread process in networks. In this chapter, we discuss applications of the PDE models in prediction of Bitcoin price and the spread of COVID and PM2.5. Part of the materials in this chapter is based on the authors' four papers, [47] on Bitcoin price prediction, [120] on quantifying prediction and intervention measures for PM2.5 in China, [142] on modeling COVID-19 in Arizona, and [157] on modeling compliance with COVID-19 mitigation policies in the US.

Mathematical Methods in Data Science
https://doi.org/10.1016/B978-0-44-318679-0.00012-0
Copyright © 2023 China Science Publishing &
Media Ltd. Published by Elsevier Inc.
All rights reserved.

In this chapter, we start with a theoretical framework for spatio-temporal modeling of diffusion in networks. The framework integrates graph clustering and embedding into Euclidean spaces with PDE modeling of diffusion process. We develop a conceptual framework that divides diffusion process in networks into two separate processes: external and internal influences. We will discuss three reaction-diffusion equation models based on the friendship hop distance and validate the models with Digg and Twitter data sets. Part of the materials in this chapter is based on the authors' papers [29,30,34,35].

6.2 Formulation of partial differential equation models

Once we embed the information propagation process into Euclidean spaces, the formulation of the spatio-temporal model for information flow is similar to that for spatial biology [24]. Spatio-temporal models are based on a mathematical formulation of the basic fact that the rate at which a given quantity changes in a given domain must equal the rate at which it flows across its boundary plus the rate at which it is created, or destroyed, within the domain.

We develop a conceptual framework that divides the information diffusion process in online social networks into two separate processes: external and internal influences, as shown in Fig. 6.1. We will see that these two processes have different spatial effects on information diffusion as the role of clusters for information diffusion in each process differs.

Because networks such as social media have rapidly gained worldwide popularity in recent years, many social media sites have experienced explosive growth in registered online users. For example, in 2019, Twitter has 1.5 billion registered users. This gives rise to extremely complex and large network graphs in online social networks. If we introduce a slightly more complex distance metric from the network's underlying topology, the number of the subsets in U can increase dramatically. Therefore the user population U will be embedded to some interval on the x-axis with more dense points. In particular, when we discuss traveling wave solutions, it is assumed that these discrete points are sufficiently dense on $(-\infty, \infty)$.

For simplicity, we assume that a constant A is the cross-sectional area of the tube. Thus the amount of information in a small section of width dx is $I(x, t)A\,dx$. Further, we let $J = J(x, t)$ denote the flux of the quantity at x, at time t. The flux measures the amount of the quantity crossing the section

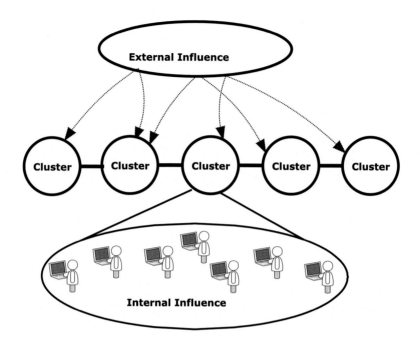

Figure 6.1 External and internal influences.

at x at time t, and its units are given in amount per unit area, per unit time. By convention, flux is positive if the flow is to the right, and negative if the flow is to the left.

Let $f = f(I, x, t)$ denote the given rate at which the information is created within the section at x at time t. Here, f represents the process within clusters in Fig. 4.5 and is a result of local growth often directly related to the underlying network structure. The process within clusters has much in common with the internal influence in [25]. In social media, f can be negative due to actions involving deletion; f is measured in amount per unit volume, per unit time. In this way, $f(I, x, t)A dx$ represents the amount of information that is created in a small width dx per unit.

We now can formulate the spatio-temporal model by considering a fixed, but arbitrary, section $a \leq x \leq b$ of the domain. The rate of change of the total amount of the information in the section must equal the rate at which it flows in at $x = a$, minus the rate at which it flows out at $x = b$, plus the rate at which it is created within $a < x < b$. In mathematical formulation, for any section $a \le x \le b$,

$$\frac{d}{dt} \int_a^b I(x, t) A dx = AJ(a, t) - AJ(b, t) + \int_a^b f(I, x, t) A dx$$

From the fundamental theorem of calculus, $J(a, t) - J(b, t) = - \int_a^b \frac{\partial I}{\partial x} dx$. Because A is constant, it may be canceled from the formula. We arrive at, for any section $a \le x \le b$,

$$\int_a^b \left(\frac{\partial I}{\partial t} + \frac{\partial J}{\partial x} - f(I, x, t) \right) dx = 0.$$

It follows that the process of a diffusion process can be formulated as

$$\frac{\partial I}{\partial t} + \frac{\partial J}{\partial x} = f(I, x, t). \tag{6.2.1}$$

J results from local diffusions. Often it flows from high density to low density and, therefore, a simple expression of flux J can be

$$J = -d \frac{\partial I}{\partial x}, \tag{6.2.2}$$

which results from a principle analogous to Fick's law ([24]) in biology or physics. The minus sign indicates the flow is down the gradient, and d represents the popularity of information that promotes the spread of the information through non-structure based activities such as search. For now, d can be viewed as an average and, therefore, is a constant. In general, it may be dependent on u, x, t. Now we obtain the following PDE model to describe a diffusion process:

$$\frac{\partial I}{\partial t} = d \frac{\partial^2 I}{\partial x^2} + f(I, x, t). \tag{6.2.3}$$

Internal influences can be viewed as the growth of population due to local growth in mathematical biology. External influences is similar to the diffusion process in mathematical biology and behaves in a manner of random walk. Extending PDEs into the context of diffusion process in general networks, we capture the similarity and difference between spreading of epidemics in biology and the diffusion process in networks. This framework builds a new architecture for modeling diffusion in networks with partial differential equations. The new architecture engages transdisciplinary approaches involving mathematics, computer science, and social sciences.

In particular, clustering algorithms will be used to define abstract cyber-distance for developing partial differential equation models. In the next few chapters, we will develop more partial differential equation models based on (6.2.2) and (6.2.3).

As an example, we discuss the diffusive logistic model introduced in [29] for characterizing the temporal and spatial patterns of information cascading over social media. The model shall be validated with the data set from Digg. The logistic model is believed to be the simplest nonlinear model to capture population dynamics where the rate of reproduction is proportional to both the existing population and the number of available resources [24]. Innovation diffusion models (5.2.1) describe the diffusion of innovations within a population. In addition, they have been widely used to describe and predict various population dynamics such as bacteria and tumor growth over time [24]. The structure-based process in Fig. 6.1 is modeled with a simple nonlinear logistic equation. The logistic equation is defined as follows. Denoting with N the population at time t, with r the intrinsic growth rate, and with K the carrying capacity that gives the upper bound of N, the population dynamics are governed by

$$\frac{dN}{dt} = rN\left(1 - \frac{N}{K}\right) \tag{6.2.4}$$

where $\frac{dN}{dt}$ is the first derivative of N with respect to t. In the context of online social networks, the term $rN(1 - \frac{N}{K})$ describes the impact of the network structure on the growth of $I(x, t)$, the density of influenced users at the distance x during time t, and r reflects the decay of news influence with respect to time t.

Based on the general spatio-temporal model (6.2.3), we arrive at the following diffusive logistic equation:

$$\frac{\partial I}{\partial t} = d\frac{\partial^2 I}{\partial x^2} + rI\left(1 - \frac{I}{K}\right)$$
$$I(x, 1) = \phi(x), \quad l \le x \le L \tag{6.2.5}$$
$$\frac{\partial I}{\partial x}(l, t) = \frac{\partial I}{\partial x}(L, t) = 0, \quad t \ge 1$$

where
- I represents the density of influenced users with a distance of x at time t;

- *d* represents the popularity of information, which promotes the spread of the information through non–structure based activities such as search (external influence);
- *r* represents the intrinsic growth rate of influenced users with the same distance, and measures how fast the information spreads (internal influence);
- *K* represents the carrying capacity, which is the maximum possible density of influenced users at a given distance;
- *L* and *l* represent the lower and upper bounds of the distances between the source *s* and other social network users;
- $\phi(x) \geq 0$ is the initial density function, which can be constructed from historical data of information spreading. Each information item has its own unique initial function;
- $\frac{\partial I}{\partial t}$ represents the first derivative of *I* with respect to time *t*;
- $\frac{\partial^2 I}{\partial x^2}$ represents the second derivative of *I* with respect to distance *x*.

$\frac{\partial I}{\partial x}(l, t) = \frac{\partial I}{\partial x}(L, t) = 0$ is the Neumann boundary condition [24], which means no flux of information across the boundaries at $x = l, L$. This assumption is plausible for social media since the users are clustered in a number of groups U_x. We also assume $\phi(x) \geq 0$ is not identical to zero and the maximum principle implies that (6.2.5) has a unique positive solution $I(x, t)$ and $0 \leq I(x, t) \leq K$.

In general, we assume that the initial density function is given and can be constructed using the data collected from the initial stage of diffusion process. Specifically, ϕ is a function of distance *x*, which captures the density of an influenced user or infected at distance *x* at the initial time. In networks, it is possible to only observe discrete values for the initial density function, because the distance *x* is discrete. The initial density is the influenced or user distribution when time $t = 1$. As in [29], we apply an effective mechanism available in MATLAB® cubic spline package, called *cubic splines interpolation* [17], to interpolate the initial discrete data in constructing $\phi(x)$. Using this process, a series of unique cubic polynomials are fitted between each of the data points, with the stipulation that the obtained curve is continuous and smooth. Hence $\phi(x)$ constructed by the cubic splines interpolation is a piecewise-defined function and twice continuous differentiable. After cubic splines interpolation, we simply set the two ends to be flat to satisfy the second requirement since in this way the slopes of the density function $\phi(x)$ at the left and right ends are zero.

6.3 Bitcoin price prediction

This section is based on the authors' work [47] on Bitcoin price prediction with PDEs. Bitcoin is currently the world's leading cryptocurrency and the blockchain is the technology that underpins it. The concept of bitcoin was first suggested in 2008 by Satoshi Nakamoto, and it became fully operational in January 2009 [48]. By May 2018, the market capitalization of Bitcoin had arrived at nearly $115 billion dollars. In contrast to the traditional financial asset, whose records of everyday monetary transactions are considered highly sensitive and are kept private, Bitcoin has no financial intermediaries and a complete list of its transactions is publicly available in a public ledger. This publicly distributed ledger creates opportunities for people to observe all the financial interactions on the blockchain network, and analyze how the assets circulate in time.

In this section, we aim to propose a partial differential equation (PDE) model to forecast bitcoin price movement. As indicated in [56], the predictive utility of different types of transactions for the bitcoin price dynamics may be different. As a result, we apply spectral analysis to aggregate bitcoin transaction subgraphs (chainlets) into clusters with similar types of transaction patterns. We embed the clusters of chainlets into a Euclidean space and develop a PDE model to incorporate the bitcoin market sentiment with the Google Trends Index. The framework of PDE models developed by the authors for information diffusion in online social networks in [111,152,169] is adapted to the bitcoin transaction network for characterizing the effect of the chainlet clusters. The PDE model enables us to describe the influence of the clusters on the price over time. To assess the forecasting ability of our model, hit ratio and relative accuracy are applied to measure the forecasting accuracy in the perspectives of bitcoin price direction and bitcoin price. Numerical results demonstrate the PDE model is capable of forecasting bitcoin price movement. The work was the first attempt to apply a PDE model on bitcoin transaction network for forecasting bitcoin price movement.

Bitcoin value (i.e., the price of a bitcoin) often undergoes large swings over short periods. For instance, at the beginning of 2013, the price started at nearly $13 per bitcoin and then rocketed to $230 on April 9, yielding almost 1700% profit in less than 4 months; In 2017, the value of a single bitcoin increased 2000%, going from $863 on January 9, 2017, to a high of $17,550 on December 11, 2017.

Given the high volatility and the difference from traditional currencies, the price of bitcoin is extremely difficult to forecast. A few studies have been conducted on forecasting or estimation for bitcoin prices. Regression models are the mostly used methods for bitcoin price forecasting by considering some potential price-affecting factors. For instance, Ciaian et al. [49] forecast bitcoin price with a linear regression model by considering some factors in macro-finance and attractiveness for investors. Jang et al. [50] introduce blockchain information (such as hash rate and block generation rate) to increase the forecasting accuracy by a Bayesian neural network. Researchers also apply machine learning techniques to make bitcoin price forecasting [51–54]. Atsalakis et al. [54] use "a hybrid neuro-fuzzy controller, namely PATSOS, to forecast the direction in the change of the daily price of bitcoin." Cretarola et al. [55] propose an ordinary difference equation to describe the behavior of bitcoin price by considering investors' attention for bitcoin. As the publicly available ledger of the Bitcoin network can be represented by a directed graph, some work exists to make bitcoin forecasting through network analysis [52,56]. Kurbucz et al. [52] forecast the price of bitcoin by the most frequent edges of its transaction network. This study shows the utility of global graph features can be used to forecast bitcoin price.

It is generally accepted that bitcoin price is significantly affected by attention or sentiment about the Bitcoin system itself [57–59]. The frequency of searches for the term "bitcoin" in Google Trends has proved to be a good measure of interest [55,57,60]. Cretarola et al. [55] regard the Google Trends index as a proxy for the attention measure, and thus propose a bivariate model in continuous time to describe the behavior of bitcoin price. Kristoufek et al. [57] demonstrate quantitatively that not only are the Google Trends Index and the prices connected but a pronounced asymmetry also exists between the effect of increased interest in the currency while it is above or below its trend value.

Recently, Akcora et al. [56] studied the influence of local topological structures on bitcoin price dynamics. They combined "chainlets" of the Bitcoin transaction networks with statistical models to forecast bitcoin price. Essentially, chainlets are special forms of network motifs or subgraphs in the address-transaction bitcoin graph. Chainlets describe transactions occurring in a blockchain and each chainlet represents a trading decision or transaction pattern. In [56], Akcora et al. find that certain types of chainlets exhibit an important role in bitcoin price forecasting. It has been found that bitcoin price is mainly and strongly linked with transaction activities [59,61]. Analysis of motifs of the bitcoin transaction networks has been found to be an indispensable tool to unveil hidden mechanisms of Bitcoin networks for the bitcoin price dynamics.

6.3.1 Network analysis for bitcoin

A blockchain is a distributed ledger that records transactions in blocks without requiring a trusted central authority. Each block contains a set of transactions and it has a hash link to its previous block, thus creating a chain of chronologically ordered blocks. When transactions happen at the same time, they will be recorded in the same block.

Bitcoin addresses are used for receiving bitcoins. A transaction represents the flow of bitcoins from input address to output addresses over time. A transaction is multi-input and multi-output, which means that a transaction may have more than one input address and more than one output address. Users take part in the bitcoin economy through addresses and a user can have two or more addresses at the same time.

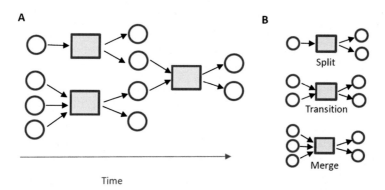

Figure 6.2 (A) A transaction-address graph; (B) Split ($C_{1\rightarrow2}$), Transition ($C_{2\rightarrow2}$), and Merge ($C_{3\rightarrow2}$) chainlets. The three types, Merge, Transition, and Split are determined according to the relative number of input addresses and output addresses, and correspond to the state that the former is greater than, equal to, or less than the latter, respectively. Addresses and transactions are shown with circles and rectangles, respectively. An arrow indicates a transfer of bitcoins.

The transaction–address graph [56,62] is a directed graph, which is vitally important for knowing bitcoins' flowing state. In this graph, the set {*Address, Transaction*} consists of vertices and edges, in which an edge represents the bitcoin's transfer between and address node and a transaction node as in Fig. 6.2. As transactions are the only means to manage bitcoins, so bitcoins can be divided or aggregated only by being spent. For instance, a transaction involves multiple addresses and every user can have different addresses, so the user can use a transaction to split, merge, or move bitcoins between its own addresses. Therefore, each transaction with its input and output addresses represents a decision, encoded by a subgraph in the transaction-address graph.

The subgraph, composed of a transaction with its input and output addresses, is called *1-chainlet*, or simply may be called *chainlet*, which is a novel graph data model, proposed in 2018 [56] for studying bitcoin price dynamics. A chainlet with x inputs and y outputs is often noted as $C_{x \to y}$. Chainlets have distinct shapes that reflect their role in the network. They are the building blocks in blockchain analysis; they represent different transaction patterns, and reflect different decisions. In this section, we analyze bitcoin chainlets and forecasting bitcoin price dynamics.

Different transactions (transactions with distinct inputs and outputs) contribute differently for the bitcoin price formation. Four hundred distinct chainlets exist in the chainlet network G and each chainlet represents a type of transaction form. However, intuitively, it is not necessary to distinguish all chainlets. For example, the transaction patterns $\mathbb{C}_{3 \to 1}$ and $\mathbb{C}_{4 \to 1}$ have no meaningful difference. Therefore, we cluster chainlets by spectral clustering, which divides the graph by using the eigenvectors of Laplacian matrix [63]. Thus, each chainlet cluster represents certain similar types of transaction pattern, which may have different predictive utilities for the bitcoin price. Our PDE model proposed in the next subsection is capable of capturing the influence of these chainlet clusters and integrating the effects of all clusters for bitcoin price forecasting.

As an example, we apply the daily transaction volumes of the 400 kinds of chainlets from December 1, 2016, to December 30, 2016 (denoted here it as Data-set 1), to build the chainlet network G with a Pearson Correlation threshold $\theta = 0.6$, which is an empirical value to ensure that most of chainlets in the chainlet network are connected and not isolated. In fact, we can use data in other time periods to build the network as well, as long as the time interval of Data-set 1 is earlier than the period for which we want to make forecasting for bitcoin price. For example, if we want to forecast the bitcoin price in February 2017, we can first build the network based on the data in January 2017. We obtain 10 chainlet clusters by applying the spectral clustering method to the above chainlet network G. Our forecasting period is from January 1, 2017, to December 31, 2017 (denoted it as Data-set 2). Fig. 6.3 shows the average transaction volumes of all the chainlet clusters for this period. Bitcoin price is mainly and strongly linked with transaction activities, especially transaction volumes [59,61]. Fig. 6.3

shows that the chainlet clusters we obtain have different levels of transaction volumes.

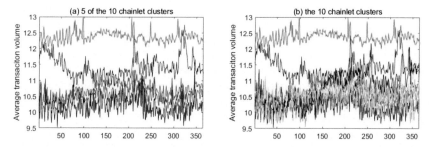

Figure 6.3 (a) Average transaction volumes for 5 of the 10 chainlet clusters; (b) The 10 chainlet clusters obtained by the spectral clustering method. Each color represents a cluster. The time period is from January 1, 2017, to December 31, 2017.

A transaction with inputs and outputs composes a chainlet. Just as in [56], we denote $C_{x \rightarrow y}$ as a chainlet if this chainlet has x inputs and y outputs. Different chainlets have different values of x and y (x and y are positive integers). Though the Bitcoin protocol limits the number of input and output addresses for a transaction, the number of inputs and outputs can still reach thousands. As a result, millions of different chainlets occur (e.g., $C_{2000 \rightarrow 20}$ and $C_{2000 \rightarrow 120}$). However, an analysis of the entire bitcoin history shows that 97.57% of the chainlets have fewer than 20 inputs and outputs [56]. This means that in bitcoin blocks, a sufficiently large number of chainlets satisfy $1 \leq x < 20$, $1 \leq y < 20$. Therefore, we build a weighted graph $G(V, E)$ with 400 nodes, where each node in V is a kind of chainlet or chainlet set and the graph node set $\{C_{x \rightarrow y}, 1 \leq x \leq 20, 1 \leq y \leq 20\}$ is defined as

$$
\mathbb{C}_{x \rightarrow y} = \begin{cases}
C_{x \rightarrow y}, & \text{if } x < 20 \quad \text{and} \quad y < 20; \\
\{C_{x \rightarrow j}, 20 \leq j < +\infty\}, & \text{if } x < 20 \quad \text{and} \quad y = 20; \\
\{C_{i \rightarrow y}, 20 \leq i < +\infty\}, & \text{if } x = 20 \quad \text{and} \quad y < 20; \\
\{C_{i \rightarrow j}, 20 \leq i < +\infty, 20 \leq j < +\infty\}, & \text{if } x = 20 \quad \text{and} \quad y = 20.
\end{cases}
$$

An edge between i and j in E and its weight are determined by the Pearson correlation coefficient of relative historical daily transaction volumes, with a correlation threshold θ.

6.3.2 PDE modeling

In this section, we establish a PDE model for bitcoin price forecasting. This PDE model is based on chainlets and the Google Trends Index for the bitcoin price. Different types of chainlet clusters represent different transaction patterns and transaction decisions; thus, they provide different predictive utility for bitcoin price. The PDE model proposed below captures the influence of the chainlet clusters and combines the effects of all the clusters for forecasting bitcoin price. We use chainlets as the building blocks for bitcoin price forecasting, and each chainlet represents a type of immutable decision. To make a better forecasting, we use spectral clustering to aggregate chainlets into clusters with similar type of transactions. We apply the authors' framework of PDE models for information diffusion in online social networks [111,152,169] to the Bitcoin transaction network for characterizing the influence of the chainlet clusters on bitcoin price.

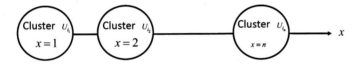

Figure 6.4 Embedding of chainlet clusters into the x-axis.

To apply a PDE model to describe the interactions of the chainlet clusters, one must embed the chainlet clusters $U_1, U_2, \ldots, U_n$ (n is the number of chainlet clusters) into a Euclidean space and arrange them in a meaningful order. In this section, the chainlet clusters are mapped onto a line such that connected clusters stay as close as possible, as in Fig. 6.4. Specifically, we now treat each chainlet cluster as a node in a new graph G_{new} where the strength of an edge is the summation of all the weights between the two clusters. The Fiedler vector (the eigenvector corresponding to the second smallest eigenvalue) of the Laplacian matrix of the new graph G_{new} can map these chainlet clusters onto a line, showing the order as $U_{i_1}, U_{i_2}, \ldots, U_{i_n}$ [152]. On this line, connected nodes stay as close as possible, ensuring that the continuous model can capture the influence of these chainlet clusters.

Having embedded chainlet clusters to the Euclidean space, let $u(x,t)$ represent the effect of chainlet cluster x on the bitcoin price. The formulation of the spatio-temporal model for the bitcoin network follows the balance law: the rate at which a given quantity changes in a given domain must equal the rate at which it flows across its boundary plus the rate at which it is created, or destroyed, within the domain. The PDE model can be conceptually divided into two processes: an internal process within each chainlet cluster and external process among chainlet clusters. Similar derivation for the PDE model has been used in our previous work for PDE models for information diffusion in online social networks in [111,152,169]. Our proposed PDE-based model is

$$\frac{\partial u(x,t)}{\partial t} = \frac{\partial}{\partial x}\left(d(x)\frac{\partial u(x,t)}{\partial x}\right) + r(t)u(x,t)h(x), \qquad (6.3.1)$$

where $r(t)u(x,t)h(x)$ describes the rate of change of bitcoin price within the cluster x; $r(t)$ represents the rate of change with respect to t; $h(x)$ describes the spatial heterogeneity of different chainlet clusters or transaction patterns. $\frac{\partial}{\partial x}\left(d(x)\frac{\partial u(x,t)}{\partial x}\right)$ reflects the rate of change of the bitcoin price among chainlet clusters, $d(x)$ describes the interaction of chainlet clusters. Because $u(x,t)$ represent the influence of chainlet cluster x on the bitcoin price, we have

$$\text{Forecasted bitcoin price} = \int u(x,t)dx. \qquad (6.3.2)$$

Investor sentiment about bitcoin, which can be represented by the Google Trends Index, is a key factor for determining bitcoin price. It is plausible to assume that

$$u(x,t) \equiv b_0 m(x,t) + \alpha(x), \qquad (6.3.3)$$

where $m(x,t)$ is the predictive utility of the Google Trends Index of chainlet cluster x; b_0 is a scale factor to bitcoin price. $\alpha(x)$ describes the heterogeneity of different chainlet clusters on bitcoin price. In this way, chainlet clusters with larger trading volumes do not necessarily have more influence on the bitcoin price.

We derive a PDE model with respect to $m(x,t)$. Note both $h(x)$ and $\alpha(x)$ represent the spatial heterogeneity of different chainlet clusters and, therefore, we can assume that $h(x) = k\alpha(x)$ with a constant k. Substituting (6.3.3) for (6.3.1) and (6.3.2) and assuming $d(x) \equiv d > 0$, d is a constant, the forecasting model of bitcoin price is

$$\begin{cases} \frac{\partial m(x,t)}{\partial t} = d\frac{\partial^2 m}{\partial x^2} + k\alpha(x)r(t)\left(m(x,t) + \frac{1}{b_0}\alpha(x)\right) + \frac{d}{b_0}\alpha''(x), \\ m(x,1) = \phi(x), L_1 < x < L_2, \\ \frac{\partial m}{\partial x}(L_1,t) = \frac{\partial m}{\partial x}(L_2,t) = 0, t > 1, \\ \text{Forecasted bitcoin price at time } t = \int_{L_1}^{L_2}\left(b_0 m(x,t) + \alpha(x)\right)dx, \end{cases} \qquad (6.3.4)$$

where

- $\alpha(x)$ satisfies $\alpha(x_i) = \alpha_i$, $i = 1, 2, \ldots, n$, where α_i describes the heterogeneity of the cluster at location x_i and n is the number of clusters; we construct $\alpha(x)$ by cubic spline interpolation [64] with the condition of $\frac{\partial \alpha}{\partial x}(L_1) = \frac{\partial \alpha}{\partial x}(L_2) = 0$. Therefore, the second derivative $\alpha''(x)$ exists and is continuous; $r(t)$ satisfies exponential decay with time. In this work, $r(t)$ is assumed the form of $r(t) = b_1 + e^{-(t-b_2)}$.
- Neumann boundary condition $\frac{\partial m}{\partial x}(L_1, t) = \frac{\partial m}{\partial x}(L_2, t) = 0$, $t > 1$ is applied and it has been assumed no flux of information flow across the boundaries at $x = L_1, L_2$; Initial function $m(x, 1) = \phi(x)$ describes the influence of every chainlet cluster and it is constructed from the historical data by cubic spline interpolation [64].
- Parameters $d, b_0, b_1, b_2, \alpha_i, i = 1, 2, \ldots, n$ are determined by the known historical data of $m(x_i, t_j)$ with a best fitting program.
- The historical forecasting utility of the Google Trends Index on bitcoin price

$$m(x_i, t_j), \quad i = 1, 2, \ldots, n; j = 1, 2, \ldots, N$$

can be obtained by computing

$$m(x_i, t_j) = (\text{Google Trends Index on "Bitcoin" at time } t_j) * P_0(x_i, t_j),$$

where

$$P_0(x_i, t_j) = \frac{\text{bitcoin transaction volume of chainlet cluster } x_i \text{ at time } t_j}{\text{total bitcoin transaction volume of all chainlet clusters at } t_j}.$$

6.3.3 Bitcoin price prediction

Bitcoin price is related to the transaction volumes and the investors' attention measured by Google [58]. The daily bitcoin transaction volumes of all transactions and the daily bitcoin price (here it refers to the intra-day open price, denominated in USD in our work) are downloaded from https://github.com/cakcora/coinworks. The time period is from January 1, 2017, to December 31, 2017. These data sets are extracted from the original bitcoin data, which are all publicly available at the Bitcoin Core page (https://bitcoin.org/en/download). The Google Trends Index on "bitcoin" captures the attention of retail/uniformed investors [60]. These data can be obtained from https://trends.google.it/trends/?geo=IT with a keyword "bitcoin."

We chose the year of 2017 for validating our model mainly because there was some huge price fluctuation in 2017. Specifically, the value of a single bitcoin increased 2000%, going from $863 on January 9, 2017, to a high of $17,550 on December 11, 2017. Thus, our model is actually also validated in time windows with a structural break in data. To forecast the bitcoin price at time t_{N+1}, the forecasting process consists in determination of parameters in (6.3.4) using known historical data $\{m(x_i, t_j), i = 1, 2, \ldots, n; j = 1, 2, \ldots, N\}$, and solving the PDE-model (6.3.4) to make a one-step forecasting for $m(x, t_{N+1}), x \in [L_1, L_2]$. Thus, the forecasted bitcoin price at time t_{N+1} is given by

$$Price(t_{N+1}) = \int_{L_1}^{L_2} \left(b_0 m(x, t_{N+1}) + \alpha(x) \right) dx. \qquad (6.3.5)$$

Specifically, we combine a tensor train (TT) global optimization approach [177] and Nelder–Mead simplex local optimization method [131] to train the PDE parameters. After each determination of the model parameters, we apply the "pdepe" function in MATLAB to compute the PDE for one-step forward in time dimension numerically.

In this work, we obtain 10 chainlet clusters therefore $n = 10$, $L_1 = x_1 = 1$, $L_2 = x_{10} = 10$. Further, we use one-step sliding window of length 3 to perform forecasting process. Namely, we use historical data of $m(x_i, t_j)$ during each 3 days to forecast the bitcoin price of the 4th day. Specifically, data of days 1–3, 2–4, 3–5, ... are used as the training set for forecasting the bitcoin price of days 4, 5, 6, ..., successively. We make a forecasting for the whole year of 2017 and the forecasting results cover 362 days from January 4, 2017, to November 31, 2017. The predictions are shown in Fig. 6.5.

In general, forecasting "bitcoin price direction" (or the "direction of bitcoin price movement") is preferred than forecasting "bitcoin price" [54]. In this present study, we measure the predictive ability of our model with hit ratio and relative accuracy (RA). Hit ratio measures the model ability for forecasting "bitcoin price direction," defined as

$$Hit\ ratio = \frac{1}{n} \sum_{1}^{n} D_i, \quad i = 1, 2, \ldots, n,$$

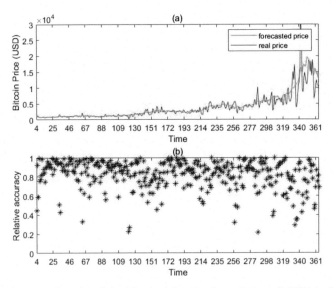

Figure 6.5 Forecasted results of the bitcoin daily price from January 4, 2017, to December 31, 2017. (a) Forecasted values versus the real observations. (b) The relative accuracy for bitcoin price forecasting. Here, the relative accuracy (RA) is the conventional definition as RA = $1 - \frac{|P_{real} - P_{forecast}|}{P_{real}}$, where P_{real} is the real bitcoin price at every data collection time point and $P_{forecast}$ is the forecasted bitcoin price through (6.3.4).

where $\sum_1^n D_i$ denotes the number of correct forecasts of the bitcoin price direction;

$$D_i = \begin{cases} 1, & \left(P_{real}(i+1) - P_{real}(i)\right)\left(P_{forecast}(i+1) - P_{real}(i)\right) > 0, \\ 0, & \text{otherwise,} \end{cases}$$

n is the number of tests. We compute the hit ratios each 3 months (shown as Table 6.1). The number of 3 months usually corresponds to a 3-month investment–trading horizon and this period has been suggested as benchmark period for evaluating a trading strategy [65,66].

Table 6.1 With a sliding window of length 3, the statistics of the forecasting results for bitcoin price direction from January 4, 2017, to December 31, 2017.

		Hit ratio (%)
2017	Jan. 4–Mar. 31	52.22
	Apr. 1–Jun. 30	56.32
	Jul. 1–Sep. 30	54.35

The relative accuracy (RA) for the ith trading day, defined as

$$\text{RA}(i) = 1 - \frac{|P_{real}(i) - P_{forecast}(i)|}{P_{real}(i)}$$

is used to measure the forecasting accuracy of bitcoin price, where $P_{real}(i)$ is the real bitcoin price for the ith trading day, and $P_{forecast}(i)$ is the forecasted bitcoin price for the ith trading day.

In our forecasting time period, though the observed real price range is large from \$ 775.98 to \$19498.68, the forecasted values of our proposed forecasting model will capture the trend of the real bitcoin price, as in Fig. 6.5(a). As expected, the forecasting performance of the proposed model deteriorates as the observed real data series is skyrocketing, as in November and December of 2017 in Fig. 6.5(a). However, as Fig. 6.5(b) shows, through statistical analysis of the forecasting results, in the last 3 months of 2017, the hit ratio is still above 50% of the 61 days in the last 2 months of 2017. There exist 25 days and 37 days whose relative accuracies were more than 0.8 and 0.7, respectively.

Specifically, Table 6.1 shows that the overall hit ratios (i.e., the percentage of accurate forecasts for the direction of price movement) are all higher than the threshold of 50% by chance (i.e., flip of a coin). In [53], it illustrates that by flipping a fair and random coin, an investor has a 50% chance to be right or wrong about the market direction. Although the hit ratios we obtained are not too much larger than 50%, the entire story will be different if we are interested in a sequence of events. Table 6.2 also shows that the overall average forecasting accuracy of 362 consecutive days in 2017 can reach 0.82. All the forecasting results are shown in Fig. 6.9(b). Of the 362 consecutive days in 2017, 82% ($296/362 \approx 82\%$), 65% ($237/362 \approx 65\%$) and 37% ($134/362 \approx 37\%$) of the days achieve an accuracy of above 0.7, 0.8, and 0.9, respectively. These statistics for the forecasting results are summarized in Table 6.2.

Table 6.2 With a sliding window of length 3, the statistics of days for the forecasting results of bitcoin price from January 4, 2017, to December 31, 2017. 362 and 134 mean that during the forecasting period of 362 days, there are 134 days whose relative accuracy of the forecastings are above 0.9.

Total days	362	Average Relative Accuracy (RA) = 0.82
days of RA > 0.9	134	(days of RA > 0.9)/(total days) = 37%
days of RA > 0.8	237	(days of RA > 0.8)/(total days) = 65%
days of RA > 0.7	296	(days of RA > 0.7)/(total days) = 82%

Table 6.3 With a sliding window of length 6, the statistics of the forecasting results for bitcoin price direction from January 7, 2017, to December 31, 2017.

		Hit ratio (%)
2017	Jan. 7–Mar. 31	51.19
	Apr. 1–Jun. 30	52.75
	Jul. 1–Sep. 30	51.09
	Oct. 1–Dec. 31	52.17

Table 6.4 With a sliding window of length 6, the statistics of days for the forecasting results of bitcoin price from January 7, 2017, to December 31, 2017. 359 and 108 mean that during the forecasting period of 359 days, there are 108 days whose relative accuracy of the forecastings are above 0.9.

Total days	359	Average Relative Accuracy (RA) = 0.77
days of RA > 0.9	108	(days of RA > 0.9)/(total days) = 30%
days of RA > 0.8	194	(days of RA > 0.8)/(total days) = 54%
days of RA > 0.7	267	(days of RA > 0.7)/(total days) = 74%

To further calibrate our model, we also apply sliding windows of lengths 6 and 9 to perform one-step forward out-of-sample forecasting, in the present analysis. The statistics of days for the forecasting results are shown in Tables 6.3 and 6.4 (using sliding windows of length 6) and Tables 6.5 and 6.6 (using sliding windows of length 9). With the increasing of the window length from 3, 6 to 9, both hit ratios and RA have decreasing trend. This may be due to high fluctuation of daily bitcoin price. Nevertheless, the forecasting results for the three windows are acceptable. Here, we also emphasize that the lengths of the sliding windows considered by us are for illustrative purposes. One can easily change the length of the window according to different types of data. However, empirical results demonstrate that data of only several days are needed for an acceptable forecasting.

6.3.4 Remarks

In this section, a PDE model is developed for forecasting bitcoin price dynamics based on daily bitcoin transaction volumes and Google Trends Index. Experiment results demonstrate that the forecasting accuracy of bitcoin price direction (measured by hit ratio) is above 50% in each of the 3 months of 2007; the average forecasting accuracy (measured by relative accuracy) of our model is 0.82 for 362 consecutive days in 2017. Because of different data sets, it may be not comparable with other works. Nevertheless, Kur-

Table 6.5 With a sliding window of length 9, the statistics of the forecasting results for bitcoin price direction from January 10, 2017, to December 31, 2017.

		Hit ratio (%)
2017	Jan. 10–Mar. 31	51.85
	Apr. 1–Jun. 30	51.65
	Jul. 1–Sep. 30	51.09
	Oct. 1–Dec. 31	51.09

Table 6.6 With a sliding window of length 9, the statistics of days for the forecasting results of bitcoin price from January 10, 2017, to December 31, 2017. 356 and 89 mean that during the forecasting period of 356 days, there are 89 days whose relative accuracy of the forecastings are above 0.9.

Total days	356	Average Relative Accuracy (RA) = 0.74
days of RA > 0.9	89	(days of RA > 0.9)/(total days) = 25%
days of RA > 0.8	161	(days of RA > 0.8)/(total days) = 45%
days of RA > 0.7	199	(days of RA > 0.7)/(total days) = 56%

bucz [52] achieves an accuracy of approximately 60.05% during daily price movement classifications between November 25, 2016, and February 5, 2018. Jang et al. [50] obtain an acceptable forecasting accuracy through selecting different relevant features of blockchain information and comparing the Bayesian neural network with benchmark models on modeling.

This work differs from the previous forecasting models with chainlets. Akcora et al. [56] introduce "chainlet" on blockchain for bitcoin price forecasting, but they focus only on the effects of certain types of chainlets on bitcoin price. Our proposed PDE model emphasizes the combined effects from all the different types of chainlet clusters. Further, the continuous PDE model describes the influence of these chainlet clusters over time.

In addition, the PDE model differs from the previous PDE models on social networks for forecasting information diffusion [152], air pollution of 189 cities in China [111], and influenza prevalence [169]. The PDE model in this section is developed to capture the combined effect of chainlets from the Bitcoin transaction network and their influence on bitcoin price. In particular, the Google Trends Index is incorporated in the model to reflect the effect of market sentimental. Unlike the base linear or logistic models in [111,152,169], the PDE model in this section has additional terms to describe the spatial heterogeneity of chainlet clusters. As a result, chainlet clusters with larger trading volumes do not necessarily have more influence on the bitcoin price. In fact, the forecasting of bitcoin price is based on the combined influence of all chainlet clusters.

6.4 Prediction of $PM_{2.5}$ in China

6.4.1 Introduction

This section is based on the authors paper [120] on quantifying prediction and intervention measures for $PM_{2.5}$ and aims to develop a specific PDE model between city clusters for forecasting daily $PM_{2.5}$ concentrations and further quantifying the influences of local reduced emissions on the changing number of polluted days. The forecasting model intuitively and comprehensively incorporates $PM_{2.5}$'s local emission and regional transportation, and human's intervention on local emission. In general, the development of a forecasting model is a more challenging task than the estimation an explanatory model, as out-of-sample and out-of-time high accuracy prediction is of paramount importance. Our work relates to several strands of literature, and in the discussion that follows, we outline how our research differs from each one of these groups of studies.

Various forecasting approaches have been applied in the prediction of $PM_{2.5}$ concentration. These methods are roughly divided into statistical models and machine learning methods. As discussed in [124], multiple linear regression and geographically weighted regression models have been used for $PM_{2.5}$ prediction. Though the statistical approaches often have high computational efficiency and simple modeling principles, they only adapt to local spatial location. Therefore, the fact of transboundary pollution is not considered. Owing to the effective employment in ambiguous time series, machine learning methods are believed to be the preferred approach for air quality prediction. For instance, Li and Zhang [133] apply Random Forest, one of machine learning models, to assist in $PM_{2.5}$ prediction. However, the disadvantage of the machine learning method is also very prominent, that is, the main mechanism behind the accuracy prediction results could not be explained ([122]). Thus, it is often insufficient to convince a key decision-maker.

The study relates to the existing works on the determinants of $PM_{2.5}$. However, most of these studies need more of knowledge to understand the physico-chemical and meteorological processes. More precisely, using GeogDetector methods, satellite sensing techniques, etc., their aim is to reveal the factors of affecting $PM_{2.5}$ concentrations, such as the chemical composition of $PM_{2.5}$ ([139]), meteorological conditions for instance of wind, temperature, pressure ([128]), and the socioeconomic factors for instance of economic growth, urbanization, and industrialization ([127,129]). Others focus on the association between $PM_{2.5}$ concentration and regional transport ([36]). In general, the studies discussed above focus on the influence of specific factors on $PM_{2.5}$ concentration; most of them are of an explanatory nature, and not on the prediction.

In addition, the study also relates to studies that use dynamic models to forecast air pollution with promising results. Presently, chemical kinetic ordinary differential equations (ODEs) and chemical transport model (for instance, the Unified Danish Eulerian model, a PDE system mathematically) are two widely used air pollution models ([125,141]). They both depict the nonlinear coupling between multiple chemical species and need knowing of the temporal dynamic emission quantities of various pollutants. The timeliness of data acquisition and the large scale computation caused by multiple species have always been vexing problems. In our previous work, a specific PDE model was first proposed to describe the spatial-temporal characteristics of $PM_{2.5}$, and thus to make predictions for air pollution ([111]). This model needs only data of a single species on $PM_{2.5}$ concentration and large scale computation is avoided by clustering. Also, PDE not only depicts the temporary dynamics, but also can describe the spatial interactions. Thus, diffusion process of $PM_{2.5}$ between city clusters can be incorporated into the PDE model. This proposes a new idea for prediction. However, this is only a primary study, and the prediction accuracy and model descriptive ability needs to be improved.

This work is also related to the literature on quantifying the influences of potential pollution reductions. Among other things, these studies successfully estimate the air pollution health impacts of emission reductions and other potential interventions ([138]), the influence of future climatic changes on some high pollution levels ([141]), and discuss the efficiency problem of air pollutant emissions reduction in China ([134]). Besides, many works discuss and quantify varies pollution problem, resulting from emissions related to food transportation ([136]), anthropogenic activities ([121]), and zinc and copper contamination ([121]). However, none of these studies quantify the influence of potential local emission reduction in the perspective of city clusters existing in China. Chinese government has published a series of national policies and action plans to vigorously implement the strategy of joint prevention and control of air pollution. Further, [132] and [123] demonstrate that the most cost-effective method for prediction thus for further joint regional air pollution control is to treat these cities in the same cluster as a whole. We aim to bring together all these strands of literatures.

Here, considering local emission, transboundary pollution, and the effects of human intervention, we develop a more specific PDE model to predict $PM_{2.5}$ concentration of each city cluster in China. The influence of local emission reductions with varies intensities are investigated in three scenarios (joint-intervention for all city cluster, part-of-joint-intervention, intervention on a single city cluster). Specifically, this model has the following advantages: (1) This PDE model can quantify the spatial and temporal dynamics of air pollution; (2) Out-of-sample prediction demonstrates that only several days of history data are needed for a acceptable prediction; (3) The PDE model can make policy modeling to some extent by changing the local emission term. Specifically, it allows us to examine and quantify the effect of enhancing interventions to control $PM_{2.5}$. Model-based simulation results illustrate the importance of joint governance.

6.4.2 PDE model for $PM_{2.5}$

A high $PM_{2.5}$ concentration at a geographical location can result from road dust, vehicle exhaust, biomass burning, industrial emission, agriculture activities, and regionally transported aerosols. Hypothetically, local emission and regional transport result in the air pollution of a place. Besides, $PM_{2.5}$ can be cleared by vegetation or dispersion from natural environmental factors and human intervention. Let $F(x, t)$ represent the $PM_{2.5}$ concentration city cluster x at time t. Below we propose the specific spatio-temporal PDE to depict the dynamics of $PM_{2.5}$ concentration:

$$\frac{\partial F(x, t)}{\partial t} = \frac{\partial}{\partial x}\left(d(x)\frac{\partial F(x, t)}{\partial x}\right) + c(x, t) - \mu(t)F(x, t),$$

$$F(x, 1) = \varphi(x), l < x < L, \qquad (6.4.1)$$

$$\frac{\partial F}{\partial x}(l, t) = \frac{\partial F}{\partial x}(L, t) = 0, t > 1,$$

where the spatial variable is x, which represents city cluster x. These city clusters in the x-axis are as the order of geographical north–south direction.

- $\frac{\partial}{\partial x}\left(d(x)\frac{\partial F(x,t)}{\partial x}\right)$ describes the transboundary pollution of $PM_{2.5}$ between different city clusters; it has been used for describing the spatial transport of air pollution in [111] and spatial spreading of infectious disease in [46]. Based on Fick's law ([156]), $-d(x)\frac{\partial F(x,t)}{\partial x}$ measures the $PM_{2.5}$ quantity crossing the section at x, where $d(x)$ measures how fast $PM_{2.5}$

transports between different city clusters. In the present study, we assume $d(x) \equiv d > 0$.

- $c(x, t) - \mu(t)F(x, t)$ presents the local pollution process in a local cluster, which denotes the rate of local emission and dissipation of $PM_{2.5}$. Specifically,

  - $c(x, t)$ is the rate of inflow of $PM_{2.5}$ into the air from the local emission at location x and time t. There exists various local emission sources in each city cluster, including road dust, vehicle exhaust, biomass burning, and industrial emissions and so on. Different city clusters have different levels of economy, essentially leading to different $PM_{2.5}$ emission amounts. In this section, $c(x, t)$ is built by cubic spline interpolation, which satisfies $c(x_i, t) \equiv c_i(t)$, $i = 1, 2, \ldots, 9$ (x_i represents the location of cluster i), and $c_i(t) \equiv b_i$ at fixed time t. The dynamic parameters $b_i, i = 1, 2, \ldots, 9$ are determined by the latest concentration data of $PM_{2.5}$.

  - $\mu(t)F(x, t)$ denotes the dissipation amount of $PM_{2.5}$ within a local cluster at location x and time t. Similar to [137], $\mu(t)$ is the dispersion rate of $PM_{2.5}$, regulated by meteorological conditions, and is given as

$$\mu(t) = \mu_0 + (\mu_1 + \mu_2 t)sin(wt + \phi_0),$$

where $w = 2\pi/365$, assuming 365 days in a year; μ_0 is a basic clearance rate of $PM_{2.5}$; $\mu_1 + \mu_2 t$ depicts the slow increasing duration of dates with high $PM_{2.5}$ concentrations ([137]). $PM_{2.5}$ concentration changes with seasonal factors; therefore we use $sin(wt + \phi_0)$ to describe the seasonal effects for the clearance rate. Here, parameters μ_0, μ_1, μ_2, and ϕ_0 are determined by real data.

- $\frac{\partial F}{\partial x}(l, t) = \frac{\partial F}{\partial x}(L, t) = 0$, $t > 1$ is the Neumann boundary condition ([156]), assuming no flux of $PM_{2.5}$ accrossing the boundaries at $x = l, L$.

- $F(x, 1) = \varphi(x)$ describes the initial amount of $PM_{2.5}$ in each city cluster and it is constructed using the history concentrations of $PM_{2.5}$ via spline interpolation.

6.4.3 Data collection and clustering

The $PM_{2.5}$ data in this section are retrieved from the web of http://www.pm25.in/, a third-party website of the China National Environmental Monitoring center. The data set consists of daily $PM_{2.5}$ concentration during continuous 180 days from January 1, 2016, to June 28, 2016, covering heavy polluted winter and ordinary days. Also, 189 priority pollution-monitoring cities, covering all 34 provincial-level regions in mainland of China, are all included. Note that due to the fact that the larger value input may overwhelm smaller value inputs in the computational process, which will decrease the prediction accuracy. Therefore, we make linear scaling on the $PM_{2.5}$ concentration value and change the data to a specific range. Specifically, "Ambient Air Quality Standards" (GB3095-2012) of China ([135]) stipulates that $PM_{2.5}$ concentration is now officially categorized into 6 levels, responding to excellent (0–35); good (36–75); light polluted (76–115); moderately polluted (116–150); heavily polluted (151–250); and severely polluted (greater than 250 µg), respectively. We use the daily $PM_{2.5}$ concentration data to illustrate the construction of a PDE model for air pollution prediction. We only need the data of the latest several days to build the models and predict the concentration on the following day. Therefore our proposed prediction model has the advantage of requiring only a few kinds of and fewer data.

As we aim to detect the global transport of $PM_{2.5}$ in China, some basic preparation work for the PDE model is needed. We first divide all the observed cities into different city clusters. Then we compute the daily average concentration level of each cluster by averaging the daily $PM_{2.5}$ concentration levels of all the cities belonging to this cluster. Further, these clusters are projected into Euclidean space. The specific process is presented in our previous work ([44]). We briefly illustrate the main process below:

- A pollution-transport network is first built to describe the directional transport relationships of $PM_{2.5}$ among the 189 cities by an adjacency matrix. Then each city is specifically regarded as a network node. Whether the transport of $PM_{2.5}$ exists or not between any two cities is mainly determined by geographical distance between cities, monthly prevailing wind direction, monthly average wind speed, and so on.
- Choose subgraph, motif M_8 (in Fig. 6.6), as the basic unit of the pollution-transport network and then divide all the 189 cities into nine clusters via the higher-order spectral clustering method in [45]. Here, subgraph M_8 is selected as it reflects the movements of $PM_{2.5}$ from pollution source to target.
- Projecting these city clusters, geographically located in the north–south direction of China, onto the y-axis of the Cartesian coordinates, as shown in Fig. 6.6. We project these city clusters as the order of geographical north–south direction instead of east–west direction and this mainly considers the following facts: Air transport is mainly influenced

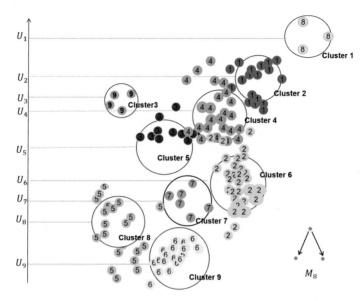

Figure 6.6 M_8-based generated clusters and their projections on the Cartesian coordinates. The map is created by software "Tableau Public 10.3" (https://public. tableau.com/).

by wind. China's monsoon wind determines that most of the time the wind blows in north-to-south direction or in the south-to-north direction.

6.4.4 $PM_{2.5}$ prediction

In view of many standard textbooks of PDE, the existence and uniqueness of the proposed PDE model (6.4.1) have been established as the standard theorems of parabolic PDEs ([176]). In this section, we validate the proposed PDE model from the perspective of model prediction accuracy and model descriptive ability. The parameters in the PDE model are determined numerically with real $PM_{2.5}$ concentration data. Essentially, the identification of parameters comprises a list of multi-parameter inverse problems of parabolic equations. A tensor train global optimization method ([177]) is first used to explore the parameter space, which provides the starting points for further local optimization. Then Nelder–Mead simplex local optimization method ([131]), corresponding to fminsearch function in MATLAB, is used to train model parameters. Numerical experiments also demonstrate that the initial value of the model parameters varying ±5% will not change the finial parameters.

To demonstrate that, we obtain a better prediction accuracy through the proposed model (6.4.1). We adopt the same accuracy measures as in [111]. In [111], mean absolute increment accuracy (MAIA) and mean relative accuracy (MRA) are defined as

$$\text{MAIA} = \frac{1}{n}\sum_{t=1}^{n}\left(1 - \frac{|F_t - \hat{F}_t|}{5}\right), \quad \text{MRA} = \frac{1}{n}\sum_{t=1}^{n}\left(1 - \frac{|F_t - \hat{F}_t|}{F_t}\right),$$

where $n = 9$ represents 9 city clusters, F_t and $\hat{F}_t$ are real observations and predicted values of $PM_{2.5}$ concentrations of each city cluster, respectively. Besides, in the present work, we also propose "Perfect rate" to quantitatively measure how better the accuracy of model (6.4.1) is than that of the model in [111]. The "Perfect rate" of each city cluster is defined as

$$\text{Perfect rate} = \frac{\text{the number of days that satisfy condition A}}{\text{the total number of days during the forecasting period}},$$
(6.4.2)

where condition A means that the prediction accuracy is above the MRA (or MAIA) of the model in [111] during the forecasting period.

We first make out-of-sample and out-of-time forecasting using our model (6.4.1) and compare them with the real $PM_{2.5}$ concentration; then we compare the prediction accuracy of this new model with the previous model in [111].

In this section, we use one-step sliding window of length 3. Namely, each three days data (3 observations) are used to predict the concentrations of the following day (1 observation); then the window of training set slides one day forward and continues to predict the following day. Specifically, $PM_{2.5}$ concentrations of days 1–3, 2–4, 3–5, ... are used as the training data for predicting $PM_{2.5}$ concentration of the following days 4, 5, 6, ..., respectively. For instance, we can obtain parameters of PDE using the history date of days 1, 2, 3, and construct the initial function $\varphi(x)$ via the $PM_{2.5}$ concentration on day 3. Then we use the fourth-order Runge–Kutta algorithm ([126]) to compute PDE for one-day forward prediction of the $PM_{2.5}$ concentration on day 4. Fig. 6.7 presents the forecasting process.

Fig. 6.7 shows that the predictions of Model (6.4.1) well capture the trend of the real observations. Specifically, as shown in Fig. 6.8 (or 6.9), in each city cluster and during the whole prediction period the red snowflakes in each city cluster are above the horizontal line with height of 0.9 (or 0.8), which mean that the prediction accuracy of all city clusters are almost above 90% (or 80%), based on the accuracy measure AIA (or RA).

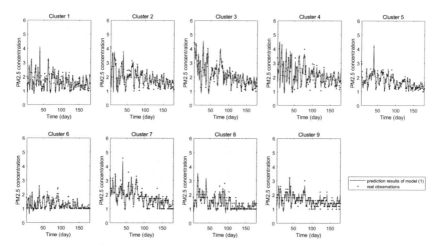

Figure 6.7 Real $PM_{2.5}$ concentrations versus predicted results of our proposed model (6.4.1). The prediction period lasts 177 days from January 4, 2016, to June 28, 2016.

Further, in Table 6.7, during the prediction period the mean AIA (MAIA) and mean RA (MRA) of each city cluster through our proposed model (6.4.1) are *all* above 95% and 90%. The red snowflake marks in Fig. 6.9 are more dispersed than that in Fig. 6.8, indicating the accuracy variance are larger under the RA measure than under the AIA measure. This is because that RA and AIA measure the prediction accuracy for $PM_{2.5}$ concentration value and for $PM_{2.5}$ concentration level, respectively.

Further, "perfect rate" (defined as (6.4.2)) is used to quantitatively measure how better the accuracy of Model (6.4.1) than that of the old model in [111]. All the perfect rates are shown in Table 6.7, and the lowest perfect rate has reached 80.79% existing in city cluster 6. Based on MAIA, the perfect rate of Region 6 is 80.79% (i.e., $143/187 \approx 80.79\%$); this means that for Cluster 6 and during the prediction period of continuous 187 days, the ratio of days whose forecasting accuracy of each day from the new model (6.4.1) is above the average prediction accuracy 95.64% from the model in [111].

6.4.5 Remarks

In this section, the proposed PDE model is built on an intercity pollution transmission network proposed in [44], and the building of the network considers various atmosphere factors. Transboundary pollution between city clusters are depicted by our PDE model. Besides, the PDE model can

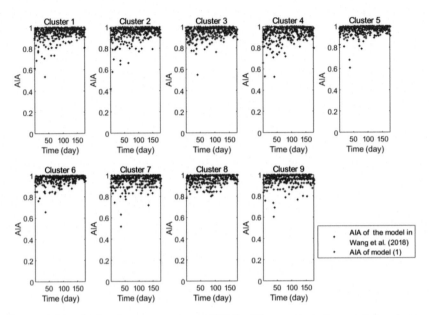

Figure 6.8 The absolute increment accuracy (AIA) for $PM_{2.5}$ concentration prediction during 177 days from January 4, 2016, to June 28, 2016.

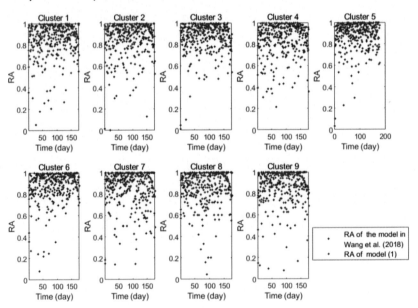

Figure 6.9 The relative accuracy (RA) for $PM_{2.5}$ concentration prediction during 177 days from January 4, 2016, to June 28, 2016.

Table 6.7 The prediction accuracy of our proposed model (6.4.1) versus that of the model in [111], where MAIA and MRA are the mean absolute increment accuracy and mean relative accuracy of each city cluster, respectively. Perfect rate quantitatively measures that during the prediction period of continuous 187 days the ratio of days whose forecasting accuracy of each day from the new model is above the average prediction accuracy from the old model in [111].

	MAIA (model (6.4.1))	MAIA (model in [111])	Perfect rate	MRA (model (6.4.1))	MRA (model in [111])	Perfect rate
Cluster 1	97.06%	92.47%	94.35%	90.65%	77.05%	91.53%
Cluster 2	97.16%	92.02%	93.79%	91.76%	78.65%	90.96%
Cluster 3	96.78%	92.88%	89.83%	91.73%	80.57%	90.40%
Cluster 4	96.28%	90.98%	91.53%	90.07%	77.75%	89.27%
Cluster 5	97.47%	94.98%	85.31%	92.31%	84.42%	87.01%
Cluster 6	97.65%	95.64%	80.79%	91.07%	83.51%	81.79%
Cluster 7	96.92%	93.34%	88.14%	90.62%	80.30%	85.88%
Cluster 8	97.28%	94.57%	83.05%	90.69%	81.90%	82.49%
Cluster 9	97.38%	93.91%	88.14%	91.43%	79.70%	86.44%

make policy modeling to some extent by changing the local emission term $c(x, t)$.

We also quantitatively compare the prediction accuracy of Model (6.4.1) and the PDE model in [111]. As in Table 6.7, regardless of the accuracy measure of MAIA or MRA, in each city cluster the mean prediction accuracy of Model (6.4.1) is obviously better than that in [111]. Also, as seen from Figs. 6.8 and 6.9, the distribution of blue snowflakes are more scattered than that of the red snowflakes. It means that for each city cluster and during the prediction period, if the daily prediction accuracy is considered as a variable, the variance of prediction accuracies of the new model (6.4.1) is smaller than that of the model in [111].

City clusters are the spatial variables in the PDE model. Cities in the same cluster are mostly adjacent to each other. Therefore the most cost-effective method for prediction thus for further joint regional air pollution control is to treat these cities in the same cluster as a whole. This is consistent with the idea of [132] and [123]. Besides, clustering are useful to avoid large-scale computation.

Simulation results of the new model (6.4.1) demonstrate that joint intervention is more efficient than local measures, which is consistent with the work of [140]. However, the extent of controlling emission is an optimal problem on economic development and environmental protection, which should be considered by multiple factors.

Another attractive feature of the model is that experimentally only several days of history data are needed for forecasting $PM_{2.5}$ concentration at the following day. Additionally, when tested in the out-of-sample period, the accuracies of the predictions are acceptable. This demonstrates our proposed model can be assisted in decision making to some extent. Actually, there exist standard meteorological models, such as the Unified Danish Eulerian model ([141]), describing air pollution by a system of PDEs. However, this kind of model accompanied with large-scale computation ([130]), as the temporal dynamic processes of the emission quantities of various chemical species involves in this model and a multiple equations are needed to be solved. Model (6.4.1), proposed in the present study, concentrates on globally describing the temporal-spatial characters of specific air pollution for different city clusters, thereby only requiring data from specific chemical species, such as case of $PM_{2.5}$ in this section.

6.5 Prediction of COVID-19 in Arizona

6.5.1 Introduction

This section is based on the authors' paper [142] on modeling COVID-19 in Arizona. Arizona emerged as one of the country's newest COVID-19 hot spots with an alarming resurgence of COVID-19 after the stay-at-home order was lifted in the middle of May 2020. The number of people hospitalized is also climbing. On June 15, Arizona reported 2,497 new COVID-19 cases, a new all-time high record, up from the previous highest number of cases of 2,140 cases in a single day on June 12. Previously, Arizona experienced the first rapid rise in the number of confirmed cases of COVID-19 infection on March 16 with a total of 1,157 confirmed cases including 20 deaths, according to the Arizona Department of Health Services ([143]). The spike of the new COVID-19 case is believed to result from the fact that Arizona took a more aggressive approach to reopen the state in the middle of May. In addition, there is also no state-level requirement for everyone to wear face masks. Many Arizonians have different views on practicing social distancing, which is the only way to prevent infections in the absence of a vaccine. Although under Arizona's reopening plan, businesses are only advised to follow federal guidance on social distancing, the trade-offs between health and the economy have forced many businesses to choose not fully implementing the social distancing requirements during the COVID-19 pandemic. Therefore, quantifying the impact of social distancing on minimizing the epidemic impact can make governments and convince more people to better understand the significance of social distancing and personal precautions. In the present paper, we examine the COVID-19 situation in the state of Arizona in the United States and predict the number of cases in Arizona after the reopening of the economy.

In this section, we present a spatio-temporal model, specifically, a partial differential equation (PDE) model, of COVID-19 based on county-level clusters. The proposed model describes the combined effects of transboundary spread among county clusters in Arizona and human activities on the transmission of COVID-19. This is, in particular, important for Arizona as well as the other states in the US. because new COVID-19 cases in the US are still continuing to head upward after the lockdown ended while most countries had peaked their new cases after lockdowns. One of the factors contributing to the continued spike of the US cases is that personal precautions are not consistent across the US once the lockdown ends. In Arizona, the face mask requirement is implemented at the local government level. A number of counties in Arizona do not require face masks. We divided the counties in Arizona into three regions. The three regions represent different geographical and social characteristics in terms of the spread of COVID-19. These disparities, which reflect differing regional levels of risk, can be better modeled by a spatio-temporal model. As a result, the characteristics of the PDE model make it suitable for COVID-19 prediction. The localized results of the spatio-temporal model provide more useful information for the local governments to closely monitor new COVID-19 clusters and quickly reinstating lockdowns at the local level when epidemic spikes.

Many spatio-temporal models characterize infectious diseases by PDEs, describing the dynamics of susceptible, infected, and recovered populations (e.g., [148–151]). Our previous work ([150,152,169]) applies PDE models to make a regional level of influenza with geo-tagged data. The PDE model we develop in the present work focuses on the spread of COVID-19 and incorporating social distancing factors. While there is a rich literature on the application of PDE to modeling the spatial spread of infectious diseases, to the best of our knowledge, this work is the first attempt to apply PDE models on COVID-19 prediction with real-data validation.

In addition, the PDE model in this section is different from the existing models in that we include the data from the Google Community Mobility Report ([174]), which reflects the effects of human activities. To help to combat the spread of COVID-19, Google releases the COVID-19 Community Mobility Reports, which provide daily, county-level aggregated data on time spent at different categories of activities, compared with a baseline period before the epidemic. These activities include retail and recreation, groceries and pharmacies, parks, transit stations, workplaces, and residential areas. Mobility trends obtained from location history are dynamic in time and reflect real-time changes in social behavior, making them a crucial factor in analyzing COVID-19 spread and its countermeasure. There are several ODE and statistical models, which utilize the COVID-19 Community Mobility data ([153–155]). To the best of our knowledge, this is the first PDE model incorporating COVID-19 Community Mobility data to predict the number of COVID-19 cases.

6.5.2 Arizona COVID data

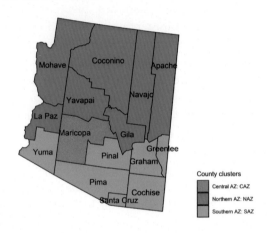

Figure 6.10 Three regions in Arizona.

There are 15 counties in the US state of Arizona. In general, Arizona is divided into northern, central, and southern Arizona. Although the boundaries of the regions are not well-defined, as we aim to predict COVID-19 cases in Arizona. We group the counties of Arizona into the three regions in Fig. 6.10. The three regions have better balanced COVID-19 cases because Maricopa County, where the city of Phoenix is located, and has about 60% of the population in Arizona. More importantly, they represent different geographical and social characteristics in terms of the spread of COVID-19. Much of the northern region is National Forest Service land, parkland, and includes part of Navajo reservations. For the per-capita COVID-19 infection rate in the US, the Navajo Nation, which spans parts of Arizona, New Mexico, and Utah, is greater than that of New York City in May

2020. Southern Arizona includes the city of Tucson and several other small cities close to the border of the US and Mexico. In the following, we will use NAZ (Region 1), CAZ (Region 2), and SAZ (Region 3) to denote the clusters of the Arizona counties.

- NAZ (Region 1) = [Mohave County, Coconino County, Yavapai County, La Paz County, Gila County, Navajo County, Apache County];
- CAZ (Region 2) = [Maricopa County];
- SAZ (Region 3) = [Yuma County, Pima County, Pinal County, Graham County, Santa Cruz County, Greenlee County, Cochise County].

We compute the daily new cases of each region by adding the new COVID-19 cases of all counties belonging to a region. We use the COVID-19 data from the New York Times at the state and the county level over time. The New York Times is compiling the time series data from state and local governments and health departments in an attempt to provide a complete record of the ongoing outbreak. The data can be downloaded from https://github.com/nytimes/covid-19-data and https://www.nytimes.com/article/coronavirus-county-data-us.html.

In addition, we incorporate the Google Community Mobility Report into our model. These Community Mobility Reports provide insights into how people's social behaviors have been changing in response to policies aimed at combating COVID-19. The reports provide the changes in movement trends compared to baselines overtime at the US county level, across different categories of activities. These activities include retail and recreation, groceries and pharmacies, parks, transit stations, workplaces, and residential. The relevant data can be downloaded from https://www.google.com/covid19/mobility/. Then we compute the daily changes of each region by adding the changes of all counties belonging to a region.

We create two time series from the Google Community Mobility Report. We accumulate the data for retail and recreation, groceries and pharmacies, parks, transit stations, workplaces, which are believed to increase the number of COVID-19 cases. On the other hand, the data from Google mobility for residential activities describes stay-at-home activities that are believed to prevent COVID-19 epidemics. In some cases, the increase of residential activities may result from events (such as parties) that could promote COVID-19 cases. However, the Google data only indicates residential activities compared to baselines. In our model, we use a Michaelis–Menten function to limit the effect of residential activities. Because it may take about 2 weeks for the effect of the activities to take place, we subtract the time *t* in our PDE model by 14 to reflect the incubation period of COVID-19 in most cases.

6.5.3 PDE modeling of Arizona COVID-19

In this section, we introduce a specific PDE model to characterize the spatio-temporal dynamics of COVID-19 cases. To apply a PDE model to the interaction of the dynamics of COVID-19 cases, one must embed the three regions NAZ, CAZ, SAZ into Euclidean space and arrange them in a meaningful order. In this section, the three regions are mapped onto a line where the locations of NAZ, CAZ, SAZ are 1, 2, 3, respectively. The arrangement will make the three regions stay as close as possible for ensuring that the continuous model can capture the spread of COVID-19 cases between the three regions. Projecting the three regions, geographically located in the north–south direction of Arizona, onto the x-axis of the Cartesian coordinates, as shown in Fig. 6.11. We project the three regions as the order of geographical north–south direction instead of other orders mainly due to the following fact: Maricopa county has much more population than any other county in Arizona. It is more likely that COVID-19 spreads from the metro Phoenix area to both northern and southern counties, at least at the beginning of 2020.

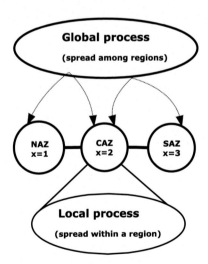

Figure 6.11 Embedding of three regions into the *x*-axis and two spreading processes.

Having embedded the three regions to the Euclidean space, we will develop the spatio-temporal model for the spread of COVID-19 cases according to the balance law: the rate at which a given quantity changes in a given domain must equal the rate at which it flows across its boundary plus the rate at which it is created, or destroyed, within the domain. The PDE model can be conceptually divided into two processes: an internal process within each region and an external process among regions. Similar derivation for the PDE model has been used in our previous work for PDE models for information diffusion in online social networks in [152].

Let $C(x, t)$ represent the cumulative COVID-19 cases in Arizona region x at a given time t. The changing rate of $C(x, t)$ depends on two processes as in Fig. 6.11:

- Global process: the social interactions of people between regions, such as traveling and commuting between regions, that contribute to the spread of COVID-19;
- Local process: in each Arizona region, people become newly infected through social interactions with infected people within a region; and people may take personal precautions to reduce and mitigate COVID-19 spread.

Combining the two processes, the dynamics of COVID-19 cases can be captured by Eq. (6.5.1):

$$
\begin{cases}
\frac{\partial C(x,t)}{\partial t} = \frac{\partial}{\partial x}\left(d(x)\frac{\partial C(x,t)}{\partial x}\right) + r(t)l(x)a(x, t-14)C(x, t) \\
\qquad - c\frac{h(x,t-14)C(x,t)}{k+C(x,t)}, \\
C(x, 1) = \psi(x), \ 1 < x < 3, \\
\frac{\partial C}{\partial x}(1, t) = \frac{\partial C}{\partial x}(3, t) = 0, \ t > 1,
\end{cases} \tag{6.5.1}
$$

where

- The term $\frac{\partial}{\partial x}\left(d(x)\frac{\partial C(x,t)}{\partial x}\right)$ denotes the spread of COVID-19 cases between different Arizona regions, where $d(x)$ measures how fast COVID-19 spreads across different Arizona regions. In epidemiology ([148] and [156]), the term $\frac{\partial}{\partial x}\left(d(x)\frac{\partial C(x,t)}{\partial x}\right)$ has been widely used for describing the spatial spread of infectious diseases. Here, we assume $d(x)$ to be constant, that is, $d(x) \equiv d > 0$.
- $r(t)l(x)a(x, t-14)C(x, t)$ represents the COVID-19 cases from a local Arizona region at location x and time t. This type of function is widely used to describe the growth of bacteria, tumors, or social information over time ([156]).

- The function $r(t) > 0$ represents the growth rate of COVID-19 cases at time t for all Arizona regions. For simplicity, we assume that $r(t)$ increases with time t as the COVID-19 cases increase. Therefore, we choose $r(t) = g(b_1 + b_2 t)$ and $g(u) = 1/(1 + exp(-u))$ to describe the pattern with parameters $b_1 > 0, b_2 > 0$ to be determined by the collected COVID-19 data.

- The location function $l(x)$ describes the spatial heterogeneity of COVID-19, which depicts different infection rates in the three Arizona regions. The function $l(x)$ is built through a cubic spline interpolation, which satisfies $l(x_i) \equiv l_i, i = 1, 2, 3$, where x_i represents the location of Arizona region i. $l(x)$ is determined by the collected COVID-19 data.

- $a(x, t - 14)$ is accumulated data from Google mobility for retail and recreation, groceries and pharmacies, parks, transit stations, work-places, which are believed to increase the COVID-19 cases. $t - 14$ again reflects the incubation period of COVID-19 in most cases.

- The function $c\frac{h(x,t-14)C(x,t)}{k+C(x,t)}$ is the rate of decrease of COVID-19 cases due to human efforts. During the period of the epidemic, Arizona people are advised to take COVID-19 precaution actions, such as wearing masks, staying 6 feet apart, or staying at home to reduce the contact rate. $c\frac{h(x,t-14)C(x,t)}{k+C(x,t)}$ to describe the potential reduction in COVID-19.

- In most cases, the data from Google mobility for residential activities are believed to prevent the spread of COVID-19. In some cases, they may result from events (such as home parties) that could promote COVID-19 cases. Here, we use Michaelis–Menten function to limit the effect of home activities in the spread of COVID-19.

- $c > 0$ represents the maximum reduction rate of COVID-19 cases due to government measures and personal precautions to maintain social distancing including wearing masks, staying 6 feet apart. k is the number of COVID-19 cases at which the reduction rate is $\frac{1}{2}c$. By adjusting the parameters, this model allows us to examine the effect of social distancing to prevent COVID-19 cases.

- $h(x, t - 14)$ describes home activities which are believed to prevent COVID-19 epidemics. $h(x, t - 14)$ is accumulated data from Google mobility for home activities. $t - 14$ is because it takes 2 weeks for the effect of the activity to take place.

- $a(x, t - 14), h(x, t - 14)$ are determined by Google Mobility data with the interpolation function of MATLAB.

- d, k, c, and parameters of $r(t), l(x)$ are determined by the known historical data of the COVID-19 cases with the best fitting function of MATLAB.
- Neumann boundary condition $\frac{\partial C}{\partial x}(1, t) = \frac{\partial C}{\partial x}(3, t) = 0$, $t > 1$ is applied in [156]. For simplicity, we count the cases imported from neighbor states as local Arizona cases and assume that no COVID-19 spreads across the boundaries at $x = 1, 3$.
- Initial function $C(x, 1) = \psi(x)$ describes the initial states of COVID-19 in every Arizona region, which can be constructed from the historical data of COVID-19 cases by cubic spline interpolation.

6.5.4 Model prediction

The basic mathematical properties of the proposed PDE model in Eq. (6.5.1) such as existence and uniqueness can be established from the standard theorems for parabolic PDEs in [176]. Below, we evaluate the robustness of our PDE-based predictive model and validate if the model has acceptable prediction performance with the COVID-19 case report in Arizona. The procedure of predictive modeling for the COVID-19 case in Arizona is summarized as follows:

- **Prediction Procedure:** In the prediction process of the research time period, the model parameters are to be determined by the historical aggregated data of COVID-19 cases in the three regions under the same structured PDE. In the current experiment, we predict the COVID-19 cases 3 days ahead. In order to forecast the COVID-19 of a given day, we first train the parameters of the PDE model and then solve the PDE model for prediction. For example, days 1–7, 2–8, ..., are used as the training data, and we predict the number of COVID-19 cases for the following days 10, 11, ..., respectively.

  The process of performing the prediction can be divided into two major processes. We first use an optimization method to fit parameters in the PDE model with historical data of COVID-19 cases. In essence, this is a multi-parameter inverse problem of parabolic equations. We integrate the local and global methods to search for the best fitting parameters. In the present work for COVID-19 modeling problems, we take a hybrid approach: first, a tensor train global optimization ([177]) is used to explore the parameter space thus to locate the starting points and then the Nelder–Mead simplex local optimization method ([131]) is used to search for the local optimization of COVID-19 modeling problem. The Nelder–Mead simplex method is implemented in the fminsearch function in MATLAB. Once the model parameters are determined, we use the fourth-order Runge–Kutta method to solve the PDE for one-step forward prediction numerically.

- **Accuracy Measurement:** We need to quantify the accuracy of model prediction of the COVID-19 cases by comparing the predicted COVID-19 cases with the observed aggregated COVID-19 cases for three regions, which are the ground truth. The mean absolute percentage error

$$1 - \left| \frac{x_{real} - x_{predict}}{x_{real}} \right|$$

is applied to measure the prediction accuracy, x_{real} is the observed COVID-19 cases at every data collection time point, and $x_{predict}$ is the predicted cases.

Fig. 6.12 illustrates predictions of COVID-19 cases in Arizona from April 24, 2020, to June 19, 2020, for three regions. The period covers the period of the end of stay-home order when the COVID-19 case started to increase quickly. The blue lines represent the predicted COVID-19 cases and red lines represent the actual COVID-19 cases. Note that we normalize the data to be between $[0, 1]$. Parameters in each prediction step are different. Here, we just provide the parameters in the last prediction for June 19. The parameters for prediction on June 19 are: $d = 0.013556543719$, $k = 4.655312010389$, $b_1 = 0.503402937243188$, $b_2 = 0.236417906835504$, $c = 0.821575737918722$ and $l_1 = 0.0826411111659247$, $l_2 = 0.347970638795282$, and $l_3 = 0.28107732159028$. Fig. 6.13 illustrates the prediction accuracy in NAZ, CAZ, and SAZ every day from April 24, 2020, to June 19, 2020. The Arizona stay-home order started on March 31, 2020, and ended on May 15, 2020. The average relative accuracy of three regions with 3 days prediction are 94%, 97%, and 95%, respectively. Clearly, the PDE-based prediction model has a good short-term prediction ability during active COVID-19 epidemics.

6.5.5 Remarks

In this section, the proposed PDE model is built on three regions in Arizona for the prediction of COVID-19 cases. The PDE model is capable of capturing the effects of various geographical and social factors. To ensure high accuracy predictions of COVID-19 cases, daily cases of COVID-19, and the effects of social distancing are included in the prediction model.

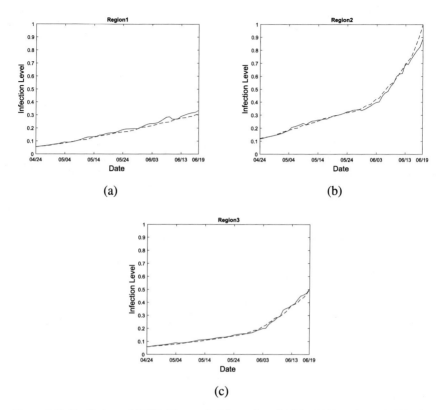

Figure 6.12 Predictions of COVID-19 cases in Arizona from April 24, 2020, to June 19, 2020, for three regions. The blue lines represent the predicted COVID-19 cases and red lines represent the actual COVID-19 cases.

In addition, Google Community Mobility data is incorporated to reflect the effects of human activities. As a result, the PDE model can be useful in making localized policies for reducing the spread of COVID-19.

We regroup 15 counties in Arizona into three regions: northern Arizona, central Arizona, and southern Arizona. One may be able to use ordinary differential equations on multiple patches for the prediction of COVID-19 cases in Arizona. Here, we choose partial differential equations instead of ordinary differential equations mainly because of the geographical and social characteristics in Arizona in terms of the spread of COVID-19. The three regions are geographically located in the north–south direction of Arizona and can be naturally projected onto the x-axis of the Cartesian coordinates. In addition, central Arizona, home to the metro Phoenix area, has about 60% of the population in Arizona. As a result, the spread

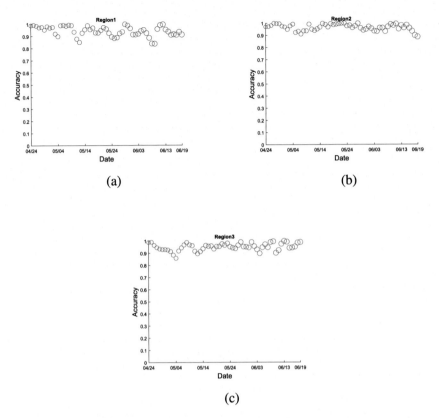

Figure 6.13 The relative accuracy in each region: NAZ (Region 1), CAZ (Region 2), and SAZ (Region 3) from April 24, 2020, to June 19, 2020.

of COVID-19 between central Arizona and other two regions are more likely predominant in terms of transboundary spread. These geographical characteristics, along with the disparities of social distancing and face mask requirements among the Arizona counties, fit squarely into the framework of reaction–diffusion equations for the spread of COVID-19.

While capturing the trend of the spread of COVID-19, we were able to avoid large scale computation by regrouping the counties, which allowed us to use a computational-heavy PDE model. Thus the diffusion process of COVID-19 between county regions as well as the increase of COVID-19 cases within a region are incorporated into the PDE model. The present paper aims to develop, for the first time in the literature, a specific PDE model between county regions for forecasting daily COVID-19 cases and further quantifying the influences of the mobility of the community on the changing the number of COVID-19 cases in the state of Arizona. In addition, In the present study, we study the effectiveness of human precautions such as face masks and social distancing on decreasing COVID-19 cases and hope to provide analytical results to help slow the spread of COVID-19 in Arizona.

In this section, we choose three regions of counties in Arizona for the spatial model because of the availability of both COVID-19 data and Google Community Mobility data. To gain more meaningful predictions with finer granularity, one may use zip codes or cities for the construction of regions or clusters. We could choose clustering algorithms to determine appropriate regions to ensure the connected zip codes stay as much as possible. However, the Google Community Mobility data is not available at the zip code level. Therefore our model for prediction for regional COVID-19 is based on three regions of counties, which is the most cost-effective method for prediction of COVID-19 in Arizona.

Arizona has emerged as a COVID-19 hot spot since the stay-home orders were lifted in mid-May. It is important to study how to slow the virus' spread. This section presents a PDE model to describe COVID-19 cases from community transmission, transboundary transmission between regions, and human activities. We apply this model for the prediction of COVID-19 cases to see the effect of social distancing on COVID-19 cases. The numerical results show that the new method of predicting COVID-19 cases is of acceptable high accuracy and can predict the effects of social distancing. To conclude, the prediction accuracy and the policy simulation suggest that a combining PDE model with real data can provide substantial information on COVID-19 spatio-temporal dynamics.

6.6 Compliance with COVID-19 mitigation policies in the US

6.6.1 Introduction

This section is based on the authors' paper [157] on modeling compliance with COVID-19 mitigation policies in the US. The US has become the center of the unprecedented global crisis of the Coronavirus Disease 2019 (COVID-19). By December 20, 2020, the total number of reported COVID-19 cases exceeded 17,000,000, with over 300,000 deaths in the US alone [158]. As the number of confirmed COVID-19 cases in the US continued to rise in early 2020, many states declared states of emergency and issued shutdown orders or stay-at-home orders to slow the spread of COVID-19 [159]. Many schools, workplaces, and public gathering spaces across the US were closed for an extended time. Although such measures might have saved lives, they have come at a high cost socially and economically. To balance various health, economic, and social concerns, governors across the US made decisions to gradually reopen the economy in summer 2020, which resulted in the increase of the number of COVID-19 cases in many states. While the first wave of COVID-19 in the early spring was mainly in coastal cities, the second wave was observed among the states in the Sun Belt. Although the geographic location was one of the main factors to identify the epidemic trend, almost all the states are still setting weekly records for new cases.

As the third wave of COVID-19 threatens communities' health across the nation, governors are considering another round of lockdowns. However, because of trade-offs between health and economy, when and how a state should impose and/or ease restrictions are not trivial. Different states have taken very different approaches to tackle the pandemic. Because businesses are only advised to follow federal guidance on social distancing, many businesses do not fully implement social distancing measurements. The absence of a national level mask mandate is thought to be escalating the spread of the virus. As delays in policy implementation could produce significant harm to public health, rigorous quantification of the non-pharmaceutical interventions to slow the spread of the disease is urgently necessary.

As a result, it is important to determine the levels of compliance at a state level. Bargain and Aminjonov [160] show that compliance with policies depends on the level of trust in institutions and decision-makers in the time of COVID-19. However, people in the US experienced the absence of a cohesive national strategy and conflicting messaging around their social distancing measures, especially during the US election campaign. Each state has experienced the policy difference and the difference in compliance level. Thus, it is crucial to quantify the temporal and geographical differences in policy implementation, together with the level of compliance.

In this section, we quantify compliance with the COVID-19 mitigation policies at a regional level during the first two waves of the pandemic, which is peaked on April 10 and July 24 (Fig. 6.14). We use a spatio-temporal model, specifically a partial differential equation (PDE) model. Our analysis is based on 10 regions defined by the US Department of Health and Human Services (HHS) because the clusters represent different geographical and social characteristics regarding the spread of COVID-19. The proposed model describes the combined effects of transboundary spread among regional clusters and human activities on the transmission of

COVID-19, enabling us to model the regional risk disparities and validate the COVID-19 spread. The localized results of the spatio-temporal model could provide valuable information to the local governments and public health officials to closely monitor new COVID-19 outbreaks and quickly reinstating mobility restrictions.

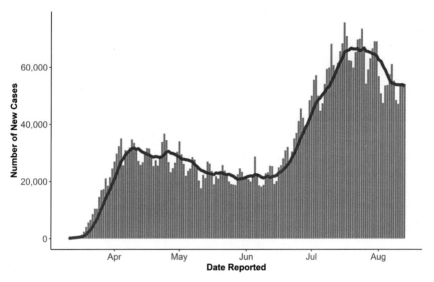

Figure 6.14 COVID-19 daily new reported cases in the US. The bars show the number of new COVID-19 cases reported each day in the US. The red line represents the 7-day rolling average of the cases between March 11, 2020, and August 18, 2020.

In response to the current COVID-19 pandemic, many mathematical models have been proposed. Many of them use ordinary differential equations (ODE) ([161–164]). The classical susceptible-infectious-recovered model (SIR) ([165]) and susceptible-exposed-infectious-recovered model (SEIR) ([145,166,167]) are the most widely adopted ones for characterizing the outbreak of COVID-19. The extension of the classical SEIR model with the age-stratified model ([146]) and the metapopulation model ([147]) were also introduced. Our previous work ([168–170]) applies PDE models to make a regional level of influenza with geo-tagged data. The PDE model we develop in this section focuses on the spread of COVID-19 and incorporating social distancing factors. While there is a rich literature on the application of PDE to model the spatial spread of infectious diseases ([148,170–172,227]), it is interesting to apply PDE models on COVID-19 short-term prediction incorporating COVID-19 mitigation policies and its compliance together with human mobility data.

In addition, the PDE model incorporates several open-source empirical data: social distancing policy dataset from the University of Washington ([173]), and the Google Community Mobility Reports (GCMR) ([174]). Mobility trends obtained from location history are dynamic in time and reflect real-time social behavior changes, making them a crucial factor in analyzing COVID-19 spread and its countermeasure. Several models utilize the GCMR, including our previous studies ([153–155]). This study extends our previous studies ([164,227]), which focused on Arizona, to the US national level as well as considering compliance to provide a more accurate prediction of the COVID-19 cases.

6.6.2 Data set sources and collection

We divide the country into 10 regions defined by the HHS, with a regional office located within each of the regions (Fig. 6.15). There are several reasons for us to use the 10 regions: (i) this enables us to capture the geographical and social characteristics regarding the spread of the virus while avoiding the high computational cost, (ii) the Centers for Disease Control and Prevention (CDC) uses the 10 regions to report weekly influenza activities. We compute three time-series data of each region by accumulating the data of all states belonging to a region.

Figure 6.15 The US Department of Health and Human Services (HHS) 10 regions. 51 states were clustered into 10 regions according to the HHS.

First, we compute each region's daily cumulative cases by adding the COVID-19 cases of all states belonging to a region. We use the COVID-19 data from the New York Times at the state level over time. The New York Times compiles the time-series data from state and local governments and health departments to provide a complete record of the ongoing outbreak. The data can be downloaded from https://github.com/nytimes/covid-19-data and https://www.nytimes.com/article/coronavirus-county-data-us.html.

Second, we create a time-series data of COVID-19 mitigation policy for each region using the data from https://github.com/COVID19StatePolicy/SocialDistancing. The data set is developed and maintained by researchers at the University of Washington, Seattle, WA, USA. The policies include emergency declarations, gathering restrictions and recommendations, school closures, restaurant restrictions, bar restrictions, business closures (including non-essential business closures), stay-at-home orders and advisories, travel restrictions and travel-based quarantine orders, case-based isolation orders, and public mask mandates. To quantify the policies, we set each policy as score one and calculate the region's daily policy scores by summing the score belonging to a region and dividing by the number of states in the region. Fig. 6.16 shows the calculated time series of the policy index of the 10 regions.

Third, human mobility data set was created based on the GCMR [174]. GCMR provides insights into how people's social behaviors have been changing in response to policies aimed at combating COVID-19. The reports provide the changes in movement trends compared to baselines overtime at the US county level, across different categories of activities. These activities include retail and recreation, groceries and pharmacies, parks, transit stations, workplaces, and residential. The relevant data can be downloaded from https://www.google.com/covid19/mobility/. Then we compute each region's daily changes by adding the changes of all states belonging to a region. We generated two time series of data sets from the GCMR; one is for the activities outside of the home, and the other is for stay-at-home activities. Former is the sum of five categories (i.e., retail and recreation, groceries and pharmacies, parks, transit stations, workplaces), and the latter is the data of residential activities.

6.6.3 PDE model for quantifying compliance with COVID-19 policies

This section introduces a specific PDE model to characterize the spatio-temporal dynamics of the US COVID-19 cases at a regional level. To apply a PDE model to the interaction of the dynamics of COVID-19 cases, one needs to embed the 10 regions into Euclidean space in such a way that the 10 regions stay as close as possible to ensure that the continuous model can

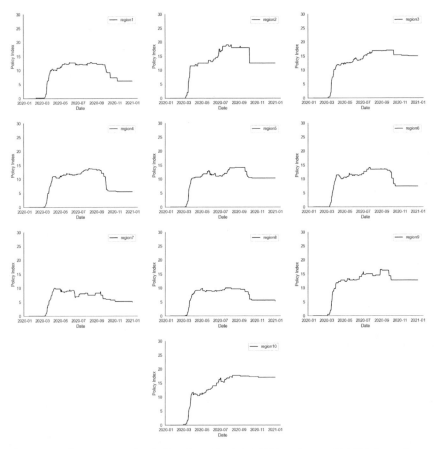

Figure 6.16 The average policy indices from March 11, 2020, to August 18, 2020, for each region. Policy indices were computed using the data on social distancing policy for each region.

capture the spread of COVID-19 cases between them. Here, we embed the 10 regions onto the x-axis of the Cartesian coordinates at $x = 1, 2, \cdots, 10$ in the east–west direction of US as shown in Fig. 6.17. One might use some algorithms discussed in [168] for a slight improvement. Because the accuracy of the prediction is acceptable in this section, we take the embedding for simplicity. According to the balance law, we will develop the spatio-temporal model for the spread of COVID-19 cases: the rate at which a given quantity changes in a given domain must equal the rate at which it flows across its boundary plus the rate at which it is created, or destroyed, within the domain. The PDE model can be conceptually divided into two processes: an internal (local) process within each region and an external (global) process between different regions. Similar derivation for the PDE model has been used in our previous work for PDE models for COVID-19 infection in Arizona and information diffusion in online social networks ([168,227]).

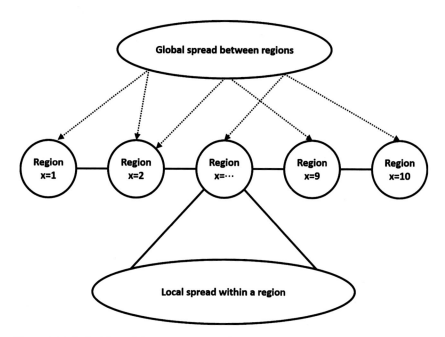

Figure 6.17 Embedding of the 10 regions into the x-axis and two spreading processes: global spread between regions and local spread within a region.

Let $C(x, t)$ represent the cumulative number of the reported COVID-19 cases in the US region x at a given time t. The changing rate of $C(x, t)$ depends on two processes as in Fig. 6.17:

- Global process: the social interactions of people between regions, such as traveling and commuting between regions, that contribute to the spread of COVID-19;
- Local process: in each US region, people become newly infected through social interactions with infected people within a region; and people may take personal precautions to reduce and mitigate COVID-19 spread.

Combining the two processes, the dynamics of COVID-19 cases can be captured by Eq. (6.6.1):

$$
\begin{cases}
\frac{\partial C(x,t)}{\partial t} = \frac{\partial}{\partial x}\left(d(x)\frac{\partial C(x,t)}{\partial x}\right) + r(t)l(x)m(x, t-10)C(x, t) \\
\qquad - p(x, t-10)E(x)C(x,t), \\
C(x, 1) = \psi(x), \; 1 < x < 10, \\
\frac{\partial C}{\partial x}(1, t) = \frac{\partial C}{\partial x}(10, t) = 0, \; t > 1.
\end{cases}
\tag{6.6.1}
$$

Among those functions, $m(x, t-10)$, $p(x, t-10)$, and $\psi(x)$ takes data and $d(x)$, $r(t)$, $l(x)$, and $E(x)$ are to be estimated. The following is a detailed explanation of each term:

- The term $\frac{\partial}{\partial x}\left(d(x)\frac{\partial C(x,t)}{\partial x}\right)$ denotes the spread of COVID-19 cases between different regions, where $d(x)$ measures how fast COVID-19 spreads across different regions. In epidemiology ([148] and [175]), the term $\frac{\partial}{\partial x}\left(d(x)\frac{\partial C(x,t)}{\partial x}\right)$ has been widely used for describing the spatial spread of infectious diseases. Here, we assume $d(x)$ to be constant, that is, $d(x) \equiv d > 0$.

- $r(t)l(x)m(x, t-10)C(x, t)$ represents the new COVID-19 cases from a local region at location x and time t. This type of function is widely used to describe the growth of bacteria, tumors, or social information over time ([175]).

  - The function $r(t) > 0$ represents the growth rate of COVID-19 cases at time t for all regions. For simplicity, we assume that $r(t)$ increases with time t as the COVID-19 cases increase. Therefore, we choose $r(t) = g(b_1 + b_2 t)$ and $g(u) = 1/(1 + \exp(-u))$ to describe the pattern with parameters $b_1 > 0, b_2 > 0$ to be determined by the collected COVID-19 data.

  - $l(x)$ describes the spatial heterogeneity of COVID-19, which depicts different infection rate of each region.

  - $m(x, t-10)$ takes the data from GCMR outside of the home activities. $t - 10$ of 10 reflects the incubation period of severe acute respiratory syndrome coronavirus 2 and reporting delay [164].

- The term $E(x)p(x, t-10)C(x, t)$ is the rate of decrease of COVID-19 cases due to human efforts such as wearing masks or social distancing to reduce the transmission rate.

  - $E(x)$ describes the spatial heterogeneity of the effectiveness of mitigation strategies to COVID-19.

  - $p(x, t-10)$ represents policy indices for each region.

- $l(x)$ and $E(x)$ are piecewise linear functions, which satisfy $l(x_i) \equiv l_i$ and $E(x_i) \equiv E_i$ for the location x_i, where l_i, E_i are determined by the fitting procedure, $i = 1, ..., 10$.

- Neumann boundary condition $\frac{\partial C}{\partial x}(1, t) = \frac{\partial C}{\partial x}(10, t) = 0$, $t > 1$ is applied in [175]. For simplicity, we count the cases imported from neighbor states as local US cases and assume that no COVID-19 spreads across the boundaries at $x = 1, 10$.
- Initial function $C(x, 1) = \psi(x)$ describes the initial states of COVID-19 in every US region, which can be constructed from the historical data of COVID-19 cases by cubic spline interpolation.

6.6.4 Model prediction

The basic mathematical properties of the proposed PDE model in Eq. (6.6.1), such as existence and uniqueness, can be established from the standard theorems for parabolic PDEs in [176]. Below, we evaluate the robustness of our PDE-based predictive model and validate if the model has acceptable short-term prediction performance with the COVID-19 case report in the US. In the current experiment, we predict the COVID-19 cases 1, 7, and 14 days ahead. It is not to predict the number of future COVID-19 cases, rather to retrospectively validate that our model can explain the COVID-19 dynamics. The procedure of predictive modeling for the COVID-19 case is summarized as follows:

- **Parameter Estimation:** The process of performing the estimation can be divided into two major processes. We first use an optimization method to fit parameters in the PDE model with historical data of COVID-19 cases. In essence, this is a multi-parameter inverse problem of parabolic equations. We integrate the local and global methods to search for the best-fitting parameters. We take a hybrid approach: first, a tensor train global optimization ([177]) is used to explore the parameter space thus to locate the starting points and then Nelder–Mead simplex local optimization method ([131]) is used to search the local optimum. The Nelder–Mead simplex method is implemented in the fminsearch function in MATLAB. Once the model parameters are determined, we use the fourth-order Runge–Kutta method to solve the PDE for one-step forward prediction numerically.
- **Prediction Procedure:** In order to estimate the cumulative number of COVID-19 cases of a given day, we first train the parameters of the PDE model and then solve the PDE model for prediction. For example, for one day ahead prediction, using data for days 1–4, 2–5, ..., we train the PDE model (i.e., estimate the best-fitted parameter values for the PDE model), and then using those estimated parameter values, we predict the number of COVID-19 cases for the following days 5, 6, ...,

Table 6.8 The parameters for prediction with one day ahead on August 18. The parameters were estimated for the each prediction step. The value on this table shows the estimated parameters for the last prediction step.

Region (x)	$l(x)$	$E(x)$
1	0.50988	0.53263
2	0.54703	0.30095
3	0.50936	0.40965
4	0.53135	0.21784
5	0.48461	0.41442
6	0.63504	0.35492
7	0.47371	0.57967
8	0.35630	0.63066
9	0.60115	0.20417
10	0.34531	0.65291

respectively. The blue lines represent the estimated COVID-19 cases and the red lines represent the cumulative of the reported COVID-19 cases. Note that we normalize the data to be between [0, 1] by dividing by the maximum value. Parameters in each prediction step are different; here, we provide the parameters in the last prediction for August 18: $d = 4.56129$, $b_1 = 0.15022$, $b_2 = 0.00736$. Values for l_i and E_i are shown in Table 6.8. The results of COVID-19 cases prediction from March 11, 2020, to August 18, 2020, for the 10 regions are shown in Fig. 6.18.

- **Accuracy Measurement:** We need to quantify the accuracy of model prediction of the COVID-19 cases by comparing the predicted COVID-19 cases with the observed COVID-19 cases for the 10 regions, which are the ground truth. The mean absolute percentage error

$$1 - \left| \frac{x_{real} - x_{predict}}{x_{real}} \right|$$

is applied to measure the prediction accuracy, where x_{real} is the observed COVID-19 cases at every data collection time point and $x_{predict}$ is the predicted cases. The average relative accuracy of the 10 regions with one day prediction are well acceptable with 93% and above as in Table 6.9. To further justify the model, we also perform 7 and 14 days ahead predictions as in Table 6.9. As demonstrated in the table, the average accuracy for 7 and 14 days ahead are about 86% and 69%, respectively.

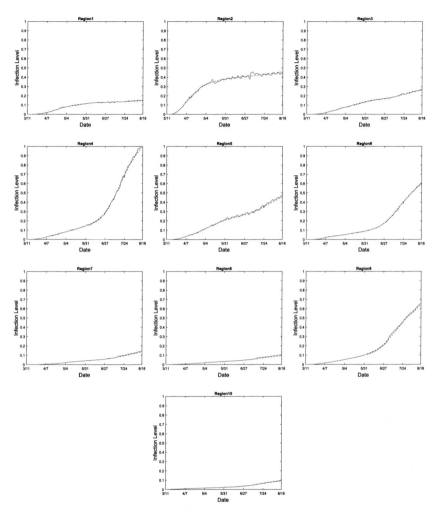

Figure 6.18 One day ahead predictions of COVID-19 cases from March 11, 2020, to August 18, 2020, for 10 regions. The blue lines represent the predicted COVID-19 cases and red lines represent the observed cumulative number of COVID-19 cases.

- **Pseudo-code:**
  - Begin with first time frame for prediction
    - Input data to update $m(x, t-10)$, $p(x, t-10)$ and $\psi(x)$. Initialize $d(x)$, $r(t)$, $l(x)$, and $E(x)$
      · MATLAB solves PDE for $C(x, t)$
      · fitting parameters of $d(x)$, $r(t)$, $l(x)$, and $E(x)$ to minimize the differences between $C(x, t)$ and COVID-19 data

Table 6.9 The prediction accuracy of our proposed model. The average relative accuracy for the entire period calculated using the mean absolute percentage error (MAPE).

	R1	R2	R3	R4	R5	R6	R7	R8	R9	R10
1 days ahead	98%	98%	98%	98%	98%	98%	96%	93%	99%	96%
7 days ahead	89%	87%	86%	86%	86%	86%	81%	80%	90%	87%
14 days ahead	71%	66%	71%	74%	71%	68%	59%	57%	77%	71%

    · repeat until accuracy is satisfied.
   – Use the parameters to solve PDE for prediction
  • Move to next time frame. Repeat the same procedure until the desired time frame reached. End.

6.6.5 Analysis of compliance with the US COVID-19 mitigation policy

The mitigation strategies such as social distancing, public mask-wearing, and stay-at-home orders have been considered as effective measures to slow the spread of COVID-19 by CDC. These actions are especially important before a vaccine becomes widely available ([178]). For example, the New York Times report that states with stronger mitigation policies over the long run are experiencing comparatively smaller outbreaks and better situations during the second or third waves of the new coronavirus ([179]). Thus to build a robust and accurate model the level of voluntary compliance has to be taken into consideration to quantify the mitigation policies. We have estimated the compliance level from the empirical COVID-19 cases and the policy indices that we have calculated.

In this section, we use parameter $E(x)$ to reflect the effectiveness of the state mitigation policies (i.e., how people comply with mitigation policies) in each region. The results of estimated $E(x)$ between March 11, 2020, and August 18, 2020 are shown in Fig. 6.19. The curves in Fig. 6.19 all start with about the same values in at the beginning of March. Around the middle of March, many states issued public health emergency declarations and various mitigation measures. As a result, we can see the curves in Fig. 6.19 increase or decease. High values of the curves indicates better compliance indices.

For example, while Fig. 6.16 indicates that the policy index of the region 9 (Arizona, California, Hawaii, and Nevada) is the average of 10

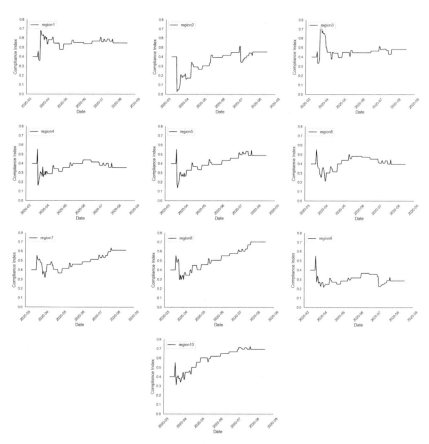

Figure 6.19 Compliance indices with the US mitigation policies in 10 regions from March 11, 2020, to August 18, 2020. The curves represent the estimated time-series values of $E(x)$ which indicated the effectiveness of the state mitigation policies (i.e., how people comply with mitigation policies).

regions, the compliance index is lower than the average throughout the period. This might result from the fact that the people in this region are less likely to comply with the ordinance and precaution measures to stop the spread of COVID-19.

We also find that region 1 (Connecticut, Maine, Massachusetts, New Hampshire, Rhode Island, and Vermont) and region 4 share similar policy scores, but the infection level of region 4 significantly exceeds that of region 1. The main reason is that the compliance index of region 1 is greater than region 4, which means the mitigation strategies in region 1 get more social support. Another example can be found by comparing region 3 (Delaware, District of Columbia, Maryland, Pennsylvania, Virginia, and West Virginia) and region 10 (Alaska, Idaho, Oregon, and Washington) from March 2020 to August 2020. They share similar policy indices, but the average compliance index of region 3 is around 0.45 while region 10 is around 0.65. As a result, region 10 shows a better COVID-19 situation during that period of time.

The growth rate of case number of COVID-19 in region 4 (Alabama, Florida, Georgia, Kentucky, Mississippi, North Carolina, South Carolina, and Tennessee) is the greatest among the 10 regions after May. The compliance index is among the lowest in the 10 regions. Moreover, Fig. 6.16 indicates that region 4 has the lowest policy index in the 10 regions. That is, the state governments do not issue strict mitigation policies, and the people in the region did not comply. Both the compliance index and the policy index of region 6 (Arkansas, Louisiana, New Mexico, Oklahoma, and Texas) are low. Contrary, the case number of COVID-19 in this region is high. This implies that the people in the region do not effectively follow the guidelines to contain the virus.

Our analysis shows that there is a significant correlation between compliance index and COVID-19 cases in many regions. We hope that the compliance index will plays an important role in disease control by quantifying policy compliance levels. Public health policies can be more effective if they gain the wide social support and are implemented in a context of social cohesion.

6.6.6 Remarks

In this section, we have built a COVID-19 prediction model incorporating social distancing policies, compliance, and human mobility. The states in the US were clustered into 10 regions to understand the epidemic dynamics of COVID-19 better. For each of the 10 regions, the parameters of the PDE model were trained and used to solve the PDE for the prediction of COVID-19 cases. The proposed model captures the spatio-temporal signals at both the national and state level. Our results agrees with other studies [180] about the importance of spatial heterogeneity to understand the progression of the COVID-19 dynamics. The average relative accuracy of the 10 regions with 3 days prediction were well acceptable with 95% and above.

In the US, there was a large degree of heterogeneity in the social distancing policy and its compliance throughout the states, cluster level analysis captured the trend while saving the computational cost. The results highlight that social distancing policy and its compliance can reduce the number of cases and help end the epidemic more quickly. The effectiveness of mitigation measures also vary in different areas due to many social factors. Every precautionary measure needs time for citizens to accept. For example, public mask-wearing is now widely viewed as a low-cost and effective measure for reducing COVID-19 transmission; however, it was not until April 3 that the CDC formally recommended mask-wearing to the general public. Moreover, while COVID-19 has become a partisan issue in the US, political beliefs and social trust have affected the compliance with the mitigation policies ([119]). Across the US, voluntary following to the CDC's mask recommendation has been uneven. Unlike some other nations, mask-wearing is not a cultural norm in the US. The absence of such a standard or a national mask mandate has resulted in considerable policy variation across states. One additional complication is that people are often unaware of hurting others when violating social distancing policies because many infected individuals are asymptomatic and unaware of being positive.

In conclusion, we have discussed a specific PDE model taking into account social distancing policy, its compliance, and human mobility—all issues which are crucial to disentangle the COVID-19 epidemic. The model fits the current data remarkably well with 1, 7 and 14 day ahead predictions. We believe that the model can help inform policymakers as they decide how to react to future pandemic waves.

Bibliography

[1] R.A. Horn, Matrix Analysis, Cambridge University Press, 2012.

[2] D.C. Lay, Linear Algebra and Its Applications, Pearson, 2011.

[3] M.P. Deisenroth, Mathematics for Machine Learning, Cambridge University Press, 1920.

[4] G. James, D. Witten, T. Hastie, R. Tibshirani, An Introduction to Statistical Learning, Springer, 2017.

[5] I. Markovsky, Low-Rank Approximation: Algorithms, Implementation, Applications, Springer, 2012.

[6] D.P. Bertsekas, J.N. Tsitsiklis, Introduction to Probability, Athena Scientific, 2008.

[7] J.L. Devore, Probability and Statistics for Engineering and the Sciences, Cengage Learning, 2015.

[8] J. Stewart, Calculus, Cengage Learning, 2015.

[9] A.I. Khuri, Advanced Calculus with Applications in Statistics, Wiley-Interscience, 2002.

[10] S. Boyd, L. Vandenberghe, Convex Optimization, Cambridge University Press, 2004.

[11] P. Wilmott, Machine Learning: An Applied Mathematics Introduction, illustrated edition, Panda Ohana Publishing, 2019.

[12] M. Belkin, P. Niyogi, Laplacian eigenmaps for dimensionality reduction and data representation, Neural Comput. 15 (2003) 1373–1396, https://doi.org/10.1162/089976603321780317.

[13] F. Brauer, C. Castillo-Chvez, Mathematical Models in Population Biology and Epidemiology, second edition, Springer, New York, 2012.

[14] F. Brauer, P. Van den Driessche, J. Wu, Mathematical Epidemiology, Springer, Heidelberg, 2008.

[15] F. Chung, Spectral Graph Theory, vol. 92, American Mathematical Society, 1997.

[16] S. Dhillon, Co-clustering documents and words using bipartite spectral graph partitioning, in: Proceedings of the 7th ACM SIGKDD International Conference on Knowledge Discovery and Data Mining, ACM, 2001, pp. 269–274.

[17] C.F. Gerald, P.O. Wheatley, Applied Numerical Analysis, Addison-Wesley, California, 1994.

[18] J. Heesterbeek, J. Metz, The saturating contact rate in marriage and epidemic models, J. Math. Biol. 31 (1993) 529–539.

[19] E.L. Ince, Ordinary Differential Equation, Dover, New York, 1927.

[20] W.O. Kermack, A.G. McKendrick, A contribution to the mathematical theory of epidemics, Proc. R. Soc. Lond. Ser. B 115 (1927) 700–721.

[21] K. Kwon, W. Xu, H. Wang, J. Chon, Spatiotemporal diffusion modeling of global mobilization in social media: The case of Egypt revolution 2011, Int. J. Commun. 10 (2016) 73–97.

[22] K. Kwon, H. Wang, W. Xu, R. Raymond, A spatiotemporal model of Twitter information diffusion: An example of Egyptian revolution 2011, in: Proceedings of Social Media and Society, Toronto, CA, July 27–29, in: ACM International Conference Proceeding Series (ICPS), 2015.

[23] J. Mena-Lorca, H.W. Hethcote, Dynamic models of infectious diseases as regulators of population sizes, J. Math. Biol. 30 (1992) 693–716.

[24] J.D. Murray, Mathematical Biology I: An Introduction, Springer-Verlag, New York, 1989.

[25] S. Myers, C. Zhu, J. Leskovec, Information diffusion and external influence in networks, in: Proceedings of the 18th ACM SIGKDD International Conference on Knowledge discovery and Data Mining, ACM, 2012, pp. 33–41.

[26] M. Newman, The structure and function of complex networks, SIAM Rev. 45 (2003) 167–256.

[27] E.M. Rogers, Diffusion of Innovations, 4th edition, Free Press, New York, 1995.

[28] X-S. Wang, H. Wang, J. Wu, Traveling waves of diffusive predator-prey systems: Disease outbreak propagation, Discrete Contin. Dyn. Syst. Ser. A 32 (2012) 3303–3324.

[29] F. Wang, H. Wang, K. Xu, Diffusive logistic model towards predicting information diffusion in online social networks, in: 2012 32nd International Conference on Distributed Computing Systems Workshops (ICDCSW), IEEE, 2012, pp. 133–139.

[30] F. Wang, H. Wang, K. Xu, J. Wu, J. Xia, Characterizing information diffusion in online social networks with linear diffusive model, in: 2013 33nd International Conference on Distributed Computing Systems (ICDCS), IEEE, 2013, pp. 307–316.

[31] E. Chong, S. Zak, An Introduction to Optimization, Wiley, 2013.

[32] X. Zhang, G-Q. Sun, Y-X. Zhu, J. Ma, Z. Jin, Epidemic dynamics on semi-directed complex networks, Math. Biosci. 246 (2013) 242–251.

[33] L. Zhang, X. Zhong, L. Wan, Modeling structure evolution of online social networks, in: 2012 8th International Conference on Information Science and Digital Content Technology (ICIDT), IEEE, 2012, pp. 15–19.

[34] L. Zhu, H. Zhao, H. Wang, Bifurcation and control of a delayed diffusive logistic model in online social networks, in: Proceedings of the 33rd Chinese Control Conference, Nanjing, July 2014.

[35] L. Zhu, H. Zhao, H. Wang, Complex dynamic behavior of a rumor propagation model with spatial-temporal diffusion terms, Inform. Sci. 349–350 (2016) 119–138.

[36] D. Chen, X. Liu, J. Lang, Y. Zhou, L. Wei, X. Wang, Estimating the contribution of regional transport to PM 2.5 air pollution in a rural area on the North China Plain, Sci. Total Environ. 583 (2017) 280–291.

[37] M.T. Chuang, Y. Zhang, D. Kang, Application of WRF/Chem-MADRID for real-time air quality forecasting over the Southeastern United States, Atmos. Environ. 45 (34) (2011) 6241–6250.

[38] K. Yahya, Y. Zhang, J.M. Vukovich, Real-time air quality forecasting over the southeastern United States using WRF/Chem-MADRID: Multiple-year assessment and sensitivity studies, Atmos. Environ. 92 (2014) 318–338.

[39] C. Li, N.C. Hsu, S.C. Tsay, A study on the potential applications of satellite data in air quality monitoring and forecasting, Atmos. Environ. 45 (22) (2011) 3663–3675.

[40] N. Benas, A. Beloconi, N. Chrysoulakis, Estimation of urban PM10 concentration, based on MODIS and MERIS/AATSR synergistic observations, Atmos. Environ. 79 (2013) 448–454.

[41] X. Mao, T. Shen, X. Feng, Prediction of hourly ground-level PM 2.5 concentrations 3 days in advance using neural networks with satellite data in eastern China, Atmos. Pollut. Res. (2017).

[42] E. Emili, C. Popp, M. Petitta, M. Riffler, S. Wunderle, M. Zebisch, PM 10 remote sensing from geostationary SEVIRI and polar-orbiting MODIS sensors over the complex terrain of the European Alpine region, Remote Sens. Environ. 114 (11) (2010) 2485–2499.

[43] Z. Ma, X. Hu, L. Huang, J. Bi, Y. Liu, Estimating ground-level PM2.5 in China using satellite remote sensing, Environ. Sci. Technol. 48 (13) (2014) 7436–7444.

[44] Y. Wang, H. Wang, S. Chang, M. Liu, Higher-order network analysis of fine particulate matter (PM 2.5) transport in China at city level, Sci. Rep. 7 (1) (2017) 13236.

[45] A.R. Benson, D.F. Gleich, J. Leskovec, Higher-order organization of complex networks, Science 353 (6295) (2016) 163–166.

[46] F. Brauer, Compartmental Models in Epidemiology. Mathematical Epidemiology, Springer, 2008.

[47] Y. Wang, H. Wang, Using networks and partial differential equations to forecast bitcoin price movement, Chaos 30 (7) (2020) 073,127.

[48] S. Nakamoto, Bitcoin: A peer-to-peer electronic cash system, http://www.bitcoin. org.

[49] P. Ciaian, M. Rajcaniova, D. Kancs, The economics of bitcoin price formation, Appl. Econ. 48 (2016) 1799–1815.

[50] H. Jang, J. Lee, An empirical study on modeling and prediction of bitcoin prices with Bayesian neural networks based on blockchain information, IEEE Access (2017).

[51] S. Velankar, S. Valecha, S. Maji, Bitcoin price prediction using machine learning, in: 2018 20th International Conference on Advanced Communication Technology (ICACT), IEEE, 2018, pp. 144–147.

[52] M.T. Kurbucz, Predicting the price of bitcoin by the most frequent edges of its transaction network, Econ. Lett. 184 (2019) 108655.

[53] Z. Chen, C. Li, W. Sun, Bitcoin price prediction using machine learning: An approach to sample dimension engineering, J. Comput. Appl. Math. 365 (2020) 112395.

[54] G.S. Atsalakis, I.G. Atsalaki, F. Pasiouras, C. Zopounidis, Bitcoin price forecasting with neuro-fuzzy techniques, European J. Oper. Res. 276 (2019) 770–780.

[55] A. Cretarola, G. Figà-Talamanca, Modeling bitcoin price and bubbles, Cryptocurrencies (2018).

[56] C.G. Akcora, A.K. Dey, Y.R. Gel, M. Kantarcioglu, Forecasting bitcoin price with graph chainlets, in: Pacific-Asia Conference on Knowledge Discovery and Data Mining, vol. 10939, 2018, pp. 765–776.

[57] L. Kristoufek, Bitcoin meets Google trends and Wikipedia: Quantifying the relationship between phenomena of the internet era, Sci. Rep. 3 (2013) 3415.

[58] J. Bukovina, M. Martiček, et al., Sentiment and bitcoin volatility, Tech. rep., Mendel University in Brno, Faculty of Business and Economics, 2016.

[59] L. Kristoufek, What are the main drivers of the bitcoin price? Evidence from wavelet coherence analysis, PLoS ONE 10 (4) (2015) e0123923.

[60] J. Engelberg, P. Gao, In search of attention, J. Finance 66 (2011) 1461–1499.

[61] D. Koutmos, Bitcoin returns and transaction activity, Econ. Lett. 167 (2018) 81–85.

[62] C.G. Akcora, M.F. Dixon, Y.R. Gel, M. Kantarcioglu, Bitcoin risk modeling with blockchain graphs, Econ. Lett. 173 (2018) 138–142.

[63] U.V. Luxburg, A tutorial on spectral clustering, Stat. Comput. 17 (4) (2007) 395–416.

[64] C.F. Gerald, P.O. Wheatley, Applied Numerical Analysis, Addison-Wesley, 1994.

[65] G.S. Atsalakis, P.V. Kimon, Forecasting stock market short-term trends using a neuro-fuzzy based methodology, Expert Syst. Appl. 36 (7) (2016) 10696–10707.

[66] G.S. Atsalakis, D. Frantzis, D. Zopounidis, Commodities' price trend forecasting by a neuro-fuzzy controller, Energy Syst. 7 (2016) 73–102.

[67] X. Guo, N.N. Xiong, H. Wang, J. Ren, Design and analysis of a prediction system about influenza-like illness from the latent temporal and spatial information, IEEE Trans. Syst. Man Cybern. Syst., https://doi.org/10.1109/TSMC.2020.3048946.

[68] C.W. Potter, A history of influenza, J. Appl. Microbiol. 91 (4) (2001) 572–579.

[69] K.D. Patterson, G.F. Pyle, The geography and mortality of the 1918 influenza pandemic, Bull. Hist. Med. 65 (1) (1991) 4–21.

[70] C.E. Mills, J.M. Robins, M. Lipsitch, Transmissibility of 1918 pandemic influenza, Nature 432 (7019) (2004) 904–906.

[71] D.T. Gilbertson, K.J. Rothman, G.M. Chertow, B.D. Bradbury, M.A. Brookhart, J. Liu, W.C. Winkelmayer, T. Stürmer, K.L. Monda, C.A. Herzog, et al., Excess deaths attributable to influenza-like illness in the ESRD population, J. Am. Soc. Nephrol. 30 (2) (2019) 346–353.

[72] V.Y. Fan, D.T. Jamison, L.H. Summers, Pandemic risk: How large are the expected losses?, Bull. World Health Organ. 96 (2) (2018) 129.

[73] C. for Disease Control and Prevention, Overview of influenza surveillance in the United States, http://www.cdc.gov/flu/weekly/overview.htm. (Accessed February 2019).

[74] M. Biggerstaff, M.A. Jhung, C. Reed, A.M. Fry, L. Balluz, L. Finelli, Influenza-like illness, the time to seek healthcare, and influenza antiviral receipt during the 2010–2011 influenza season—United States, J. Infect. Dis. 210 (4) (2014) 535–544.

[75] S. Cauchemez, A.J. Valleron, P.Y. Boelle, A. Flahault, N.M. Ferguson, Estimating the impact of school closure on influenza transmission from sentinel data, Nature 452 (7188) (2008) 750–754.

[76] P.M. Polgreen, Y. Chen, D.M. Pennock, F.D. Nelson, R.A. Weinstein, Using internet searches for influenza surveillance, Clin. Infect. Dis. 47 (11) (2008) 1443–1448.

[77] J. Ginsberg, M.H. Mohebbi, R.S. Patel, L. Brammer, M.S. Smolinski, L. Brilliant, Detecting influenza epidemics using search engine query data, Nature 457 (7232) (2009) 1012–1014.

[78] D. Butler, When Google got flu wrong, Nat. News 494 (7436) (2013) 155.

[79] D. Lazer, R. Kennedy, G. King, A. Vespignani, The parable of Google flu: Traps in big data analysis, Science 343 (6176) (2014) 1203–1205.

[80] D.A. Broniatowski, M.J. Paul, M. Dredze, Twitter: Big data opportunities, Inform. 49 (2014) 255.

[81] F. Wang, H. Wang, K. Xu, R. Raymond, J. Chon, S. Fuller, A. Debruyn, Regional level influenza study with geo-tagged Twitter data, J. Med. Syst. 40 (2016) 189.

[82] H. Hu, H. Wang, F. Wang, D. Langley, A. Avram, M. Liu, Prediction of influenza-like illness based on the improved artificial tree algorithm and artificial neural network, Sci. Rep. 8 (1) (2018) 1–8.

[83] D.J. McIver, J.S. Brownstein, Wikipedia usage estimates prevalence of influenza-like illness in the United States in near real-time, PLoS Comput. Biol. 10 (4) (2014) e1003,581.

[84] N. Generous, G. Fairchild, A. Deshpande, S. Valle, R. Priedhorsky, Global disease monitoring and forecasting with Wikipedia, PLoS Comput. Biol. 10 (11) (2014) e1003,892.

[85] K. Lee, A. Agrawal, A. Choudhary, Forecasting influenza levels using real-time social media streams, in: 2017 IEEE International Conference on Healthcare Informatics (ICHI), IEEE, 2017, pp. 409–414.

[86] M. Santillana, A.T. Nguyen, M. Dredze, M.J. Paul, E.O. Nsoesie, J.S. Brownstein, Combining search, social media, and traditional data sources to improve influenza surveillance, PLoS Comput. Biol. 11 (10) (2015) e1004,513.

[87] H. Xue, Y. Bai, H. Hu, H. Liang, Influenza activity surveillance based on multiple regression model and artificial neural network, IEEE Access 6 (2017) 563–575.

[88] W. Yang, M. Lipsitch, J. Shaman, Inference of seasonal and pandemic influenza transmission dynamics, Proc. Natl. Acad. Sci. USA 112 (9) (2015) 2723–2728.

[89] H.W. Hethcote, The mathematics of infectious diseases, SIAM Rev. 42 (4) (2000) 599–653.

[90] K.H. Degue, J. Le Ny, An interval observer for discrete-time SEIR epidemic models, in: 2018 Annual American Control Conference (ACC), IEEE, 2018, pp. 5934–5939.

[91] X. Guo, Y. Sun, J. Ren, Low dimensional mid-term chaotic time series prediction by delay parameterized method, Inform. Sci. 516 (2020) 1–19.

[92] C. Zhou, S. Huang, N. Xiong, S.H. Yang, H. Li, Y. Qin, X. Li, Design and analysis of multimodel-based anomaly intrusion detection systems in industrial process automation, IEEE Trans. Syst. Man Cybern. Syst. 45 (10) (2015) 1345–1360.

[93] Q. Zhang, C. Zhou, N. Xiong, Y. Qin, X. Li, S. Huang, Multimodel-based incident prediction and risk assessment in dynamic cybersecurity protection for industrial control systems, IEEE Trans. Syst. Man Cybern. Syst. 46 (10) (2015) 1429–1444.

[94] X. Guo, X. Xie, J. Ren, M. Laktionova, E. Tabachnikova, L. Yu, W.S. Cheung, K.A. Dahmen, P.K. Liaw, Plastic dynamics of the Al0.5CoCrCuFeNi high entropy alloy at cryogenic temperatures: Jerky flow, stair-like fluctuation, scaling behavior, and non-chaotic state, Appl. Phys. Lett. 111 (25) (2017) 251,905.

[95] J. Ren, C. Chen, Z. Liu, R. Li, G. Wang, Plastic dynamics transition between chaotic and self-organized critical states in a glassy metal via a multifractal intermediate, Phys. Rev. B 86 (13) (2012) 134,303.

[96] J. Sun, Y. Yang, N.N. Xiong, L. Dai, X. Peng, J. Luo, Complex network construction of multivariate time series using information geometry, IEEE Trans. Syst. Man Cybern. Syst. 49 (1) (2017) 107–122.

[97] F. Takens, Detecting strange attractors in turbulence, in: Dynamical Systems and Turbulence, Warwick 1980, Springer, 1981, pp. 366–381.

[98] A.M. Fraser, H.L. Swinney, Independent coordinates for strange attractors from mutual information, Phys. Rev. A 33 (2) (1986) 1134.

[99] A. Wolf, J.B. Swift, H.L. Swinney, J.A. Vastano, Determining Lyapunov exponents from a time series, Physica D 16 (3) (1985) 285–317.

[100] J. Ren, C. Chen, G. Wang, W.S. Cheung, B. Sun, N. Mattern, S. Siegmund, J. Eckert, Various sizes of sliding event bursts in the plastic flow of metallic glasses based on a spatiotemporal dynamic model, J. Appl. Phys. 116 (3) (2014) 033,520.

[101] S.M. Pincus, Approximate entropy as a measure of system complexity, Proc. Natl. Acad. Sci. USA 88 (6) (1991) 2297–2301.

[102] S.M. Pincus, I.M. Gladstone, R.A. Ehrenkranz, A regularity statistic for medical data analysis, J. Clin. Monit. 7 (4) (1991) 335–345.

[103] E.R. Deyle, G. Sugihara, Generalized theorems for nonlinear state space reconstruction, PLoS ONE 6 (3) (2011) e18,295.

[104] D. Broomhead, D. Lowe, Multivariable Functional Interpolation and Adaptive Networks, Complex Systems, vol. 2, 1988.

[105] F. Girosi, T. Poggio, Networks and the best approximation property, Biol. Cybernet. 63 (3) (1990) 169–176.

[106] J. Moody, C.J. Darken, Fast learning in networks of locally-tuned processing units, Neural Comput. 1 (2) (1989) 281–294.

[107] X. Deng, Y. Zhong, L. Lü, N. Xiong, C. Yeung, A general and effective diffusion-based recommendation scheme on coupled social networks, Inform. Sci. 417 (2017) 420–434.

[108] Y. Wang, H. Wang, S. Zhang, Prediction of daily pm2.5 concentration in china using data-driven ordinary differential equations, Appl. Math. Comput. 375 (2020) 125,088.

[109] C. Xia, Z. Wang, C. Zheng, Q. Guo, Y. Shi, A new coupled disease-awareness spreading model with mass media on multiplex networks, Inform. Sci. 471 (2019) 185–200.

[110] J. Wang, C. Li, C. Xia, Improved centrality indicators to characterize the nodal spreading capability in complex networks, Appl. Math. Comput. 334 (2018) 388–400.

[111] Y. Wang, H. Wang, S. Chang, A. Avram, Prediction of daily pm 2.5 concentration in china using partial differential equations, PLoS ONE 13 (6) (2018) e0197,666.

[112] Y. Wang, Regional-level prediction model with advection PDE model and fine particulate matter (pm 2.5) concentration data, Phys. Scr. 95 (3) (2020) 035,204.

[113] H. Cao, L. Kang, Y. Chen, J. Yu, Evolutionary modeling of systems of ordinary differential equations with genetic programming, Genet. Program. Evol. Mach. 1 (4) (2000) 309–337.

[114] Y. Chen, B. Yang, Q. Meng, Y. Zhao, A. Abraham, Time-series forecasting using a system of ordinary differential equations, Inform. Sci. 181 (1) (2011) 106–114.

[115] J. Madár, J. Abonyi, F. Szeifert, Genetic programming for the identification of non-linear input–output models, Ind. Eng. Chem. Res. 44 (9) (2005) 3178–3186.

[116] M. Ashyraliyev, Y. Fomekong-Nanfack, J.A. Kaandorp, J.G. Blom, Systems biology: Parameter estimation for biochemical models, FEBS J. 276 (4) (2009) 886–902.

[117] H. Akaike, Information theory and an extension of the maximum likelihood principle, in: Selected Papers of Hirotugu Akaike, Springer, 1998, pp. 199–213.

[118] S. Roch, Mathematical methods in data science, https://sebroc.github.io/MMiDS-s20/, 2020.

[119] M. Painter, T. Qiu, Political beliefs affect compliance with COVID-19 social distancing orders, 2020.

[120] Y. Wang, H. Wang, S. Zhang, Quantifying prediction and intervention measures for PM2.5 by a PDE model, J. Clean. Prod. 268 (2020) 0959.

[121] F. Benaissa, I. Bendahmane, N. Bourfis, O. Aoulaiche, R. Alkama, Bioindication of urban air polycyclic aromatic hydrocarbons using petunia hybrida, Civ. Eng. J. 5 (6) (2019) 1305–1313.

[122] M. Buchanan, The limits of machine prediction, Nat. Phys. 15 (304) (2019).

[123] Z.Y. Chen, D.L. Chen, X.M. Xie, J. Cai, Y. Zhuang, N.L. Cheng, B. He, B. Gao, Spatial self-aggregation effects and national division of city-level pm2.5 concentrations in China based on spatio-temporal clustering, J. Clean. Prod. 207 (2019) 875–881.

[124] Y.Y. Chu, Y.S. Liu, X.Y. Li, Z.Y. Liu, H. Lu, Y.N. Lu, Z.F. Mao, X. Chen, N. Li, M. Ren, et al., A review on predicting ground pm2.5 concentration using satellite aerosol optical depth, Atmosphere 7 (10) (2016) 129.

[125] F. Feng, Z.F. Wang, J. Li, G.R. Carmichael, A nonnegativity preserved efficient algorithm for atmospheric chemical kinetic equations, Appl. Math. Comput. 271 (2015) 519–531.

[126] C.F. Gerald, P.O. Wheatley, Applied Numerical Analysis, 5th edition, Pearson Academic, 2004.

[127] D.B. Guan, X. Su, Q. Zhang, G.P. Peters, Z. Liu, Y. Lei, K.B. He, The socioeconomic drivers of China's primary pm2.5 emissions, Environ. Res. Lett. 9 (2) (2014).

[128] J.P. Guo, F. Xia, Y. Zhang, H. Liu, J. Li, M.Y. Lou, J. He, Y. Yan, F. Wang, M. Min, Impact of diurnal variability and meteorological factors on the pm2.5 − AOD relationship: Implications for pm2.5 remote sensing, Environ. Pollut. 221 (2014) 94–104.

[129] Y. Hao, Y.M. Liu, The influential factors of urban pm2.5 concentrations in China: A spatial econometric analysis, J. Clean. Prod. 112 (2016) 1443–1453.

[130] J. Karátson, T. Kurics, A preconditioned iterative solution scheme for nonlinear parabolic systems arising in air pollution modeling, Math. Model. Anal. 18 (5) (2013) 641–653.

[131] J.C. Lagarias, J.A. Reeds, M.H. Wright, P.E. Wright, Convergence properties of the Nelder–Mead simplex method in low dimensions, SIAM J. Optim. 9 (1) (1998) 112–147.

[132] H.J. Li, Y.J. Qi, C. Li, X.Y. Liu, Routes and clustering features of pm2.5 spillover within the Jing-Jin-Ji region at multiple timescales identified using complex network-based methods, J. Clean. Prod. 209 (2019) 1195–1205.

[133] X.T. Li, X.D. Zhang, Predicting ground-level pm2.5 concentrations in the Beijing-Tianjin-Hebei region: A hybrid remote sensing and machine learning approach, Environ. Pollut. 249 (2019) 735–749.

[134] Y. Li, Y. Chiu, L.H. Wang, Y. Zhou, T.Y. Lin, Dynamic and network slack-based measure analysis of china's regional energy and air pollution reduction efficiencies, J. Clean. Prod. 251 (2020) 119,546.

[135] Ministry of Environmental Protection of the People's Republic of China, China national ambient air quality standard (in Chinese; gb3095-2012), 2012.

[136] B. Striebig, E. Smitts, S. Morton, Impact of transportation on carbon dioxide emissions from locally vs. non-locally sourced food, Emerg. Sci. J. 3 (4) (2019) 222–234.

[137] S.Y. Tang, Q.L. Yan, W. Shi, X. Wang, X.D. Sun, P.B. Yu, J.H. Wu, Y.N. Xiao, Measuring the impact of air pollution on respiratory infection risk in China, Environ. Pollut. 232 (2018) 477–486.

[138] C.W. Tessum, J.D. Hill, J.D. Marshall, Inmap: A model for air pollution interventions, PLoS ONE 12 (4) (2017) e0176131.

[139] H.L. Wang, L.P. Qiao, S.R. Lou, M. Zhou, A.J. Ding, H.Y. Huang, J.M. Chen, Q. Wang, S. Tao, C.H. Chen, Chemical composition of pm2.5 and meteorological impact among three years in urban Shanghai, China, J. Clean. Prod. 112 (2016) 1302–1311.

[140] Y.J. Xie, L.J. Zhao, J. Xue, H.O. Gao, H.Y. Li, R. Jiang, X.Y. Qiu, S.H. Zhang, Methods for defining the scopes and priorities for joint prevention and control of air pollution regions based on data-mining technologies, J. Clean. Prod. 185 (2018) 912–921.

[141] Z. Zlatev, K. Georgiev, I. Dimov, Influence of climatic changes on pollution levels in the Balkan peninsula, Comput. Math. Appl. 65 (3) (2013) 544–562.

[142] H. Wang, N. Yamamoto, Using a partial differential equation with Google mobility data to predict COVID-19 in Arizona, Math. Biosci. Eng. 17 (5) (2020) 4891–4904.

[143] Arizona Department of Health Services, Confirmed COVID-19 cases by day, Available from https://www.azdhs.gov/preparedness/epidemiology-disease-control/infectious-disease-epidemiology/covid-19/dashboards/index.php, 2020.

[144] S. Lai, N.W. Ruktanonchai, L. Zhou, O. Prosper, W. Luo, J.R. Floyd, A. Wesolowski, M. Santillana, C. Zhang, X. Du, H. Yu, A.J. Tatem, Effect of non-pharmaceutical interventions to contain COVID-19 in China, Nature 585 (7825) (2020) 410–413.

[145] Z. Yang, Z. Zeng, K. Wang, S. Wong, W. Liang, M. Zanin, P. Liu, X. Cao, Z. Gao, Z. Mai, J. Liang, X. Liu, S. Li, Y. Li, F. Ye, W. Guan, Y. Yang, F. Li, S. Luo, Y. Xie, B. Liu, Z. Wang, S. Zhang, Y. Wang, N. Zhong, J. He, Modified SEIR and AI prediction of the epidemics trend of COVID-19 in China under public health interventions, J. Thorac. Dis. 12 (2020) 165–174.

[146] K. Prem, Y. Liu, T.W. Russell, A.J. Kucharski, R.M. Eggo, N. Davies, The effect of control strategies to reduce social mixing on outcomes of the COVID-19 epidemic in Wuhan, China: A modelling study, Lancet Public Health 5 (2020) e261–e270.

[147] B.S. Pujari, S.M. Shekatkar, Multi-city modeling of epidemics using spatial networks: Application to 2019-nCov (COVID-19) coronavirus in India, medRxiv, 2020.

[148] F. Brauer, C. Castillo-Chavez, Z. Feng, Mathematical Models in Epidemiology, Springer, 2019.

[149] E.E. Holmes, M.A. Lewis, J.E. Banks, R.R. Veit, Partial differential equations in ecology: Spatial interactions and population dynamics, Ecology 75 (1994) 17–29.

[150] Y. Wang, K. Xu, Y. Kang, H. Wang, F. Wang, A. Avram, Regional influenza prediction with sampling Twitter data and PDE model, Int. J. Environ. Res. Public Health 17 (2020) 678.

[151] M. Zhu, X. Guo, Z. Lin, The risk index for an SIR epidemic model and spatial spreading of the infectious disease, Math. Biosci. Eng. 14 (2017) 1565–1583.

[152] H. Wang, F. Wang, K. Xu, Modeling Information Diffusion in Online Social Networks With Partial Differential Equations, Springer, 2020.

[153] N. Picchiotti, M. Salvioli, E. Zanardini, F. Missale, COVID-19 pandemic: A mobility-dependent SEIR model with undetected cases in Italy, Europe and US, arXiv:2005.08882.

[154] R. Abouk, B. Heydari, The immediate effect of COVID-19 policies on social distancing behavior in the United States, medRxiv, https://doi.org/10.1101/2020.04.07.20057356, 2020.

[155] Z. Vokó, J.G. Pitter, The effect of social distance measures on COVID-19 epidemics in Europe: an interrupted time series analysis, GeroScience, https://doi.org/10.1007/s11357-020-00205-0.

[156] J.D. Murray, Mathematical biology. I. An introduction, Photosynthetica 40 (2002) 414.

[157] N. Yamamoto, B. Jiang, H. Wang, Quantifying compliance with COVID-19 mitigation policies in the US: A mathematical modeling study, Infect. Dis. Model. 6 (2021) 503–513.

[158] Centers for Disease Control and Prevention, Available from https://covid.cdc.gov/covid-data-tracker/#cases_casesper100klast7days.

[159] Department of Health and Human Services, Available from https://healthdata.gov/dataset/covid-19-state-and-county-policy-orders.

[160] O. Bargain, A. Aminjonov, Trust and compliance to public health policies in times of COVID-19, 2020.

[161] S. He, S. Tang, L. Rong, A discrete stochastic model of the COVID-19 outbreak: Forecast and control, Math. Biosci. Eng. 17 (2020) 2792–2804, https://doi.org/10.3934/mbe.2020153.

[162] M.T. Li, G.Q. Sun, J. Zhang, Y. Zhao, X. Pei, L. Li, Y. Wang, W.Y. Zhang, Z.K. Zhang, Z. Ji, Analysis of COVID-19 transmission in Shanxi Province with discrete time imported cases, Math. Biosci. Eng. 17 (2020) 3710–3720.

[163] L. Wang, J. Wang, H. Zhao, Y. Shi, K. Wang, P. Wu, L. Shi, Modelling and assessing the effects of medical resources on transmission of novel coronavirus (COVID-19) in Wuhan, China, Math. Biosci. Eng. 17 (2020) 2936–2949.

[164] N. Yamamoto, H. Wang, Assess the impacts of human mobility change on COVID-19 dynamics in AZ, U.S.: A modeling study incorporating Google community mobility reports, arXiv:2009.02419 [q-bio.PE].

[165] Y. Huang, L. Yang, H. Dai, F. Tian, K. Chen, Epidemic situation and forecasting of COVID-19 in and outside China, Bull. World Health Organ. (2020), E-pub: 16 March 2020.

[166] S. Lai, N.W. Ruktanonchai, L. Zhou, O. Prosper, W. Luo, J.R. Floyd, A. Wesolowski, M. Santillana, C. Zhang, X. Du, H. Yu, A.J. Tatem, Effect of non-pharmaceutical interventions to contain COVID-19 in China, Nature (2020).

[167] R. Omori, R. Matsuyama, Y. Nakata, The age distribution of mortality from novel coronavirus disease (COVID-19) suggests no large difference of susceptibility by age, Sci. Rep. 10 (2020) 16642.

[168] H. Wang, F. Wang, K. Xu, Modeling information diffusion in online social networks with partial differential equations, Springer, 2020.

[169] F. Wang, H. Wang, K. Xu, R. Raymond, J. Chon, S. Fuller, A. Debruyn, Regional level influenza study with geo-tagged Twitter data, J. Med. Syst. 40 (2016) 189.

[170] Y. Wang, K. Xu, Y. Kang, H. Wang, F. Wang, A. Avram, Regional influenza prediction with sampling Twitter data and PDE model, Int. J. Environ. Res. Public Health 17 (2020) 678.

[171] E.E. Holmes, M.A. Lewis, J.E. Banks, R.R. Veit, Partial differential equations in ecology: Spatial interactions and population dynamics, Ecology 75 (1994) 17–29.

[172] M. Zhu, X. Guo, Z. Lin, The risk index for an SIR epidemic model and spatial spreading of the infectious disease, Math. Biosci. Eng. 14 (2017) 1565–1583.

[173] N. Fullman, B. Bang-Jensen, G. Reinke, B. Magistro, R. Castellano, M. Erickson, K. Amano, J. Wilkerson, C. Adolph, State-level social distancing policies in response to COVID-19 in the US, version 1.108, Available from http://www.covid19statepolicy.org, December 17, 2020.

[174] Google, Google COVID-19 community mobility reports, Available from https://www.google.com/covid19/mobility/.

[175] J.D. Murray, Mathematical biology. I. An introduction, Photosynthetica 40 (2002) 414.

[176] A. Friedman, Partial Differential Equations, Courier Dover Publications, 2008.

[177] I.V. Oseledets, Tensor-train decomposition, SIAM J. Sci. Comput. 33 (2011) 2295–2317.

[178] Centers for Disease Control and Prevention (CDC), Implementation of mitigation strategies for communities with local COVID-19 transmission, Available from https://www.cdc.gov/coronavirus/2019-ncov/community/community-mitigation.html.

[179] The New York Times, States that imposed few restrictions now have the worst outbreaks, Available from https://www.nytimes.com/interactive/2020/11/18/us/covid-state-restrictions.html?auth=login-google1tap&login=google1tap.

[180] E.R. White, L.H. Dufresne, State-level variation of initial COVID-19 dynamics in the United States: The role of local government interventions, medRxiv, 2020.

[181] L. Zhang, D. Li, J. Ren, Analysis of COVID-19 by discrete multi-stage dynamics system with time delay, Geomat. Inform. Sci. Wuhan Univ. (2020).

[182] World Health Organization (WHO), Coronavirus disease (COVID-2019) situation reports, https://www.who.int/emergencies/diseases/novel-coronavirus-2019/situation-reports.html.

[183] X. Wang, S.Y. Tang, Y. Chen, et al., When will Wuhan and its surrounding areas return to work under novel coronavirus pneumonia epidemic? Data driven network mode l analysis, Sci. Sin. Math. (April 30, 2020) 1–10.

[184] T. Sanyi, T. Biao, N.L. Bragazzi, X. Fan, L. Tangjuan, H. Sha, R. Pengyu, W. Xia, C. Xiang, P. Zhihang, et al., Analysis of COVID-19 epidemic traced data and stochastic discrete transmission dynamic model, https://coronavirus.1science.com/item/9a631edf1c374daace5e94e78178075d92a78329, 2020.

[185] Y. Yan, Y. Chen, K. Liu, X. Luo, B. Xu, Y. Jiang, J. Cheng, Modeling and prediction for the trend of outbreak of NCP based on a time-delay dynamic system, Sci. Sin. Math. 50 (3) (2020).

[186] H. Sen-zhong, P. Zhihang, J. Zhen, Studies of the strategies for controlling the COVID-19 epidemic in china: Estimation of control efficacy and suggestions for policy makers, Sci. Sin. Math. 50 (6) (2020) 885.

[187] C. Hengjian, H. Tao, Nonlinear regression in COVID-19 forecasting, Sci. Sin. Math. (2020).

[188] H. Tian, Y. Liu, Y. Li, C.H. Wu, B. Chen, M.U. Kraemer, B. Li, J. Cai, B. Xu, Q. Yang, et al., An investigation of transmission control measures during the first 50 days of the COVID-19 epidemic in china, Science 368 (6491) (2020) 638–642.

[189] X. He, E.H. Lau, P. Wu, X. Deng, J. Wang, X. Hao, Y.C. Lau, J.Y. Wong, Y. Guan, X. Tan, et al., Temporal dynamics in viral shedding and transmissibility of COVID-19, Nat. Med. 26 (5) (2020) 672–675.

[190] W. Xiao, Q. Liu, J. Huan, P. Sun, L. Wang, C. Zang, S. Zhu, L. Gao, A cybernetics-based dynamic infection model for analyzing SARS-CoV-2 infection stability and predicting uncontrollable risks, medRxiv, 2020.

[191] A. Piunovskiy, A. Plakhov, M. Tumanov, Optimal impulse control of a sir epidemic, Optimal Control Appl. Methods 41 (2) (2020) 448–468.

[192] Y. Long, L. Wang, Global dynamics of a delayed two-patch discrete sir disease model, Commun. Nonlinear Sci. Numer. Simul. 83 (2020) 105,117.

[193] N. Tuerxun, B. Wen, Z. Teng, The stationary distribution in a class of stochastic sirs epidemic models with non-monotonic incidence and degenerate diffusion, Math. Comput. Simulation 182 (2021) 888–912.

[194] X. Zhao, X. He, T. Feng, Z. Qiu, A stochastic switched sirs epidemic model with nonlinear incidence and vaccination: Stationary distribution and extinction, Int. J. Biomath. 13 (03) (2020) 2050,020.

[195] S. Rajasekar, M. Pitchaimani, Ergodic stationary distribution and extinction of a stochastic sirs epidemic model with logistic growth and nonlinear incidence, Appl. Math. Comput. 377 (2020) 125,143.

[196] K. Wan, J. Chen, C. Lu, L. Dong, Z. Wu, L. Zhang, When will the battle against novel coronavirus end in Wuhan: A SEIR modeling analysis, J. Glob. Health 10 (1) (2020).

[197] K. Iwata, C. Miyakoshi, A simulation on potential secondary spread of novel coronavirus in an exported country using a stochastic epidemic SEIR model, J. Clin. Med. 9 (4) (2020) 944.

[198] R. Huang, M. Liu, Y. Ding, Spatial-temporal distribution of COVID-19 in china and its prediction: A data-driven modeling analysis, J. Infect. Dev. Ctries. 14 (03) (2020) 246–253.

[199] C. News, Italian officials: The number of people infected may be 10 times higher than the official statistics [eb/ol], https://baijiahao.baidu.com, March 29, 2020.

[200] Centers for Disease Control and Prevention, Transcript-CDC media telebriefing: Update on COVID-19, https://www.cdc.gov/media/releases/2020/t0309-covid-19-update.html, 2020.

[201] National Health Commission of the People's Republic of China, http://www.nhc.gov.cn.

[202] L. Deren, S. Zhenfeng, Y. Wenbo, Z. Xinyan, Z. Suhong, Public epidemic prevention and control services based on big data of spatiotemporal location make cities more smart, Geomat. Inform. Sci. Wuhan Univ. 45 (4) (2020) 475–487.

[203] Arizona Department of Health Services, Confirmed COVID-19 cases by day, https://www.azdhs.gov/preparedness/epidemiology-disease-control/infectious-disease-epidemiology/covid-19/dashboards/index.php, 2020.

[204] Office of the Governor Doug Ducey, Stay home stay healthy stay connected, https://azgovernor.gov/governor/news/2020/03/stay-home-stay-healthy-stay-connected.

[205] S. Mervosh, S. Romerom, What Arizona's tenuous virus plateau could teach us, New York Times, July 24, 2020, http://nyti.ms/3jCrcmv.

[206] M.U.G. Kraemer, C.H. Yang, B. Gutierrez, C.H. Wu, B. Klein, D.M. Pigott, Data Working Group, L. Plessis, N.R. Faria, R. Li, W.P. Hanage, J.S. Brownstein, M. Layan, A. Vespignani, H. Tian, C. Dye, O.G. Pybus, S.V. Scarpino, The effect of human mobility and control measures on the COVID-19 epidemic in China, Science 368 (6490) (2020) 493–497.

[207] J. Sun, Z. Shi, H. Xu, Non-pharmaceutical interventions used for COVID-19 had a major impact on reducing influenza in China in 2020, J. Travel Med. 27 (8) (2020) taaa064.

[208] X. Zhou, Z. Wu, R. Yu, S. Cao, W. Fang, Z. Jiang, F. Yuan, C. Yan, D. Chen, Modelling-based evaluation of the effect of quarantine control by the Chinese government in the coronavirus disease 2019 outbreak, Sci. China, Life Sci. 63 (8) (2020) 1257–1260.

[209] G.J. Tellis, A. Sood, N. Sood, How long should social distancing last? Predicting time to moderation, control, and containment of COVID-19, USC Marshall School of Business Research Paper, March 28, 2020, Available at SSRN: https://ssrn.com/abstract=3562996.

[210] E.S. Gel, M. Jehn, T. Lant, A.R. Muldoon, T. Nelson, et al., COVID-19 healthcare demand projections: Arizona, PLoS ONE 15 (12) (2020) e0242588.

[211] H.S. Badr, H. Du, M. Marshall, E. Dong, M.M. Squire, L.M. Gardner, Association between mobility patterns and COVID-19 transmission in the USA: A mathematical modelling, Lancet Infect. Dis. 20 (11) (2020) 1247–1254.

[212] N. Oliver, B. Lepri, H. Sterly, R. Lambiotte, S. Deletaille, M.D. Nadai, E. Letouzé, A.A. Salah, R. Benjamins, C. Cattuto, V. Colizza, N. Cordes, S.P. Fraiberger, T.

Koebe, S. Lehmann, J. Murillo, A. Pentland, P.N. Pham, F. Pivetta, J. Saramäki, S.V. Scarpino, M. Tizzoni, S. Verhulst, P. Vinck, Mobile phone data for informing public health actions across the COVID-19 pandemic life cycle, Sci. Adv. 6 (23) (2020) eabc0764.

[213] Y. Zhou, R. Xu, D. Hu, Y. Yue, Q. Li, Jizhe Xia, Effects of human mobility restrictions on the spread of COVID-19 in Shenzhen, China: A modelling study using mobile phone data, Lancet Dig. Health 2 (8) (2020) e417–e424.

[214] E. Pepe, P. Bajardi, L. Gauvin, F. Privitera, B. Lake, C. Cattuto, M. Tizzoni, COVID-19 outbreak response, a dataset to assess mobility changes in Italy following national lockdown, Sci. Data 7 (2020) 230.

[215] D. Delen, E. Eryarsoy, B. Davazdahemami, No place like home: Cross-national data analysis of the efficacy of social distancing during the COVID-19 pandemic, JMIR Public Health Surveill. 6 (2) (2020) e19862.

[216] P. Gigliotti, E.G. Martin, Predictors of state-level stay-at-home orders in the United States and their association with mobility of residents, J. Public Health Manag. Pract. 26 (6) (2020) 622–631.

[217] A. Godio, F. Pace, A. Vergnano, SEIR modeling of the Italian epidemic of SARS-CoV-2 using computational swarm intelligence, Int. J. Environ. Res. Public Health 17 (10) (2020) 3535.

[218] L. Russo, C. Anastassopoulou, A. Tsakris, G.N. Bifulco, E.F. Campana, G. Toraldo, C. Siettos, Tracing day-zero and forecasting the COVID-19 outbreak in Lombardy, Italy: A compartmental modelling and numerical optimization approach, PLoS ONE 15 (10) (2020) e0240649.

[219] M. Sulyok, M. Walker, Community movement and COVID-19: A global study using Google's community mobility reports, Epidemiol. Infect. 148 (2020) e284.

[220] New York Times, Coronavirus (COVID-19) data in the United States, https://github.com/nytimes/covid-19-data.

[221] U.S. Census Bureau, 2011–2015 5-year ACS commuting flows, Available from https://www.census.gov/data/tables/2015/demo/metro-micro/commuting-flows-2015.html, 2015.

[222] A. Bick, A. Blandin, K. Mertens, Work from home after the COVID-19 outbreak, Federal Reserve Bank of Dallas, 2020.

[223] S. Flaxman, S. Mishra, A. Gandy, H.J.T. Unwin, T.A. Mellan, H. Coupland, C. Whittaker, H. Zhu, T. Berah, J.W. Eaton, M. Monod, Imperial College COVID-19 Response Team, A.C. Ghani, C.A. Donnelly, S. Riley, M.A.C. Vollmer, N.M. Ferguson, L.C. Okell, S. Bhatt, Estimating the effects of non-pharmaceutical interventions on COVID-19 in Europe, Nature 584 (2020) 257–261.

[224] A. Pan, L. Liu, C. Wang, H. Guo, X. Hao, Q. Wang, J. Huang, N. He, H. Yu, X. Lin, S. Wei, T. Wu, Association of Public Health interventions with the epidemiology of the COVID-19 outbreak in Wuhan, China, JAMA 323 (19) (2020) 1915–1923.

[225] M.W. Fong, H. Gao, J.Y. Wong, J. Xiao, E.Y.C. Shiu, S. Ryu, B.J. Cowling, Non-pharmaceutical measures for pandemic influenza in nonhealthcare settings—social distancing measures, Emerg. Infect. Dis. 26 (2020) 976–984.

[226] K. Prem, Y. Liu, T.W. Russell, A.J. Kucharski, R.M. Eggo, N. Davies, Centre for the Mathematical Modelling of Infectious Diseases COVID-19 Working Group, M. Jit, P. Klepac, The effect of control strategies to reduce social mixing on outcomes of the COVID-19 epidemic in Wuhan, China: A modelling study, Lancet Public Health 5 (5) (2020) E260.

[227] H. Wang, N. Yamamoto, Using a partial differential equation with Google mobility data to predict COVID-19 in Arizona, Math. Biosci. Eng. 17 (5) (2020) 4891–4904.

[228] S.A. Lauer, K.H. Grantz, Q. Bi, F.K. Jones, Q. Zheng, H.R. Meredith, A.S. Azman, N.G. Reich, J. Lessler, The incubation period of coronavirus disease 2019 (COVID-

19) from publicly reported confirmed cases: Estimation and application, Ann. Intern. Med. 172 (2020) 577–582.

[229] D. Margaret, K.S. Vittal, T. Martin, M. Martin, M. Gerry, Mitigating the wider health effects of COVID-19 pandemic response, BMJ 369 (2020) m1557.

[230] G. Wang, Y. Zhang, J. Zhao, J. Zhang, F. Jiang, Mitigate the effects of home confinement on children during the COVID-19 outbreak, Lancet 395 (10228) (2020) 945–947.

[231] N. Yamamoto, H. Wang, Assess the impacts of human mobility change on COVID-19 dynamics in Arizona, U.S.: A modeling study incorporating Google community mobility reports, https://arxiv.org/abs/2009.02419, 2020.

Index